"*Formation for Mission* is a timely, well-researche[d] 'emerging adults' in today's context. I appreciate [...] mation that focuses on the God of mission, is gr[...] of Scripture, and leads to vibrant and engaged f[...] tantly, this publication fills a gap by addressing the changing demographics in the US, the resultant contextual realities inherent in diverse socioeconomic and ethnic backgrounds as it relates to guiding and engaging emerging adults. I look forward to making good use of this excellent resource."

—**Cas Monaco,** vice president of missiology and gospel engagement, FamilyLife

"In every generation, congregations cry out to know how to reach young people. *Formation for Mission* provides exactly this insight. Deftly weaving together the concepts of mission, spiritual formation, and emerging adulthood while accounting for the many psychological, sociological, behavioral, and cultural crosscurrents that intersect them, it offers an unblinking view of what it is like to be an emerging adult in twenty-first-century America. At the same time, it offers an honest assessment of the American church, letting congregations know that if they want to meet emerging adults where they are then they must jettison inward-focused portions of the Christian subculture and recommit themselves to the self-giving mission of Jesus Christ by becoming mentoring communities that create intentional space for young adults. The authors and editors are clear that only when a congregation is willing to submit itself to being formed in God's mission can it be used by the Holy Spirit to form emerging adults as disciples. It delivers all this with exactly what we have come to expect from work published out of the Wheaton College Billy Graham Center for Evangelism: strong scholarship that is engaged with a deep bibliography, nuanced in its thinking, grounded in fresh empirical research, sensitive to the lived experience of those it addresses, faithful to the gospel, and eminently practical."

—**Mark R. Teasdale,** E. Stanley Jones Professor of Evangelism, Garrett-Evangelical Theological Seminary

"Through a deep grounding in research that uses historic developmental theories as a foundation to a current understanding of the emerging adult life, *Formation for Mission* offers a fresh perspective on incorporating emerging adults into the missional vision of the church. With the incorporation of contemporary contexts of racial and ethnic reconciliation, sexual ethics, and communal outreach, as well as the conversational encouragement of discussion questions, this book is a must-read for those leading and serving in ministry and missions as well as for those who prepare them. This will be an essential text for many years to come!"

—**Laura Barwegen,** associate professor of Christian formation and ministry, Litfin School of Mission and Ministry, Wheaton College

"This book is written for so many people. The missiologist who seeks to reach people, the planters/pastors/leaders who daily help in the spiritual formation of young adults, parents who most days feel so inadequate in understanding this new generation. Essentially, all those who care about the spiritual lives of emerging adults. In this book, the authors remind leaders that working with young adults is not an either/or situation but a both/and. Both outreach and discipleship, hand in hand. Cutting through the fog of confusion and predictions surrounding young adults, the authors remind us, where there is crisis there is also opportunity. It's a thoughtful and well-informed analysis that will be considered a primer for those working with this life stage. Do yourself a favor and add it to your 'must read' list!"

—Elizabeth "Liz" Rios, founder/president,
Passion2Plant Network

"It is no secret that increasing numbers of young people are leaving the church behind as they enter into their adult lives. But as pastors, lay leaders and others recognize, the answer to retaining and perhaps bringing them back to the church remains elusive. In *Formation for Mission*, Mary Lederleitner, Andrew MacDonald, and Rick Richardson bring together scholars and practitioners who present needed insights on the lives of emerging adults and examples of how successful 'missional development' can take place. Those who are concerned about the spiritual lives of young Christians would do well to study this book and use it to imagine new approaches to ministry with emerging adults."

—Richard Flory, executive director,
USC Center for Religion and Civic Culture

"So many reports today leave us disheartened over narratives that ensnare the lives of young adults, leading to an exodus from congregations and the relinquishment of faith commitments that historically have given meaning and coherence to the Christian life. How refreshing then to find our colleagues at Wheaton thoughtfully recrafting alternative pathways. There is so much that offers hope and so much to ponder in this text from the microcosm of the classroom to the macrocosm of transnational networks that you can't help but feel afresh the compelling invitation to give your life anew to the mission of God. I was gobsmacked to find theories I have known for decades take on new meanings; enamored to gain understanding that can take me further up and deeper in; and thrilled to find our sisters and brothers of color inviting us to missional spaces to encounter the world with different eyes. I can't wait to put this text before students and let the conversations begin!"

—Chris Kiesling, professor of discipleship and human development,
Asbury Theological Seminary

Formation for Mission

Discipleship and Identity for Emerging Adults

Formation for Mission

Discipleship and Identity for Emerging Adults

Edited by Mary T. Lederleitner,
Andrew MacDonald, and Rick Richardson

LEXHAM PRESS

Print ISBN 9781683596158
Digital ISBN 9781683596165
Library of Congress Control Number 2022933931

Series Editors: Mary T. Lederleitner, Andrew MacDonald, and Rick Richardson
Lexham Editorial: Kelsey Matthews, Abby Salinger, Claire Brubaker, Mandi
    Newell
Cover Design: Joshua Hunt, Brittany Schrock
Typesetting: ProjectLuz.com

Contents

Introduction

Mary T. Lederleitner, Andrew MacDonald,
and Rick Richardson

• • • • •

But the plans of the Lord *stand firm forever,*
the purposes of his heart through all generations.

—Psalm 33:11 NIV

One generation commends your works to another;
they tell of your mighty acts.

—Psalm 145:4 NIV

S ome might be wondering whether this book is primarily about *reaching* emerging adults or *discipling* them. The answer is both, for the two issues are inexorably linked. Each generation is commissioned to pass faith on to the next so they too might come to know and follow God faithfully. While God has been at work since the beginning of time, our focus is to highlight missional formation with the next generation of emerging adults so they are able to rise to the challenges they face to make Christ known and God's purposes a reality through their lives.

Since so much good theological work has already been written about the mission of God, our purpose in this book is not to critique those writings. We understand that ecclesial streams parse their understanding of God's mission in different ways. If you want to place this book in a theological context, we view God's mission as including both proclamation of the gospel and action, for we believe when either is missing that the witness of Christ through the people of God becomes distorted.

However, while the calling to pass on faith to the next generation remains the same, we enter this conversation realizing that the process of missional development has shifted from what was common practice in many prior generations. For this reason, our goal is to weave together insights from the social sciences, missiology, theology, education, and church and ministry practitioners to illuminate the missional formation process in a way that adds to the current conversation. We believe by weaving together these insights we will understand more clearly how to help inspire, facilitate, and support the missional growth and development of emerging adults in significant ways. Let's get started!

1

• • • • •

What Are We Talking About?

*Mary T. Lederleitner, Andrew
MacDonald, and Rick Richardson*

• • • • •

*There is something particularly powerful and poignant
about the "twenty-something" years, harboring, as
they do, both promise and vulnerability.*

—Sharon Daloz Parks

S ophia explained,

When I was at university I started going to a
Christian group on campus. I was on the leadership team but I was leading a double life. I would
attend meetings and go to Bible studies but, because
I was part of the Greek system on my campus, many
nights I would go to fraternity parties. I drank way

too much. I wasn't sleeping around, but close to it, always hoping no one would find out.

When I graduated I wanted to make a clean break. I wanted to live like a Christian. I wanted to be a true disciple. I started attending a church near where I live. They are very welcoming towards people from my generation. I have been able to grow in my understanding of the Bible and lead in some areas of ministry and outreach.

I'm so grateful for my church small group. We're all facing the same challenges and temptations. Everyone our age goes to bars, and it's easy to drink too much and do things that we deeply regret later. So, we hold each other accountable. If we go to a bar to be with other friends, we go together and we watch out for each other. I am growing so much in my faith and as a person.

THE PURPOSE OF THIS BOOK

The person who shared this story was such a talented and gifted young woman.[1] As she recounted her aspirations and the challenges she faced, her story seemed to capture the "promise and vulnerability" that often come with the journey to adulthood.[2] Our purpose for this book is to equip anyone who might have a passion to help emerging adults navigate this season of life. You might be older than they are, or you might be a peer. Whichever way you are positioned, we want to provide an opportunity for you to learn from others. We will share positive experiences, and also mistakes made, that facilitate and hinder their missional development. Our hope is that this book will be a resource that equips you to influence emerging adults in ways that help them grow to their full potential so that, in Christ, with their eyes focused on the God of mission, they can make their best contributions in the world.

The authors who have contributed to this book have shared some of the richest insights they have uncovered through their academic studies and research on emerging adults. They have translated this wisdom in ways that will help you to easily make connections between theory and practice, research and real life. For those who desire a deep dive into the academic research behind each chapter, bibliographic resources are also provided. We believe this book will be especially beneficial if you read and work through it together in groups or teams, discussing and unpacking insights and implications with your own unique contexts in mind. For that reason, questions are included at the end of each chapter to facilitate deeper reflection and problem solving, and to think strategically about next steps.

UNDERSTANDING EMERGING ADULTHOOD

There are different terms and complexities surrounding the phase of life that is frequently referred to as "emerging adulthood." For that reason, it is essential to clarify what we are talking about so we lessen confusion as we travel on this learning journey together.

AN AGE RANGE OR A GENERATION?

The conversation addressed in this book relates to the season of life between when a person ends adolescence and when they begin making long-term commitments characteristic of adulthood. For many that means it begins after they finish high school and before they get married, begin having children, and settle into professions. In some cultures that transition might be marked by other actions such as providing financial support for parents instead of being the recipient of their support. The time a person spends in this season of life varies based on their own developmental progress, sociological issues such as the availability of long-term employment in their desired professions, and other factors.

Often people reference the age span between eighteen and twenty-nine as the season of emerging adulthood, with the core period common to most being ages eighteen to twenty-five.[3]

While some might view emerging adulthood in terms of a specific generation, such as iGen/Gen Z, that is not a complete picture. The phrase emerging adulthood relates most frequently to the maturation process a person undergoes as part of their development to adulthood. Those navigating it are from diverse socioeconomic and ethnic backgrounds,[4] and those contextual realities trigger diverse challenges and issues. One of the goals of this book is to address some holes in the research, since experiences of emerging adults from diverse backgrounds are less frequently studied and understood. We wish we could highlight all of these distinctions, but that is impossible within a single text. However, our hope is that the examples shared will foster in readers curiosity and new research with diverse groups of emerging adults in the days ahead.

WHAT HAS CHANGED?

In many cultures and for generations, elders from a community would initiate younger members. There would be some form of ritual or process they would follow,[5] and at its conclusion they would be initiated into the community with adult status, accompanied by the corresponding roles and responsibilities of adulthood. The process of entering adulthood has become elongated because of a wide range of sociological factors such as globalization, growing access to information, greater financial resources, the need for higher levels of education to work in an information economy, the burden of academic debt experienced by many in order to obtain higher levels of education to function in an information economy, and older people living longer and not leaving their jobs. Entering adulthood used to be fairly straightforward: after adolescence most people would get married and begin working in a vocation handed down by a parent (or choose their vocation from a small set of options). The process is now far more complex.

Another area that has changed relates to continuity of faith and church participation. The Pew Research Center has been showing an increase in the number of people who are now religiously unaffiliated and who attend church with less frequency than prior generations.[6] Below is a graph of the Pew data on religious affiliation in the United States.[7] The unaffiliated, also called "nones," are now the most numerous religious grouping in America (26 percent, or one out of every four people). Nones are made up of atheists (4 percent of US adults), agnostics (5 percent of US adults), and "nothing in particulars" (17 percent of US adults).

The percentages are much more striking for younger adults. Among millennials ages twenty-two to thirty-five, nones make up

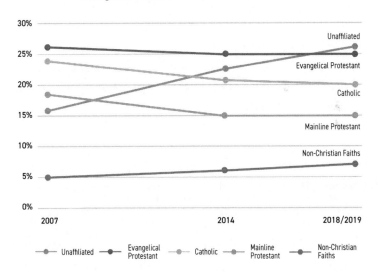

Religious Shifts Between 2007 and 2019

Unaffiliated

Evangelical Protestant

Catholic

Mainline Protestant

Non-Christian Faiths

| 2007 | 2014 | 2018/2019 |

Unaffiliated · Evangelical Protestant · Catholic · Mainline Protestant · Non-Christian Faiths

40 percent as of 2018/2019, up about 4 percent in just four years. In the same age grouping, the percentage of those who identify as Christian stands at 49 percent. The percentage of nones for people ages nineteen to twenty-nine, though we don't have exact figures, stands at about 42–43 percent. We are approaching the time when emerging adult nones will numerically surpass emerging adults who identify as some form of Christian. If the trend lines continue at about a 1 percent gain per year, we are two to three years away from that seismic shift in the majority religious identification of emerging adults in the United States transitioning from Christian to unaffiliated, with unaffiliated at more than 45 percent of the emerging adult population and Christian-affiliated emerging adults at less than 45 percent. The drift away from Christian affiliation is steady and substantial, and shows no signs of reversing. By 2026, more than half of emerging adults will likely be unaffiliated.

Prior to this latest research, others had also been sounding the alarm that many in this age range were leaving their faith.[8] Since many churches are developed primarily with families with children in mind, the elongated path of emerging adulthood, according to Robert Wuthnow, now means "it is now more likely that a teenager may drop out of his or her congregation after confirmation at age thirteen and not feel the same urgency about participating again until he or she is a parent at age thirty-five."[9] For these reasons, reaching emerging adults and aiding their faith formation has been a growing concern for parents, campus-ministry workers, pastors, and others across the country.

IS IT A NEW STAGE OF LIFE?

Jeffrey Jensen Arnett was the academic researcher who first proposed the phrase "emerging adulthood."[10] He found after adolescence young people seemed to be entering a new phase characterized by identity explorations, instability, self-focus, feeling in-between or in transition, and an age of possibility when they seemed to have "an unparalleled opportunity to transform their lives."[11] The term emerging adulthood arose out of research as the phrase people being interviewed were using to describe the process or journey they were traveling.[12] During this season, "emerging adults develop skills for daily living, gain a better understanding of who they are and what they want from life, and begin to build a foundation for their adult lives."[13]

The idea that this is a life stage has elicited debate primarily from sociologists who believe it is applicable primarily to people who have access to wealth—for example, middle and upper-class families whose children can afford to go to university. Also, some believe that it is just a transition period and not a developmental period.[14] However, despite this critique, one theme remains consistent. Academics and researchers regularly affirm that this is a season of identity formation. That process, along with its impact in the missional formation process, will be explored in the next chapter.

WHAT DOES "FORMATION FOR MISSION" MEAN?

Before delving into that topic, it is beneficial to first explain how we are using the phrase "missional formation." What does it mean? How are we defining it? What role does Christian spiritual formation play in the process when it occurs within a culture that regularly undermines Christian discipleship? We believe that Christian spiritual formation leads to vibrant followers of Jesus who are engaged in congregations and culture. In the United States this formation takes place in a cultural context that is seeking to spiritually form people into consumers, moral intuitionists, and people whose sense of identity is shaped more by postmodern secular and political culture and social media influences[15] than by Jesus, Scripture, and congregational life. Through genuine

Christian spiritual formation, as laid out by authors in the following chapters, these emerging adult disciples will then *live for Christ, enter into congregational life, and engage in mission in distinctively Christian ways.*

As such, this way of viewing emerging adults' formation for mission has affected how this book flows. The first section lays the groundwork for the conversation. The second section unpacks barriers to the Christian spiritual formation process and how ministry leaders are overcoming them. The third section highlights a variety of strategies ministries are using to connect emerging adults to God's mission so they can participate with God's people in meaningful and distinctively Christian ways, and grow through the process. The fourth section highlights a sample of unique approaches and missional insights ministry leaders are discovering when working with racially distinct groups of emerging adults. We then close the book with some final insights and reflections in light of all that has been shared. The appendix provides a historical overview of the impact this age group has made to the broader missions movement.

A REASON FOR HOPE

While the challenges facing the church in reaching and forming emerging adults for mission in this time in history are substantive, we believe there are many reasons to have hope and believe that these trends can change. A study of two thousand unchurched people across the country, including 466 Millennials (born between 1981 and 1996), showed that many were more receptive to Christian faith than expected.[16] Just a couple indicators of this receptivity include: (1) Though 75 percent of unchurched millennials left church for at least a year in their twenties, 40 percent of unchurched millennials expect to attend church regularly in the future. (2) Though 42 percent of unchurched millennials identify as unaffiliated, over half of them say they are "nothing in particular" and are far more spiritually receptive than the ones who say they are atheist or agnostic. Barna Group has also found this increased level of spiritual interest and spiritual conversation for millennials.[17]

In addition, a broad study of forty-five hundred Protestant churches, followed by an in-depth study of sixty churches that are effectively reaching emerging adults, demonstrated ten key best practices that churches reaching emerging adults are pursuing. These leaders model personal outreach, pastors preach hospitably to the unchurched and develop strong entry-point ministries for unchurched people, and there are clear next-step ministries for first-time visitors.[18] The research shows clearly that churches are able to reach and develop emerging adults when they commit to certain practices, priorities, and patterns of relating. In response, we can feel challenged but also hopeful. There are many actions that people who care about emerging adults can take. The following chapters are full of insights, examples, research, and stories to help all who care about their formation for mission!

QUESTIONS FOR DIALOGUE

1. What are the areas of promise you are seeing in emerging adults you know, and where are their areas of deepest vulnerability?

2. What are the more common paths or journeys to adulthood in your context, and how long do you see those processes unfolding?

3. If you could research any issue or question about emerging adulthood, what would you choose and why?

BIBLIOGRAPHY

Arnett, Jeffrey Jensen. "Does Emerging Adulthood Theory Apply across Social Classes? National Data on a Persistent Question." *Emerging Adulthood* 4, no. 4 (2016): 227–35.

———. "Emerging Adulthood: A Theory of Development from the Late Teens through the Twenties." *American Psychologist* 55, no. 5 (2000): 469–80.

———. *Emerging Adulthood: The Winding Road from the Late Teens through the Twenties.* Oxford: Oxford University Press, 2004.

Arnett, Jeffrey Jensen, Marion Kloep, Leo B. Hendry, and Jennifer L. Tanner. *Debating Emerging Adulthood: Stage or Process?* New York: Oxford University Press, 2011.

Arnett, Jeffrey Jensen, and Jennifer L. Tanner. "In Defense of Emerging Adulthood as a Life Stage: Rejoinder to Kloep's and Hendry's Chapters 4 and 5." Pages 121–34 in *Debating Emerging Adulthood: Stage or Process?*, by Jeffrey Jensen Arnett, Marion Kloep, Leo B. Hendry, and Jennifer L. Tanner. New York: Oxford University Press, 2011.

Barna Group. *Gen Z: The Culture, Beliefs, and Motivations Shaping the Next Generation.* Barna Group Publishers, 2018.

———. "Millennial Non-Christians Show Greater Spiritual Curiosity Than Older Adults." 2019. https://www.barna.com/research/millennial-spiritual-curiosity.

Blustein, David L., Anna P. Chaves, Matthew A. Diemer, Laura A. Gallagher, Kevin G. Marshall, Selcuk Sirin, and Kuldhir S. Bhati. "Voices of the Forgotten Half: The Role of Social Class in the School-to-Work Transition." *Journal of Counseling Psychology* 49, no. 3 (2002): 311–23.

Bois-Reymond, Manuela du. "Emerging Adulthood Theory and Social Class." Pages 47–61 in *The Oxford Handbook of Emerging Adulthood.* Edited by Jeffrey Jensen Arnett. Oxford: Oxford University Press, 2016.

Côté, James. "Emerging Adulthood as an Institutionalized Moratorium: Risks and Benefits to Identity Formation."

Pages 85-116 in *Emerging Adults in America: Coming of Age in the 21st Century*. Edited by Jeffrey Jensen Arnett and Jennifer Lynn Tanner. Washington, DC: American Psychological Association, 2006.

Côté, James, and John M. Bynner. "Changes in the Transition to Adulthood in the UK and Canada: The Role of Structure and Agency in Emerging Adulthood." *Journal of Youth Studies* 11, no. 3 (2008): 251-68.

Everts, Don, and Doug Schaupp. *I Once Was Lost: What Postmodern Skeptics Taught Us about Their Path to Jesus*. Downers Grove, IL: IVP Books, 2008.

Kinnaman, David, and Aly Hawkins. *You Lost Me: Why Young Christians Are Leaving the Church ... and Rethinking Faith*. Grand Rapids: Baker, 2011.

Kinnaman, David, and Gabe Lyons. *Unchristian: What a New Generation Really Thinks about Christianity ... and Why It Matters*. Grand Rapids: Baker, 2007.

Kloep, Marion, and Leo B. Hendry. "Rejoinder to Chapters 2 and 3: Critical Comments on Arnett's and Tanner's Approach." Pages 107-20 in *Debating Emerging Adulthood: Stage or Process?*, by Jeffrey Jensen Arnett, Marion Kloep, Leo B. Hendry, and Jennifer L. Tanner. New York: Oxford University Press, 2011.

———. "A Systematic Approach to the Transitions to Adulthood." Pages 53-75 in *Debating Emerging Adulthood: Stage or Process?*, by Jeffrey Jensen Arnett, Marion Kloep, Leo B. Hendry, and Jennifer L. Tanner. New York: Oxford University Press, 2011.

Lederleitner, Mary. "Transition Journeys in Emerging Adulthood as InterVarsity Students Seek to Connect with Faith Communities after Graduation: A Qualitative Study with Educational and Sociological Implications." PhD diss., Trinity Evangelical Divinity School, 2014.

Parks, Sharon Daloz. *Big Questions, Worthy Dreams: Mentoring Young Adults in Their Search for Meaning, Purpose, and Faith*. San Francisco: Jossey-Bass, 2000.

Pew Research Center. "America's Changing Religious Landscape." 2015. https://www.pewforum.org/2015/05/12/americas-changing-religious-landscape/.

———. "U.S. Decline of Christianity Continues at a Rapid Pace: Update on America's Changing Religious Landscape." 2019. https://www.pewforum.org/2019/10/17/in-u-s-decline-of-christianity-continues-at-rapid-pace/.

Richardson, Rick. *You Found Me: New Research on How Unchurched Nones, Millennials, and Irreligious Are Surprisingly Open to Christian Faith*. Downers Grove, IL: InterVarsity Press, 2019.

Silver, Eric. "Students' Attitudes toward College Drinking: A Moral Intuitionist Approach." *Deviant Behavior* 41, no. 8 (2020): 1033-51.

Smith, Christian, Kari Christofferson, Hilary Davidson, and Patricia Snell Herzog. *Lost in Transition: The Dark Side of Emerging Adulthood*. Oxford: Oxford University Press, 2011.

Smith, Christian, and Patricia Snell. *Souls in Transition: The Religious and Spiritual Lives of Emerging Adults*. Oxford: Oxford University Press, 2009.

Syed, Moin, and Lauren L. Mitchell. "How Race and Ethnicity Shape Emerging Adulthood." Pages 87-103 in *The Oxford Handbook of Emerging Adulthood*. Edited by Jeffrey Jensen Arnett. Oxford: Oxford University Press, 2016.

———. "Race, Ethnicity, and Emerging Adulthood: Retrospect and Prospects." *Emerging Adulthood* 1, no. 2 (2013): 83-95.

Van Gennep, Arnold. *The Rites of Passage*. 2nd ed. Chicago: University of Chicago Press, 2019.

Wuthnow, Robert. *After the Baby Boomers: How Twenty- and Thirty-Somethings Are Shaping the Future of American Religion*. Princeton: Princeton University Press, 2007.

2

· · · · ·

The Role of Identity Formation

Mary T. Lederleitner, Andrew
MacDonald, and Rick Richardson

· · · · ·

We were taught to be world changers and I believed it!
But the world is cynical. If you are not with people who
believe that, it is so easy for cynicism to leak in.

—A recent university graduate[1]

Angela is heavily involved in ministry through her local congregation and also through a Black campus ministry.[2] She
said,

> I'm high-identity African American. I looooove my
> culture. I love it! I love what we represent. I love
> who we are. I love going to a church where I can see
> people who look like me worshiping God. We're on

the same battlefield. I love to see that. I love to see
that solidarity. And it's important to me to see in a
world where we are minorities, it's important for
me to see that solidarity. It's important to see that
we are different than what people say we are. You
know, and I can see that in my church. Not everyone
in my church is a statistic. So, to me, being part of
that community combats what the world would tell
me that I am. It combats that completely.

She chuckled and said, "And so, that's why I realize I search
for these places because I do not want to believe what someone
else will say that I am. And I want to have my own identity as an
African American person. And I feel the freedom to grow in that
identity and have that identity when I'm in that place."[3]

UNDERSTANDING THE IDENTITY
FORMATION PROCESS

Whether it is growing to think of oneself as a "world changer" or
finding one's sense of self culturally and missionally by participating in a church, identity formation provides a person's foundation
for adulthood because it is "the process of claiming membership
in the social world" and "standing for something."[4] Because many
authors in the following chapters make reference to this concept,
we would like to highlight four theories that help to explain this
important aspect of human development and share implications
of each theory for the missional formation process. Since David
Setran explains narrative identity so well in a later chapter, we
will not address it at this time.

THE LIFE-CYCLE MODEL

Erik Erikson is the most frequently cited theorist in this area
because of his writing about the human life cycle.[5] He describes

it as having eight stages: infancy, early childhood, play age, school age, adolescence, young adulthood, adulthood, and old age. He says that each stage comes with a unique psychosocial crisis that is common for that specific season of life, but would be considered by society as being unusual or less acceptable in another. In his theory Erikson explains that identity formation is the normal or acceptable developmental process for adolescents and young adults.[6]

He doesn't use the phrase emerging adulthood because at the time he was developing his theory that terminology had not yet been coined. The core idea is that identity formation must be navigated well if a person in their late teens or twenties is going to be able to make adult commitments. Erikson writes that identity formation involves inner agency where various selves are brought into a composite self. He also writes that understanding one's identity becomes more necessary and problematic wherever a wide range of possibilities exists.[7]

The theory is a psychosocial model wherein an identity crisis is navigated, and it works at three levels. The first is the social aspect, rooted in the idea that people's environment is not only around them but "forever in them." The environment in which a person is raised is therefore significant in shaping identity. However, there is also a self aspect. This is composed of a person's "selves" and the "roles" the person plays in society. The third is the ego aspect, which is frequently referred to as ego identity. It is central in the identity formation process but partially unconscious. It involves the process in which each person "must at any given stage of life deal with a changing Self which demands to be synthesized with abandoned and anticipated selves."[8]

"The selves are mostly preconscious," but "they can become conscious" if "the ego agrees to it." Erikson explains there are often "shock-like transitions between these selves," but a healthy personality brings congruence and coherence to them. The reason the concept of identify formation can be challenging to understand is that it is located in the core of the individual and also in the individual's communal culture. Erikson explains that it is "a kind of psychosocial relativity because it involves a process of simultaneous reflection and observation, a process taking place on all levels of mental functioning." A person judges their self based on perceptions of others as others are doing the same.[9]

Identity formation continues throughout a person's lifetime. It is never fully established or unchanging. But it is the process of human development that is seen as normal for this season of life. The primary critique of Erikson's model is an "invisibility of women, class, race and culture,"[10] a problem linked to many theories that emerged at that time in history. However, many who critique the weaknesses of the theory also appreciate aspects of it. For example, one proponent, Sally Archer, explains, "Erikson is not attempting to find the operational definition of identity," but "as a clinician he does an exquisite job of conveying the complexity and richness of a concept that perhaps defies a single definition."[11]

IMPLICATIONS OF ERIKSON'S MODEL

Through Erikson's work, people who are passionate about emerging adults' missional formation process can gain clues and insights that are helpful. There are many paths emerging adults can choose other than following Christ wholeheartedly and caring about God's purposes in the world. How an emerging adult understands "self" and integrates their various selves and identities into a congruent whole is essential for each person who seeks to follow Christ as their Lord. Emerging adults on this journey experience a process of exploration and maturation as they move from self-centered or self-focused worldviews to seeing oneself and the world through God's eyes.

As emerging adults on the journey of missional formation attest, it is often a jarring process to keep growing and learning how to integrate faith into all facets of their lives so they embody a congruent Christlike witness. It is also challenging to learn how to navigate brokenness when their aspirations for congruency are not yet fulfilled. Seasons of reflection, observing others, being observed, and perspective taking are essential for their growth and development. So too is the need to learn how to navigate earlier environments, which Erikson explains are "forever in [emerging adults]." How they make meaning of these earlier environments and experiences they encountered often determines whether they will accept God's love, and whether they will trust, follow, and take the risks faced by all who want to participate in God's mission.

THE IDENTITY-STATUS MODEL

James Marcia builds on Erikson's work. He describes four identity statuses in the identity formation process: foreclosure, diffusion, moratorium, and achievement. A person with a foreclosed identity status is one who has never experienced the identity crisis Erikson describes, yet the person expresses commitment. Marcia explains that with these individuals it is indistinguishable where their parents' goals and values end and where those of the emerging adults begin.[12] People with foreclosed identities are threatened by the idea of deeply exploring and examining their worldviews and the assumptions and values that underpin them.

A person with a diffused identity is characterized by lack of commitment. For example, such a person has "neither decided upon an occupation nor is much concerned about it." There is also a lack of concern for ideological matters, or the person "takes a smorgasbord approach in which one outlook seems as good" as any other.[13] Not only has the person not undergone the identity crisis that Erikson describes, but the person has no interest in entering into that crisis. These individuals are more concerned about living a carefree existence and not being bogged down by commitments.

An individual who is in moratorium has launched him- or herself "into the exploration phase" and is "suffering its consequences."[14] Unlike the foreclosed or diffused identity statuses, these individuals embrace the crisis despite the pain it causes.[15] "Within the moratorium status, guilt and anxiety can become so overwhelming" that the "young person in a moratorium phase may become stuck and despair of ever finding a social choice that feels right." A complexity in this phase is navigating tension inherent in learning how society is going to respond to different choices they might make.[16]

A person who has the identity achievement status has walked through the crisis period and is now "committed to an occupation and ideology," even though the "ultimate choice may be a variation of parental wishes," as Marcia writes. The person has "reevaluated past beliefs and achieved a resolution" that enables the person to act freely in future situations. People with this status often actively seek out opportunities for growth.[17] While a common critique is that these statuses represent personality types rather than a spectrum of human development, this theory has been catalytic in the creation of "identity interventions" that help emerging adults in areas such as therapy, education, pastoral guidance, career counseling, and parenting.[18] The purpose of these identity interventions is to help emerging adults develop and form an identity that enables them to more effectively navigate challenges they face now and additional challenges they are likely to encounter in the years ahead.

IMPLICATIONS OF MARCIA'S MODEL

Regarding the missional formation process, many church and ministry practitioners express that their goal is to facilitate a process that helps emerging adults move from a state of merely believing what they did as an adolescent into a more mature phase of faith development. Many are aided by this model because it can help in discerning where emerging adults are with regard to their faith development. Are they just parroting what they were taught as kids? Are they ambivalent about faith in general and not concerned at all about it? Are they wrestling with faith commitments but not yet sure what they believe? Just as this theory aids people in other fields to create identity interventions for those who would be benefited by them, so too church and ministry practitioners create spaces for dialogue, missional experiences, and other opportunities that will be highlighted in the following chapters. In many ways discipleship is an identity intervention, as people reorient their lives and how they see themselves through the lens of Christ and God's kingdom rather than self-centered orientations. Through meaningful identity interventions, though we refer to them with different terminology, emerging adults can grow and develop a solid foundation of achieved or mature faith identity that leads to using their gifts and talents in meaningful service in ways that further God's purposes in the world.

THE BIO-ECOLOGICAL MODEL

Urie Bronfenbrenner's bio-ecological theory of human development is also referred to frequently in the literature about emerging adulthood. The first version of Bronfenbrenner's theory focused primarily on the developing person and the person's environment, but later it was adapted to also explicitly address the role of genetic inheritance in development.[19] While genetic factors are insightful for a variety of issues such as mental-health conditions that emerge in this season of life, we will highlight other aspects of the theory here.

Bronfenbrenner explains, "The developing person is viewed not merely as a tabula rasa on which the environment makes its impact, but as a growing, dynamic entity that progressively moves into and restructures" the environment in which the person resides. Development is seen as a person's growing understanding of their environment, and their "growing capacity to discover, sustain, or alter its properties."[20]

The theory has both systems and interpersonal components. The ecological environment is conceived as a set of nested structures, and as humans transition among these different nested structures, the roles they occupy change. The theory espouses that "roles have a magiclike power to alter how a person is treated, how

she acts, what she does, and thereby even what she thinks and feels."
Some systems are vast, exerting influence on a developing person,
but the person has no power to influence them in return. In other
systems there is greater mutuality, as individuals are both influenced by them and able to influence them. Bronfenbrenner asserts,
"What matters for behavior and development is the environment
as it is perceived rather than as it may exist in 'objective' reality."[21]

Interpersonal structures serve "as contexts of human development," and this "occurs when one member is paying close and
sustained attention to the activity of the other, who, in turn, at
least acknowledges the interest being shown." This can then evolve
into a situation in which the two participants perceive themselves
as doing something together. Reciprocity begins to take place,
and each person begins influencing the other. Bronfenbrenner
explains, "The optimal situation for learning and development
is one in which the balance of power gradually shifts in favor of
the developing person, in other words, when the latter is given
increasing opportunity to exercise control over the situation."
Simply noticing and paying close attention to people can become
the catalyst for development, and if "one person undergoes developmental change, the other is also likely to do so."[22]

Bronfenbenner argues that by creating quasi-experiments
in various systems it is possible to affect development and even
alter aspects of the systems. He also explains that development is
enhanced if "role demands in the different settings are compatible," and development is optimal when there are supportive links
between various systems or settings.[23]

IMPLICATIONS OF BRONFENBRENNER'S MODEL

Many aspects of Bronfenbrenner's theory will become evident in
the coming chapters. In churches where emerging adults feel seen,
and where they have roles of service and leadership, their missional development can flourish. Their development is impeded
when they lose the ability to engage and shape their environments,

or when they are viewed as leaders in a parachurch ministry context but as pseudo-adolescents until they are married with children in a church context. Being in communities where others are growing in their missional development is potent for emerging adults' own growth and transformation. Many chapters that follow are in various ways unpacking "quasi-experiments" churches and ministries implement to aid the missional formation process of emerging adults.

ETHNIC IDENTITY FORMATION MODEL

There are other theories as well, but for now we will close with the writings of Jean Phinney, the author mentioned most frequently in articles and books regarding ethnic identity formation in emerging adulthood. She writes, "The task of understanding ethnic identity is complicated" given the uniqueness which distinguishes each type of group.[24] Although the historic approach is to examine ethnicity through the lens of intergroup relations, ethnic identity formation looks at the issue with a focus on individuals and their development.[25]

Phinney examines identity formation in light of Erikson's and Marcia's work. She believes ethnic identity formation has three stages: unexamined ethnic identity, ethnic identity search, and achieved ethnic identity. Unexamined ethnic identity is marked by a lack of exploration. The searching stage involves trying to understand the "meaning of ethnicity for oneself," whereas the achievement stage is marked by a "clear" and "confident sense of one's ethnicity."[26] Phinney writes that under the lack of exploration there are two possible subtypes. These include diffusion, as characterized by a lack of interest or concern with ethnicity, and foreclosure, as marked the absorption of uncritically examined opinions of others.

She writes that although "developmental psychology has been more attentive to the role of history and culture than some other branches of psychology, the emphasis in the field remains on processes of growth and change that are assumed to be common across all people."[27] In her opinion, this approach is too simplistic, given "identity formation involves the development of both personal identity and group identity."[28] She believes studying identity formation from an ecological or systems perspective is much better. However, doing that type of research is far more difficult. Phinney writes:

> All young people must navigate complex worlds of home, school, friends, work, and leisure, in contexts that are continually changing. Yet relatively little research takes seriously the need to deal with the complexity and contextually embedded nature of human development. Even for those who accept the importance of viewing development as dynamic and contextually embedded, it is a daunting task to frame research questions and design studies that acknowledge, let alone deal with, this complexity. As a result, contextual factors are rarely addressed in depth, and much research continues to emphasize universal processes.[29]

Despite these complexities, she believes "there is a progression in normal development from an unformed or diffuse identity to a secure committed identity."[30]

IMPLICATIONS OF PHINNEY'S MODEL

Emerging adults are immersed in the milieu of ethnic diversity. Many emerging adults wrestle with making meaning of their own ethnic identities, as well as understanding themselves in communities with ethnic others. A number of chapters will highlight this as well. However, God's mission is also marked by diversity and the reality of people from every tongue, tribe, and culture worshiping and being together as they engage in God's kingdom for all eternity (Rev 5:8–9). This theory urges church and mission practitioners to not rush or minimize the racial and ethnic identity pieces in practice and in research. As such, we believe this theory is also significant as we think through our work and ministries with emerging adults.

REFLECTING FURTHER ABOUT THE MISSIONAL FORMATION PROCESS

Missional formation in emerging adulthood is significantly intertwined with the identity formation process. Pastors and ministry workers frequently emphasize spiritual formation as essential, which is a work of the Holy Spirit that "forms the life of Christ in us" and places Jesus rather than us at the center.[31] To facilitate that development, people participate in a variety of spiritual disciplines, and while these in and of themselves do not form the life of Christ in people, they foster a greater openness for the Holy Spirit to do this spiritual work in our hearts.

What is often highlighted less is that "spiritual formation mostly involves paying attention and participating in who God is—Father, Son, and Holy Spirit—and what he does."[32] That is the critical intersecting piece for understanding missional formation. By paying attention to who God is and what he is doing in the world, and by being in community with others who are relating to God and engaging in activities that encompass his purposes, emerging adults make meaning that can become foundational for how they live the rest of their lives. Through that endeavor they transform in Christlikeness, as they watch God and others on the journey.

As missiologist Christopher Wright has argued, mission is best understood asour committed participation as God's people, at God's invitation and command, in God's own mission within the history of God's world for the redemption of God's creation."[33] In that grand narrative of God's mission and what God is doing in this world, a composite self begins to emerge that has Christ at the center, and together with God's people they influence communities to have and keep Christ at the center. In that missional formation process emerging adults begin freely offering themselves and their gifts to be a blessing in the world, to further God's loving and redemptive purposes through the guidance of the Holy Spirit in community with others.

THE OPPORTUNITY BEFORE US

Those wishing to aid emerging adults on a missional journey can facilitate deep and meaningful learning communities so they can be influenced in positive ways by their peers, and better identify and understand how God is working in the world. But scholars note that finding a community of belonging that encourages intentional development can be one of the most difficult tasks emerging adults face.[34] Even though religion can be a principle source of identity strength, a longitudinal study with emerging adults indicated that when it came to participating in churches the prevailing sentiment was that they didn't feel a sense of belonging in them.[35]

Many churches continue to provide ample resources for the development of children, teens, married couples, and older adults, but "almost nothing" in comparison to help emerging adults weather this formative time of life. Congregations "could be a valuable source of support" for emerging adults, but that potential is rarely realized. Many major decisions such as which career to pursue and who to marry are often being made "after these support systems have ceased to function."[36] Our hope is that this book will enable readers to provide the support, encouragement, and challenge emerging adults need grow in missional formation so that in Christ they can wholly fulfill God's purposes for their lives and make their best contributions in the world.

QUESTIONS FOR DIALOGUE

1. Which theory of identity formation intrigues you the most and why?

2. Which roles or selves in emerging adulthood do you find most difficult to bring together into a composite "self"?

3. What "quasi-experiments" might be beneficial to try in your setting as you seek to facilitate missional formation in the lives of emerging adults?

4. Where are churches in your area strong at providing a community for emerging adult development, and where are they weakest and in need of help?

BIBLIOGRAPHY

Archer, Sally L. "A Feminist's Approach to Identity Research." Pages 25-49 In *Adolescent Identity Formation*. Edited by Gerald R. Adams, Thomas P. Gullotta, and Raymond Montemayor. Newbury Park, CA: Sage, 1992.

Arnett, Jeffrey Jensen. "Does Emerging Adulthood Theory Apply across Social Classes? National Data on a Persistent Question." *Emerging Adulthood* 4, no. 4 (2016): 227-35.

————. 2015. *Emerging Adulthood: The Winding Road from the Late Teens through the Twenties*. 2nd ed. New York: Oxford University Press, 2015.

Blustein, David L., Anna P. Chaves, Matthew A. Diemer, Laura A. Gallagher, Kevin G. Marshall, Selcuk Sirin, and Kuldhir S. Bhati. "Voices of the Forgotten Half: The Role of Social Class in the School-to-Work Transition." *Journal of Counseling Psychology* 49, no. 3 (2002): 311-23.

Bois-Reymond, Manuela du. "Emerging Adulthood Theory and Social Class." Pages 47–61 in *The Oxford Handbook of Emerging Adulthood*. Edited by Jeffrey Jensen Arnett. Oxford: Oxford University Press, 2016.

Bronfenbrenner, Urie, ed. *The Ecology of Human Development: Experiments by Nature and Design*. Cambridge: Harvard University Press, 1979.

———. *Making Human Beings Human: Bioecological Perspectives on Human Development*. Thousand Oaks, CA: Sage, 2005.

Côté, James. "Emerging Adulthood as an Institutionalized Moratorium: Risks and Benefits to Identity Formation." Pages 85–116 in *Emerging Adults in America: Coming of Age in the 21st Century*. Edited by Jeffrey Jensen Arnett and Jennifer Lynn Tanner. Washington, DC: American Psychological Association, 2006.

Côté, James, and John M. Bynner. "Changes in the Transition to Adulthood in the UK and Canada: The Role of Structure and Agency in Emerging Adulthood." *Journal of Youth Studies* 11, no. 3 (2008): 251–68.

Erikson, Erik. *Childhood and Society*. New York: W. W. Norton, 1950.

———. *Identity and the Life Cycle*. New York: W. W. Norton, 1959.

———. *Identity: Youth and Crisis*. New York: W. W. Norton, 1968.

———. *The Life Cycle Completed*. New York: W. W. Norton, 1997.

Josselson, Ruthellen. "Theory of Identity Development and the Question of Intervention." Pages 12–25 in *Interventions for Adolescent Identity Development*. Edited by Sally L. Archer. Thousand Oaks, CA: Sage, 1994.

Lederleitner, Mary. "Transition Journeys in Emerging Adulthood as InterVarsity Students Seek to Connect with Faith Communities after Graduation: A Qualitative Study with Educational and Sociological Implications." PhD diss., Trinity Evangelical Divinity School, 2014.

Marcia, James E. "Development and Validity of Ego-Identity Status." *Journal of Personality and Social Psychology* 3, no. 5 (1966): 551–58.

———. "Identity and Psychotherapy." Pages 29–46 in *Interventions for Adolescent Identity Development*. Edited by Sally L. Archer. Thousand Oaks, CA: Sage, 1994.

McKinney, John Paul. "Identity: A Construct Comes of Age and Starts to Work." Pages 245–57 in *Interventions for Adolescent Identity Development*. Edited by Sally L. Archer. Thousand Oaks, CA: Sage, 1994.

Peterson, Eugene H. "Spirituality/Spiritual Formation." In *Dictionary for Theological Interpretation of the Bible*. Edited by Kevin J. Vanhoozer. Grand Rapids: Baker Books, 2005.

Phinney, Jean. "Ethnic Identity in Adolescents and Adults: Review of Research." *Psychological Bulletin* 3, no. 3 (1990): 499–514.

———. "Identity Formation across Cultures: The Interaction of Personal, Societal, and Historical Change." *Human Development* 43 (2000): 27–31.

———. "Understanding Development in Cultural Contexts: How Do We Deal with the Complexity?" *Human Development* 53 (2010): 33–38.

Schwartz, Seth J. "The Evolution of Eriksonian and Neo-Eriksonian Identity Theory and Research: A Review and Integration." *Identity: An International Journal of Theory and Research* 1, no. 1 (2001): 7–58.

Smith, Christian, and Patricia Snell. *Souls in Transition: The Religious and Spiritual Lives of Emerging Adults*. Oxford: Oxford University Press, 2009.

Syed, Moin, and Lauren L. Mitchell. "How Race and Ethnicity Shape Emerging Adulthood." Pages 87–103 in *The Oxford Handbook of Emerging Adulthood*. Edited by Jeffrey Jensen Arnett. Oxford: Oxford University Press, 2016.

————. "Race, Ethnicity, and Emerging Adulthood: Retrospect and Prospects." *Emerging Adulthood* 1, no. 2 (2013): 83–95.

Tajfel, Henri. "Social Psychology of Intergroup Relations." *Annual Review of Psychology* 33 (1982): 1–39.

Wright, Christopher J. H. *The Mission of God's People: A Biblical Theology of the Church's Mission.* Grand Rapids: Zondervan, 2010.

Wuthnow, Robert. *After the Baby Boomers: How Twenty- and Thirty-Somethings Are Shaping the Future of American Religion.* Princeton: Princeton University Press, 2007.

Facilitating Missional Development

. . . . .

Yet you, Lord, are our Father.
We are the clay, you are the potter;
we are all the work of your hand.

—Isaiah 64:8 NIV

For we are his workmanship, created in Christ Jesus for good works,
which God prepared beforehand, that we should walk in them.

—Ephesians 2:10 ESV

If we hope to be fruitful facilitators in emerging adults' formation for mission, we need to be grounded and humble regarding
who is truly behind any and all changes that happen. It is our
Heavenly Father who is shaping and molding all of us. By "fixing
our eyes on Jesus, the author and perfector of faith," we can find
the endurance needed to bear with others through what at times
can be a painful and arduous journey (Heb 12:1-13 NASB). We are
not asked or expected to help people change through our own
strength, but we are to abide in Christ in such a way that God
works in and through us (John 15:1-11).

The "hall of faith," as Hebrews 11:1-40 is commonly referred to, is filled with people from so many different generations who followed God faithfully and sought to live out his purposes in their lives and contexts. May we be faithful in how we come alongside emerging adults as they seek to understand what God is calling them into and what faithfulness to him looks like for their own lives, their faith communities, and their generation. The following chapters provide a glimpse into four key areas where many emerging adults struggle and how others are learning to walk with them in ways that support their missional formation.

3

· · · · ·

Emerging Adult Sexuality
and Discipleship

Charles Stokes

· · · · ·

*Chastity is the most unpopular of the Christian virtues. There
is no getting away from it: the old Christian rule is, "Either
marriage, with complete faithfulness to your partner, or else
total abstinence." Now this is so difficult and so contrary to our
instincts, that obviously either Christianity is wrong or our sexual
instinct, as it now is, has gone wrong. One or the other. Of course,
being a Christian, I think it is the instinct which has gone wrong.*

—C. S. Lewis, *Mere Christianity*

One of my favorite emerging adults had a hard time emerging.
My wife and I met Callie and her two best friends, three college freshmen, when they started attending the college Bible study
we led through our church. Cassie became our regular babysitter,

and our children adored her. She and her crew seemed like they had stepped right out of a Disney Channel sitcom: a multiracial trio with a naive but optimistic view of the world. As they started college, they proudly professed to be virgins who were waiting for marriage. By the time they all graduated, their combined experiences had included drunken orgies, a broken engagement (because she cheated), the embrace of a bisexual identity, a suicide attempt, anorexia, phone calls to us in the middle of the night while having sex with a stranger, and several instances of self-mutilation.

We lost touch with Callie's friends after they left the church, but Callie, whom we continue to love dearly, stayed in touch with us throughout, even as she ignored most of our advice. We listened to and loved her over endless coffee dates. We challenged her once, "Why not try abstaining from sex for a month? Just a month. Just give your body time to calm down so that you can think straight." She sadly admitted that even if she tried, she couldn't do it. She was stuck in a cycle of casual sexual encounters. One of the hardest conversations we've ever had was telling her she could no longer nanny our children because of her drug use. It broke all three of our hearts. Believe it or not, though, after two rounds in a long-term treatment center (we wrote her encouraging letters) and countless hours of therapy (we attended with her and held her as she cried), Callie is in a pretty healthy place now and is even drawing on her struggles to help others. But, it took her longer to *recover* from college than it had taken her to complete her degree.

I learned from ministering to Callie and company to never assume anything with evangelical young adults; the sexual ethic of this world can latch onto them faster than you can catch your breath. I also learned a lesson I'll bet you already know. In the process of missional formation, there's no substitute or shortcut for loving relationships, for encountering emerging adults where they are. In that spirit of encounter, I begin by describing some of the most important features of emerging adults sexuality. For if we don't understand how to navigate this aspect of emerging adulthood, their missional development may be cut short, or, worse, they may disengage from Christian community because it doesn't address what they believe to be one of the most important parts of their lives.

SIX FEATURES OF EMERGING ADULT SEXUALITY

People wanting to facilitate the process of missional formation in the lives of emerging adults can benefit from understanding the six trends below. These trends include insights synthesized from the research of fellow sociologists Mark Regnerus, Jeremy Uecker, and Brad Wilcox—as well as my own observations from twenty-plus years of research and ministry with emerging adults.

COMPULSORY EXPRESSIVISM

This generation has fully embraced the secular idea that we are clever animals and that we must find ways to give expression to our sexual desires, lest we risk suppressing them and doing ourselves great psychological harm. Sigmund Freud would be proud. Emerging adults who are unwilling or unable to express some form of sexuality (even if it is asexuality) may be suspected of emotional impairment at best, and deception or bigotry at worst. Consider Iris Caldwell, a contestant on the reality show "Married at First Sight." Her faith-based virginity was consistently presented as a potential obstacle to her finding a match, even prompting a pastoral counselor to discuss it with her as if it were a problem.[1] In the end, her matched husband rejected her, citing that he didn't want "the responsibility" that marrying a "sexually immature" person entails. Indeed, ours is a world where emerging adult virgins find it necessary to hide or apologize for their chastity.

ORIENTING IDENTITY

Sex has long ceased to be a private, personal matter. Sexuality, then, has become a "master identity" category. Of course, LGBTQ+

persons have long had to actively wrestle with sexuality because of their minority experiences in a world where heterosexuality was taken for granted. But because available sexual categories have multiplied—and exploded in popularity—Gen Z has grown up with sexuality as an identity that *everyone* needs to wrestle with. Moreover, because sexuality is now typically portrayed as a fixed characteristic to be discovered (rather than sexual actions to be chosen), young people feel pressure to sort out their sexual identity as soon as possible (in some cases even before puberty!). Combining this trend with the previous one of compulsory expressivism creates a social environment where a primary task for young Americans is to experiment with sexual behaviors in order to discover their governing sexual identity.[2]

SELECTIVE TOLERANCE

Around 2000, researchers asked college women to rank several value statements about sex and sexuality. The statement that earned the second-highest level of agreement (83 percent) was, "I should not judge anyone's sexual conduct except my own."[3] Research interviews with men and women further revealed that emerging adults feel enormous pressure to commend their peers' sexual expression, even if it goes against their own values.[4] Agreeing to disagree is insufficient; sexual behaviors must be affirmed. Noncompliance on this matter is what is *not* tolerated. Thus, emerging adults find themselves in a wide-open sexual arena, where they are required to participate—either as actors or applauding audience. They are not allowed to reference traditional sources of sexual guidance (family, ethnic culture, religion) except in the privacy of their own heads.

Before moving to the final three trends, it's important to note that while there is plenty of trauma related to emerging adults sexuality, most sexually permissive emerging adults don't associate their choices with their unhappiness—*if* they are unhappy at all. Indeed,

Premarital Sex in America, Cheap Sex, and *The Future of Christian Marriage* provide myriad examples of emerging adults (especially college-going men) who are quite happy with the current state of affairs.[5] Some men and women feel liberated and empowered by modern sexual culture. And though a significant number of emerging adults women express dissatisfaction (especially as they get older and the "hookup culture" takes its toll), they may not view current sexual culture as the source of their relational problems. This is to say, Christian parents and ministers of emerging adults shouldn't necessarily expect many "prodigals" to return home, enlightened and ready to comply. Even after being burned by destructive sexual behaviors, some will still see the church as the *last* place to look for advice. Most of them will not be coming to us; we will have to find other ways to reach them. And now, on to the bad news.

SHAME AND CONFUSION

Teaching sociology at a Christian university, I occasionally solicit my students' opinions on sexuality and Christianity. Not much of what they tell me surprises me anymore, but one theme continues to gut me every time: *shame.* Keep in mind that many of these students are active Christians, putting their faith to work in ways that impress and inspire me. Rather than a celebration of the wonders of love and sex, or the joys of a happy romance, they tell me they feel condemned and dirty. The students say that their ministers rarely talk about sex, and that when they do, the statements feel canned, lacking real conviction. In this vacuum of leadership, shame reigns, as peers gossip about each other or anxiously confess (or cloak) their forbidden sexual desires.

Some of my secular peers would blame Christianity and its outdated morals for this sad state. But I suspect it's mostly because these Christian emerging adults (and perhaps their ministers) have been silenced and disoriented by the current sexual climate. *Their* voices rarely show up in the research, and they are certainly not accurately represented in the media! They've been told that what their faith asks of them is not only unhealthy but practically impossible. And, at least for many of the students I've talked to, churches and parachurch ministries haven't found effective ways to make biblical sexuality defensible, much less an aspiration. So my Christian students feel confused, conflicted, and most of all, ashamed.

DIVERGING DESTINIES

One of the least discussed but most important trends in America over the last thirty years has been the complete unraveling of lower-class families. College is now the site of the great family divide, as Americans who complete a college degree are much more likely to marry, have their children grow up with both married parents, and avoid divorce. Ironically, mid-twentieth-century progressives thought it would be the privileged who would cast aside the patriarchal chains of marriage for more flexible forms of family. Instead, well-educated Americans look more conventional in their families (celebrity relationships are not representative of well-educated Americans), while less-educated adults and children face the world less connected and more alone than ever before.[6] Layer systemic racial prejudice onto the challenges of social class, and less-privileged Black families face enormous obstacles. While the ethnic picture beyond Black and white is more complicated, the important takeaway from this trend is that the impact of the first three trends is experienced differently by different subcultural groups. Lower-class Asian American emerging adult sexuality is not the same as upper-class Asian American emerging adult sexuality is not the same as upper-class Latinx sexuality, and so on. I find it helpful to think of the first three trends as a massive weather system—all emerging adults are being affected by it, but some of them live in sturdy houses while others have cardboard boxes. Ministering to young adults will require sensitivity to the specific social context.

NONRELATIONAL SEXUAL ENCOUNTERS

A surprise to no one, recent sociological research tells us that "cheap" interpersonal sex is easier to come by than ever.[7] And so it may be hard to imagine, especially given the trends listed above, but emerging adults are *actually* having less sex. Well, at least, they're having less *actual* sex. Pornography-fueled masturbation is taking a growing share of the sexual-experience market. Some have blamed economic hardships for the trend, while others implicate our increased usage of electronics.[8] I suspect the culmination of some larger trends (outlined in the next section) is the main driver. While the research is still developing in the United States, if the patterns are similar to what has happened in Japan,[9] then two factors are involved. First, emerging adults view relationships though a consumer lens. Every relational interaction involves at least a subconscious cost-benefit analysis. And apparently, a growing number of emerging adults are deciding that having sex with another person isn't worth the trouble. Forget cheap sex. Sex with yourself is even cheaper. In most secular audiences, the "revelation" I just dropped would get a "[Yawn] So what?" A particularly snarky commenter might even venture, "Doesn't that just reduce the abortions that you Christians hate?"

I get it. Porn has become normalized, and masturbation is just another of the mandatorily celebrated sexual practices. But read these next sentences slowly to let them sink in: young adults at the peak of their fertility are having less sex with each other at a time when sex has never been easier for them to access. One of the most powerful and basic human drives is being subverted, exactly when it would be expected to be strongest. Our emerging adults are fasting at a feast of their own making. How did we get here?

A TALE OF TWO TECHNOLOGIES

Transforming behavior around something as basic and biological as the reproductive drive takes some pretty powerful cultural magic. Progressive ideologies about sexuality aren't enough by themselves to move the needle of normality. Technology is the real change agent.

When I was a graduate student at the university of Texas at Austin, I taught a class on romantic relationships. One day I had the class brainstorm everything they could think of associated with "sex." As you might imagine, coming from students at a large, public university, many of the things they mentioned wouldn't be suitable for mentioning in a sermon. There were some laughs, a couple of somber moments, and overall, a pretty thorough coverage of what sex means in the minds of privileged twenty-somethings. But you know what they never mentioned in about ten minutes of pretty detailed brainstorming? Babies. A class of over forty students said whatever they thought about sex until they were out of ideas and it didn't occur to one of them to connect sex with making children. What social force could so radically separate two things (sex and babies) that had been inextricably linked in human minds since the beginning? The pill.[10]

Before the pill, the social institution of family organically provided the norms for sex, because sex *might* make babies, and babies have to be cared for (by families). Across cultures, religions have almost always also had some vested interest in sex, in part because the magnitude of the moral consequences of sex was obvious so long as sex and procreation were linked. After all, anyone who has held a newborn intuitively senses the moral gravity of caring for a helpless human life. But as the taken-for-granted connection between sex and procreation rapidly became the taken-for-granted *separation* of the two, sex became *cheap*—more casual amusement than profound potential co-creation.[11] In step, the taken-for-granted moral authority of religion and family regarding sex was thus widely challenged.[12] Into this morally contested space, electronic media (e-media) has enabled social institutions other than church and family to become the authorities on sex. Two aspects of e-media are especially noteworthy for our discussion of emerging adult sexuality.

First, e-media products are removed from bodily realities but can be subconsciously interpreted as normal. In other words, purveyors of e-media can just make stuff up, and it seems so real that the *automated, emotional system of our brain* is fooled. Obviously, anyone will tell you they don't *really* believe all they watch, but this response is only true when we actively engage the *rational, deliberative part of our brain* to critically distinguish the real from fictional elements.[13] Of course, that's not how we typically consume e-media—news, maybe, but not the passive entertainment that populates our Netflix watchlist. Instead, we intuitively imagine that e-media is based on the real, normal world out there. If what we experience in reality doesn't fit our e-media-constructed world, we usually blame the gap on our limited perception. Against e-media's illusory worldview of sex, the more organically grounded institutions of family and religion seem less appealing.

Second, e-media is enabled by broadcast technologies that directly socialize viewers, without interference from intermediary institutions. Before e-media's ubiquitous screens, parents filtered the information that reached their children. And usually the information that reached parents had already been curated by other social institutions (churches, schools, governments, newspapers) that often saw themselves as having some moral responsibility for crafting a healthy society. But today, whatever sells (or generates clicks) is king for e-media. Thus, the current generation of children have been socialized (taught what is normal) about sex not by families and religious organizations, but by wizards of illusion whose moral authority is to the almighty dollar.

Social change is complicated. Chemical contraception and electronic media aren't the only causes of shifting sexual norms. But I highlight these two technologies for a couple of reasons. First, chemical contraception and e-media are so fundamentally woven into our social fabric that it should be apparent there is no going back. Subcultural groups might resist the influence of one or the other of these technologies, but the broader society, including most Christians, will continue to embrace them. Second, understanding the influence of these two technologies on emerging adult sexuality can help us better understand the emerging adult sexual worldview.

Now, on to some suggestions for how to better love emerging adults around issues of sexuality. I've picked three ideas that I think are especially countercultural while directly addressing emerging adult sexuality both in its features and causes. Also, I'm assuming that the suggestions below would be attempted in the context of loving, grace-filled relationships with emerging adults.

THREE RADICAL, REDEMPTIVE IDEAS

So how do those who care about the missional formation of emerging adults respond to the challenges of modern sexual culture? Cultivating compassionate, grace-filled personal relationships will always in vogue. Building on the foundation of those relationships, the following three ideas are able to draw emerging adults deeper into radical, missional discipleship.

RECOVERING AND PRACTICING THEOLOGY OF THE BODY

Like so many emerging adults, Callie had body issues. Popular culture simultaneously idolizes and despises human bodies. On the one hand, we are told we are essentially slaves to our bodily passions (we must act on our desires or risk losing our identities), while on the other we are encouraged to technologically modify the natural operation of our (presumably inadequate) bodies. The early church had body issues, too. Several early heresies (often collectively called Gnosticism) taught that the human body was an inferior shell that contained our true spiritual selves. Debates around these heresies were not a sideshow;

they directly affected the church's understanding of the identity of Christ. Could a purely spiritual God *really* be united with a fleshly human body? The orthodox Christian teaching that emerged from the debates[14] holds that God (the Son) indeed had, even still has, a body. What's more, redeemed humans, after the resurrection, will have bodies like that of the risen Christ. These are not esoteric doctrines, relegated to dusty tomes of church history. Misunderstanding of our bodies is actually at the root of all dysfunctional sexuality.

To quickly summarize a set of ideas that would take (and deserves) volumes,[15] the big idea here is that what we do with our bodies matters. Even secular brain science supports the profound body-mind connection.[16] How we think changes our bodies, and how we act changes our minds. This is no more profoundly illustrated than in sexual intercourse. No wonder Paul says, "Flee from sexual immorality. All other sins a person commits are outside the body, but whoever sins sexually, sins against their own body. ... Therefore, honor God with your bodies" (1 Cor 6:18, 20 NIV).[17] Emerging adults are immersed in a popular culture that tells them "What happens in Vegas [or, really, anywhere among consenting adults], stays in Vegas." Christian doctrine says that what we do with our bodies has temporal and potentially eternal consequences.

It is critical to find compelling ways to present Christian doctrines more effectively and at younger ages.[18] Waiting until young adulthood is too late. Many emerging adults are attracted to the organic and are showing signs of becoming fatigued with the electronic technologies they can't escape. My son, upon reaching age eighteen and receiving our permission to open social media accounts, decided none of them were worth the headaches he had witnessed among his friends. He's very social and loves a party, but he sticks with texting and GroupMe (and secretly, I couldn't be more pleased). Emerging adults long for the authentic in a world of ephemera, and a few can sense the emptiness of consumerism, even as they are swept along by it. Christianity has a meta-story that combats all of these toxic elements, if only we can learn to tell it well.

The theology of the body cannot be simply talked about, however. Baked into the doctrine itself is the necessity of practice. When we worship God, we do it with our bodies, not just our minds. We love others by practical acts of service and, especially, our attentive presence.

Our bodies are worth our tender care and should never be despised. Our bodies are capable of reproduction, and this is a profound honor, not to be casually discarded. Even those "bodies" who seemingly can do nothing (the unborn, the severely impaired, the dying) are worthy of respect. Whatever ills emerging adult sexuality can be redeemed in a proper theology of the body.

ENDORSING SACRED SINGLENESS

Looking back, I think one of the things that haunted Callie and her friends was that they had no idea how to orient their sexual feelings toward honoring God. They knew what not to do—have sex. But church didn't have much to say about what they could say yes to, other than heterosexual marriage. For many emerging adults, heterosexual marriage is a scary or distant prospect because of the fear of divorce, an apparent lack of suitable or interested partners, or the (perceived) need for economic stability that may never come. For others, heterosexual marriage seems impossible because they are same-sex attracted, gender nonconforming, or simply uninterested in sex. Essentially, for one reason or another, heterosexual marriage is not a present reality for most young adults. But their sexual feelings are *very* present. If the Christian theology of the body is so comprehensively helpful, shouldn't it speak to the situations of these emerging adults?

Jesus said some strange things about marriage. He took a hard line against divorce, and when his listeners balked, he replied, "Not everyone can accept this word, but only those to whom it has been given. For there are eunuchs who were born that way, and there are eunuchs who have been made eunuchs by others—and there are those who choose to live like eunuchs for the sake of the kingdom of heaven. The one who can accept this should accept it" (Matt 19:11-12 NIV). I argue that without integrating this teaching from Jesus, we won't be able to present a coherent Christian sexuality to this generation. Here's why.

Jesus is solemnly stating that we can love, serve, and know God wholly and completely without ever acting on sexual desires. Eunuchs were people who couldn't have sex, either naturally ("born that way") or because they had been castrated by people who wished to use them as household slaves. The link here between sex and reproduction—and between sex and marriage—would have been obvious to Jesus's listeners (and to generations of pre-1960s Christians, who didn't live in a birth control–saturated world). The third group of people Jesus mentions *live like* eunuchs, meaning they don't have sex, on purpose, in order to best serve God. This state of life had been "given" to them, suggestive of a gift.

Paul assumes the same link between marriage and sex when he teaches the Corinthians (the promiscuity of Corinth, as you may know, would have embarrassed Vegas), "if they cannot control themselves, they should marry, for it is better to marry than to burn with passion." And he uses the same gift-giving language when he talks about his own celibacy: "I wish that all of you were as I am [single and not having sex]. But each of you has your own gift from God" (1 Cor 7:7-9). Paul himself served God as unmarried and chaste—and he makes it clear later that this was by his choice (1 Cor 9:5). In the same way, countless Christians through the centuries have dedicated their sexuality to God. Flowing from a Christian theology of the body, sacred (chaste) singleness is a way of honoring God in our bodies that *embraces* our sexuality (whatever those sexual feelings, desires, or abilities are) by offering our whole selves as a gift to God. But the teaching of and living witness of chaste singleness is missing in large parts of Christianity.[19]

Recovering a robust, living witness of chaste singleness in our churches offers two critical benefits. First, all of the other biblical teachings on sexuality only make sense if it is possible to be fully, healthily human while *not* acting on our sexual desires. Otherwise, it would be cruel to proscribe any consensual sexual behaviors at all. Chaste singleness says we don't need sexual relationships— *or* the nonrelational "sex" growing in popularity—in order to be fully realized humans. In fact, eschewing these is both a sacrifice pleasing to God, and a gift *from* God.

A second benefit of recovering chaste singleness is that it beautifully reminds us that we love God with our whole selves, which necessarily includes our bodies. Recall the earlier discussion on the theology of the body. What we do, how we act, is an essential part of our worship. As Christians, every part of our embodied human experience is to be offered to God, including our sexuality. As Jesus emphasizes with his discussion of the different kinds of eunuchs, there is a diverse range of human sexual feeling, desire, and ability, but *everyone* is still able to offer their sexuality as a gift to God. Of course, Jesus doesn't assume that such an offering is easy. Orienting any of our passions toward God is difficult. It's why, after reminding them of God's incredible love for them, Paul calls the Roman Christians to "offer your bodies as living sacrifices" (Rom 12:1). This is nothing less than a call to total surrender of our whole selves. Such a "living sacrifice" is only possible by God's grace, a grace capable of covering every faulty attempt we make at surrender.

TEACHING TIME-BOUND COMMITMENTS

As Callie (and friends) would occasionally share about their struggles with their sexual relationships, one of the most striking aspects was how fleeting, even disposable, their experiences were. It was almost compulsive for them to "move on" without wrestling with the consequences of their actions. And based on what I've seen in the research, they were hardly extreme examples. Making and keeping commitments is not exactly a strength of many emerging adults. By contrast, I've often seen the opposite problem from very devout emerging adults. Determined not to participate in the hookup culture, they either completely avoid romantic relationships or prematurely overcommit in the first "good" romance they encounter. The results of either of these strategies can be just as sexually frustrating, if not as damaging, as sexual experimentation. I believe one of the major underlying issues is that the pop-cultural script for romantic relationships is deeply flawed.

To the degree that any kind of cultural norms and directives still exist for dating, the prescription is to experimentally grow in intimacy with the potential partner until either confirming a deeper commitment[20] or breaking up because the relationship is no longer a good fit. This isn't too different from how we treat consumer goods. As every "as seen on TV" product company can attest, customers love to hear, "100 percent satisfaction guaranteed or return for a full refund!" But as relational strategies go, it's difficult to think of a better way to condition our souls for instability. I call it "divorce training." Surely we can do better?

A much more sensible approach is to make time-bound commitments as we move through romantic relationships. The commitment length and purpose should be tailored to the specific situation. For instance, a couple in the early stages of a relationship may decide to stay open to seeing other people, but promise not to enter into an exclusive relationship with anyone else either for three months. At the end of three months, they can reevaluate and decide what to do: make another time-bound commitment (the same kind again, or maybe more serious this time), or go their separate ways, with no blame placed on either party (assuming everyone kept the previous promise). On the other hand, a couple who are sure they are in love could commit to date one another exclusively for six months, while praying for wisdom about whether to get engaged. They might even want to get more specific: commit to going out at least once a week, taking turns planning the date, perhaps. Or they can commit to talking through a list of ten important topics. Couples should definitely discuss their commitments to physical boundaries and how they will support these commitments through accountability and support. Making and keeping these promises, which are important but much less profound than marriage, is practice in the all-important skill of fidelity. After all, even Christian marriage is a kind of time-bound commitment, except that the length of time is uncertain. As opposed to "divorce training," I call this the "breakup-free" approach, and it comes with a big payoff. It helps emerging adults trade in their commitment phobia for a gently growing confidence.

Often this stage can help open the eyes of an emerging adult who watches their potential "soulmate" fail at even lower-level promises. My wife and I have mentored many couples through these time-bound commitments. We've seen most thrive and grow closer and more confident. Two of our couples crashed and burned simply because one of the two people couldn't even keep the first commitment. It was much better for them to learn early in the dating process than a year into marriage.

When suggesting time-bound commitments, I sometimes hear the concern that they are unromantic. My answer is that they are infinitely more romantic than relational insecurity or breaking up. I think most of the resistance here is that we are emotionally attached to a romantic narrative that is more Hollywood than reality. Time-bound commitments need not remove spontaneity or romantic gestures; those elements are totally up to the couple's creativity. Also, I'm not suggesting that time-bound commitments could ever replace offering our sexuality as part of our living sacrifice to God. They are merely one sensible way to do it.

FINAL THOUGHTS

Callie and her friends illustrate only one part of the story of emerging adult sexuality. As noted above, the sexual experiences of young adults vary widely by social class and ethnicity. And, though they are a minority, there are also emerging adults who are striving to align their sexuality with the teaching of Scripture. I've been blessed to know, and sometimes counsel, some of these devout emerging adults. They are a living witness that—just as it did in the early church—Christianity still has the resources to guide emerging adults through a high-risk sexual landscape. Among these resources are a robust theology of the body, the possibility of chaste singleness as a healthy way of expressing sexuality, and using time-bound commitments to sensibly pace romantic relationships.

Having an effective approach for addressing sexuality is a critical piece in the missional formation process. The strategy we choose will either attract or repel emerging adults; it will provide a bridge that enables them to keep growing in their faith and witness, or create a chasm that will be hard for them to cross on their journeys. As G. K. Chesterton said, "The Christian ideal has not been tried and found wanting. It has been found difficult; and left untried."[21] May the Lord help us love and serve both those who are struggling like Callie and those who are trying the narrow, difficult way.

QUESTIONS FOR DIALOGUE

1. In what ways (if any) are you integrating conversations about sexuality into outreach or discipleship endeavors with emerging adults?

2. What has been the fruit or impact of your current approach?

3. Which of the six features of emerging adult sexuality do you think are most prevalent in your context? Provide examples or stories to support your choice, but please use pseudonyms to honor people's privacy.

4. Which redemptive idea(s) do you believe would be most effective in your context and why?

BIBLIOGRAPHY

Blankenhorn, David. *The Future of Marriage.* New York: Encounter Books, 2007.

Bogle, Kathleen A. *Hooking Up: Sex, Dating, and Relationships on Campus.* New York: New York University Press, 2008.

CanaVox. "Tips for Talking to Your Kids about Sex." CanaVox, 2020.

Chesterton, G. K. *"What's Wrong with the World?"* New York: Dodd, Mead & Co, 1910.

Edin, Kathryn, and Maria Kefalas. *Promises I Can Keep: Why Poor Women Put Motherhood before Marriage.* Berkeley: University of California Press, 2005.

Haworth, Abigail. "Why Have Young People in Japan Stopped Having Sex?" *The Observer*, October 19, 2013.

Kahneman, Daniel. *Thinking, Fast and Slow.* New York: Farrar, Straus, and Giroux, 2011.

Kuruvilla, Abraham. "Celibacy and the Gospel." In *Sanctified Sexuality.* Edited by Sandra Glahn and C. Gary Barnes. Grand Rapids: Kregel Academic, 2020.

Kwiatkowski, Elizabeth. "'Married at First Sight' Star Iris Caldwell: I Get So Much Hate and Feel Misjudged, When Did Virginity Become a Bad Thing?!" RealityTVWorld. com, November 18, 2019.

Lewis, C. S. *Mere Christianity.* New York: Simon and Schuster, 1984.

Regnerus, Mark D. *Cheap Sex: The Future of Christian Marriage.* New York: Oxford University Press, 2020.

——. *The Transformation of Men, Marriage, and Monogamy.* New York: Oxford University Press, 2017.

Regnerus, Mark D., and Jeremy Uecker. *Premarital Sex in America: How Young Americans Meet, Mate, and Think about Marrying*. New York: Oxford University Press, 2010.

Stokes, Charles, and Elizabeth Stokes. "Biblically Grounded Video Teaching on Emotional and Relational Health." ChuckandBetsy.com.

Van Der Kolk, Bessel. *The Body Keeps the Score: Brain, Mind, and Body in the Healing of Trauma*. New York: Penguin, 2014.

West, Christopher. *Theology of the Body for Beginners: Rediscovering the Meaning of Life, Love, Sex, and Gender*. North Palm Beach, FL: Beacon, 2018.

Wilcox, Brad. "When Marriage Disappears: The New Middle America." Report by Institute for American Values and National Marriage Project. 2010.

Wilcox, Brad, and Lyman Stone. "The Happiness Recession." *The Atlantic*. April 4, 2019.

Wright, N. T. *Surprised by Hope: Rethinking Heaven, the Resurrection, and the Mission of the Church*. New York: HarperCollins, 2008.

Yarhouse, Mark. *Understanding Sexual Identity: A Resource for Youth Ministry*. Grand Rapids: Zondervan, 2013.

4

· · · · ·

Tackling What Impedes
Church Involvement

Mary T. Lederleitner

· · · · ·

*I would say, if there is a hole in the transition, there's a bigger hole in
the transition of minorities. You know what I mean? My experience
was definitely like massively supported and then completely on
my own. There's no soft incline. We don't have people to talk
about it with or people to go through it with. We're so isolated.*

—Xander[1]

A shley said, "When I was at university, I had a ridiculous
amount of support. If I was tired someone would come by
and knock on my door, and encourage me to go to Bible study. It
was a shock to my system when I graduated. Sometimes I wake up
and make myself go to church, but sometimes I just don't. Nobody
will call or know if I don't go." Ashley's tone and demeanor were

filled with sadness and a level of despair. She was having a very difficult time reconciling the incredible disparity between her experiences in Christian community during her time at university and what she was experiencing after graduation. She wondered why the contrast was so great and why there could not be more consistency in the process.[2]

JARRING TRANSITIONS
AFTER UNIVERSITY

Christian Smith and Patricia Snell write, "Religious faith and practice generally associate with settled lives and tend to be disrupted by social, institutional, and geographical transitions."[3] However, emerging adulthood is a phase of life filled with "unsettledness." Many churches, parachurch ministries, and Christian universities focus on helping high school students transition well into university so their spiritual formation will continue. Many academic institutions focus on helping them find employment after graduating so their professional formation will continue. However, far fewer people are paying attention to providing an easier or more seamless transition to faith communities after graduation from university so emerging adults' missional formation process will continue in an unimpeded way. That process in the lives of emerging adults is often far more haphazard and disconnected.

The focus of this chapter is to share important insights from transition research conducted with missional twenty-somethings as they sought to find their places in churches after graduation. The reason this research is being highlighted is that it provides a model that can be easily replicated in a variety of contexts by campus ministries and Christian universities who want to know what their graduates are encountering. Several theories were especially beneficial for understanding their experiences, and out of the research a number of findings emerged that can be quite beneficial for people who care about emerging adults' ongoing missional development. Insights from additional researchers will be shared as well,[4] with the goal of helping readers understand the hurdles emerging adults are having to overcome in order to engage with congregations.

THE RESEARCH PROCESS

Although research indicates the trend in emerging adulthood has been "away from religious beliefs and religious participation," in rare instances it goes "in the other direction, toward greater faith."[5] InterVarsity Christian Fellowship students are some of the "rare cases" mentioned by researchers who examine trends in emerging adulthood.[6] InterVarsity is a parachurch campus ministry that draws ethnically diverse students. At the time the research was conducted, the organization's vision was "to see students and faculty transformed, campuses renewed, and world changers developed."[7] They express faith through evangelism, whole-life stewardship, engaging in cross-cultural mission, ethnic reconciliation and justice, and partnering with churches in ways that will enable students, faculty, and staff to be equipped "to be lifelong active members in local congregations."[8] A critical emphasis of the ministry is missional formation. The organization focuses on helping students develop their own internal voices and find their own unique callings so after graduation, as they follow Christ, they will make a difference in the world.

The research was conducted in the Chicago area but was designed so the study could be replicated easily in other cities and with different populations of missional twenty-somethings.[9] Participants in the research were split evenly along gender lines. Half of each gender were from minority cultures and half from the majority culture. The sample was selected from the broad population of InterVarsity alumni based on three criteria. (1) Each research participant self-identified as being active or fairly active in their InterVarsity chapter during the last two years of their university experience, or they self-identified as being moderately active in InterVarsity and very active in a local faith community during this period. (2) Each graduated from university two to four years before the research was conducted. (3) Each lived within a sixty-mile radius of the designated landmark in downtown Chicago.

Given emerging adults capacity for self-reflection, interviews were used. The central concern of this research was to determine how "people in this setting constructed reality"[10] about their own transitions and what helped and hindered them in the process. I offered to buy them lunch, dinner, or coffee near where they worked or lived if they would be willing to share their stories and insights. I conducted the interviews using semistructured, open-ended questions so they could "cast their stories in their terms."[11] With their permission, interviews were recorded and transcribed to accurately capture what they shared.

THE TRANSITION IN
THEIR OWN WORDS

These emerging adults regularly spoke about things such as disconnected experiences, marginalization in churches because they were not yet married with children, lacking support to live a Christian life when there was so much pressure to go backwards, and a general sense of feeling invisible. For example, Cole described the period since graduating as being "like little blocks of time." He explained that he had a wide variety of different experiences, but none of them were connected. Nothing related to anything else. Adam used the word "challenging" to describe what the transition process had been like for him. He explained that during his time in InterVarsity he was deeply committed and faithful when it came to practicing spiritual disciplines, and as a result he experienced a great deal of spiritual growth. He said, "I felt if I didn't do something, if I wasn't doing what I was supposed to be doing there, I wasn't just letting myself down; I was letting a lot more people down." But, he said, "Now no one really notices." He explained that he had learned how to pretend to have a vibrant relationship with God when in reality that was not the case at all. He said he hardly ever prayed now but no one knew.

In Adam's faith community a man was not considered an adult who can influence the congregation until he is married with children, and Adam was still single. Dawn explained how painful it was to try to get involved in a couples Sunday school class at her church. She said it was like she was invisible because she and her husband did not have children. They kept persevering because they didn't want their commitment to only be based on getting their own needs met, but she was losing heart and wondering whether to keep going.

Cassie told the story of being away from the faith community where she and her husband were baptized and married for months before anyone noticed. She said, "Remembering people and being remembered" is critical because "that's the first step for community to be created." She said, "I feel like that's the spark that starts the fire." Andrew talked about visiting his parents' faith community, a megachurch. It was the faith community he attended faithfully before going to university. He believed his experience was likely the same for many people between eighteen and thirty-two years old. He said, "I felt like I was completely ignored in the sermon. Really, from fourteen to thirty-two, anywhere in between that, we're not going to really talk about you in the sermon because we don't think you're here."

Lilly explained that she came to faith through the ministry of InterVarsity, but after graduating she was now back with a lot of her old friends. She said, "I was very atheistic so when I reconnect with my friends, all of my friends are not Christians. My boyfriend isn't Christian. I feel like I'm standing in two very different buckets. And it's actually, considering all the things, it's amazing that I did not just fall off and not continue to be a Christian anymore.

But I feel pulled in two different directions." Lilly said for much of the time she has felt all alone in her search for a faith community because she attended university in a different part of the country.

Hannah was deeply involved in Christian community through InterVarsity, but the loneliness of the transition has led her to date a non-Christian. She said, "We are trying to break up and we can't break up. It's so hard for me now to figure out, to navigate the space of, what is it that is really important to me? And really to face myself in the mirror and find yourself at this crossroads. Is this a choice now?" She never thought she would consider dating and possibly marrying a guy who wasn't a Christian. Lilly is still occasionally trying to find a church, but Hannah stopped trying after a few years of discouraging experiences.

Paul described it this way. "There were people who were there. There were staff workers that guide and help you out, but all of the sudden [he clicked his fingers] that's gone. Within the course of twenty-four hours it feels like, wow, you are starting over. Not starting over, but wow, I'm all alone." He seemed to express sadness yet acceptance that this is simply the way it is.

THEORIES THAT INTERSECT WITH EMERGING ADULTS' EXPERIENCES

As I started looking for theories and models that could explain what they were experiencing, I found myself reflecting a great deal on the insights of Urie Bronfenbrenner, Nancy Schlossberg, and Alexander Astin. I believe each adds ideas and concepts that are critical for this discussion.

BRONFENBRENNER'S INSIGHTS

Urie Bronfenbrenner's bio-ecological theory of human development was mentioned in the first chapter of this book. The theory focuses on transitions or "shifts in role or setting, which occur throughout the life span." Bronfenbrenner explains that development "occurs when one member is paying close and sustained attention to the activity of the other, who, in turn, at least acknowledges the interest being shown." The simple act of paying close attention to people then becomes catalytic for development. If one member "undergoes developmental change, the other is also likely to do so." These emerging adults revealed through many of their responses how demotivating and detrimental it was to their formation when no one seemed to notice their presence or cared whether they stayed involved in a faith community. Bronfenbrenner also explains that "what matters for behavior and development is the environment as it is perceived rather than as it may exist in 'objective' reality."[12] People in those congregations might have cared deeply about these emerging adults, but their sentiment alone was not sufficient. There needed to be clear ways of conveying care and concern so twenty-somethings could experience and believe it.

Further, Bronfenbrenner explains that development is enhanced if "role demands in the different settings are compatible." I saw a pattern that, when roles were present in the new faith communities that were similar to those in prior ones, emerging adults' growth continued largely unimpeded. Roles especially around leadership were critical. Seeing oneself as a leader of ministry often caused emerging adults to feel a greater sense of responsibility to keep growing, for not doing so could hurt others in their communities. Bronfenbrenner explains that development is optimal when there are supportive links between microsystems or settings.[13] Emerging adults who were able to connect with congregations through networks and relationships from their campus ministries also experienced transitions that were more likely to be marked by ongoing growth in missional formation.

Bronfenbrenner's theory also speaks of "quasi-experiments" and how they are to be encouraged.[14] However, it was most often the churches that were started in order to reach twenty-somethings that were intentional about experimenting with new ways to engage them. Occasionally traditional churches became passionate about emerging adults and began to try new things that proved to be fruitful in their contexts. Much of the time, however, emerging adults were being asked to fit into ministries designed primarily, if not exclusively, for married people with children.

SCHLOSSBERG'S INSIGHTS

Nancy Schlossberg discovered that in times of transition, people "often feel marginal and that they do not matter."[15] Others have written about this as well. *Mattering* is the idea that a person is significant in the world and can "somehow make a difference."[16] It also refers to "the feeling that others depend" on the person, are interested in the person, are concerned with the person's fate, and "that one commands the interest or notice of another person."[17] It is the sense that people care about what the person thinks, wants, or does. Perceptions regarding marginality or mattering are critical, for they cause people to be motivated or unmotivated to engage.[18]

Core in Schlossberg's theory is the idea that "every time an individual changes roles or experiences a transition, the potential for feeling marginal arises."[19] Someone can begin by feeling marginal, such as when they begin university as a freshman, and later become part of that community. However, that same person can feel marginal again after graduating, when the person moves. "People moving from one city to another often feel marginal," for they are "often nagged by the question, do I belong in this new place," or would anyone notice if I disappeared?[20] "Often people in the midst of one transition experience other transitions, which makes coping especially difficult."[21]

Many aspects of this theory intersect with this research data about missional twenty-somethings. Transitions are a time of liminality that often feel like periods of invisibility.[22] Schlossberg believes people who care about emerging adults need to prepare them for anticipated and unanticipated transitions they will be facing not just during their time in higher education but also as they leave

university.[23] She states that developmental mentors are especially
helpful in this season, asking questions and helping emerging
adults to integrate knowledge and what they are learning.[24]

ASTIN'S INSIGHTS

The appeal of Alexander Astin's theory of involvement, by his own
admission, lies in its simplicity. The crux of the theory is that "students learn by becoming involved."[25] As a theory it has its "roots in
a longitudinal study of university dropouts."[26] The broad concept
is that involvement will foster development, and great care and
attention must be paid as to why people drop out, because that
outcome so greatly hinders development. A person's involvement,
or their lack of involvement, in a faith community after graduation seemed to indicate whether or not a person would continue
to grow in their missional development. Yet many churches were
not intentional about making this a strategic investment or focus
of their congregations, even though so much had been invested in
these emerging adults during prior seasons in their lives.

ADDITIONAL INSIGHTS FROM
OTHER RESEARCHERS

Additional themes arose that mirror writings of recent scholars in
the field as well. While space is limited, I want to highlight three
areas that keep rising to the surface.

A HOSPITABLE PLACE TO LAND

While physically silent, implicit messages from church processes
and practices come across quite loudly.[27] Emerging adults who
visit congregations are often sifting through what they experience
through this lens: Is someone expecting me, and do they want me
to be here? Being warm and welcoming is the new cool for emerging adults, and in the book *Growing Young* there is much written
about the many small and big actions churches can take to create

a hospitable church culture.[28] If changing church culture seems overwhelming, effective gatekeepers can be developed who are able to greet and orient emerging adults into subcultures and subgroups in a church that are warm and welcoming. Since many people who work with larger campus ministries across the nation raise financial support (often from their church's mission program or from people within their congregation), these individuals are usually well-equipped to help church leaders learn how to develop hospitable places for emerging adults.

I often find myself wondering, given all the money and time invested by staff serving with campus ministries at public and private universities and those serving at Christian colleges, what would happen if each of these people invested 2–3 percent of their time toward equipping churches to be more fruitful in their work with emerging adults? It seems like such a wise investment to provide this type of scaffolding for emerging adult transitions, as it better ensures that what has been invested in their development to date will truly bear fruit in the years to come.

A MEANINGFUL WAY TO SERVE

It is also essential to have a way for emerging adults to very quickly be able to use their gifts and talents to serve others in the church and needs in the surrounding communities. Wisdom is needed to discern what areas are appropriate depending on their level of spiritual maturity. However, that transition to service needs to take place very quickly.[29] In the past congregations often waited much longer before integrating emerging and young adults into service, but that has to change. By the time they arrive at your church they have likely already led in a variety of ways. Their missional development will continue as they can find ways to use their skills and talents to serve others.[30] Even for those who might arrive at a church with immature attitudes of entitlement, engaging them quickly in service and mission can help them grow past these attitudes that hinder their development.[31]

TAKING DISCIPLESHIP SERIOUSLY

The other piece that regularly emerges in research is a desire for genuine discipleship. In my research over and over again emerging adults explained that they wanted to keep growing. They didn't want to go backwards. They didn't want their spiritual and missional development to wither. The *Growing Young* research shows that they take Jesus's message quite seriously.[32] They want and need to see the connection between evangelism, discipleship, and mission.[33] They want to learn how to integrate their faith with their professions so they can make a genuine difference in the world.[34] This is a season of challenge where people want to engage with deep questions that have long-lasting implications for who they will become and how they will live the rest of their lives.[35] Teaching and discipleship need to take this into consideration. It is not a time to water down the message of the gospel or fall into thinking you have to entertain people. Emerging adults are coming to a church because they want to grow spiritually and missionally.

INTENTIONALITY OR LAISSEZ-FAIRE APPROACH?

In the midst researching I came across a quote that seemed to capture what is so often the situation when it comes to emerging adults navigating important transitions. The authors explain that "in naturally occurring resilience, luck may play a significant part"; however, for stakeholders who care about "the successful transitions of young people to adulthood, it would be desirable to rely less on lucky conjunctions and more on thoughtful scaffolding of this transition."[36] In other words, intentionality is needed to overcome the obstacles in churches that are impeding emerging adults missional formation. May we care about the transitions they are facing and address these roadblocks in the months and years ahead so their missional development might continue. Surely the world needs the contribution they have to make!

QUESTIONS FOR DIALOGUE

1. What are the more challenging transitions emerging adults in your context are navigating? What steps could you take to better ensure that their missional formation will continue in the next leg of their journey?

2. How do the theories mentioned in this chapter relate to what you are seeing and hearing from emerging adults?

3. What are some creative and effective ways to equip gatekeepers in local congregations in your community so emerging adults have hospitable places to land when they visit churches?

4. What type of research would be beneficial for your context? (For example, what issues do you need to understand better? What processes might help you to get better data or information about those things? Are there ways to free up time and space for one or more people on your team to engage in research in these areas? And so on.)

BIBLIOGRAPHY

Ammerman, Nancy, Carroll Jackson, Carl S. Dudley, and William McKinney, eds. *Studying Congregations*. Nashville: Abingdon, 1998.

Arnett, Jeffrey Jensen. *Emerging Adulthood: The Winding Road from the Late Teens through the Twenties*. Oxford: Oxford University Press, 2004.

Astin, Alexander. "Involvement in Learning Revisited: Lessons We Have Learned." *Journal of College Student Development* 40, no. 5 (1999): 587–98.

————. *Preventing Students from Dropping Out*. San Francisco: Jossey-Bass, 1975.

————. "Student Involvement: A Developmental Theory for Higher Education." *Journal of College Student Personnel* 25, no. 4 (1984): 297–308.

Blustein, David L., Anna P. Chaves, Matthew A. Diemer, Laura A. Gallagher, Kevin G. Marshall, Selcuk Sirin, and Kuldhir S. Bhati. "Voices of the Forgotten Half: The Role of Social Class in the School-to-Work Transition." *Journal of Counseling Psychology* 49, no. 3 (2002): 311–23.

Bronfenbrenner, Urie, ed. *The Ecology of Human Development: Experiments by Nature and Design*. Cambridge: Harvard University Press, 1979.

————. *Making Human Beings Human: Bioecological Perspectives on Human Development*. Thousand Oaks, CA: Sage, 2005.

Charmaz, Kathy. "Grounded Theory: Objectives and Constructivist Methods." Pages 509–535 in *Handbook of Qualitative Research, Second Edition*. Edited by N. K. Denzin and Y. S. Lincoln. Thousand Oaks, CA: Sage, 2000.

InterVarsity Press. "About InterVarsity Press." 2020. http://www. ivpress.com/about/.

————. "About InterVarsity Press." 2013. http://www.ivpress. com/about/.

Kinnaman, David, and Mark Matlock. *Faith for Exiles: Five Ways for a New Generation to Follow Jesus in a Digital Babylon*. Grand Rapids: Baker Books, 2019.

Lederleitner, Mary. "Transition Journeys in Emerging Adulthood as InterVarsity Students Seek to Connect with Faith Communities after Graduation: A Qualitative Study with Educational and Sociological Implications." PhD diss., Trinity Evangelical Divinity School, 2014.

Masten, Ann S., Jelena Obradovic, and Keith B. Burt. "Resilience in Emerging Adulthood: Developmental Perspectives on Continuity and Transformation." Pages 173–90 in

Emerging Adults in America: Coming of Age in the 21st Century,. Edited by Jeffrey Jensen Arnett and Jennifer Lynn Tanner. Washington, DC: American Psychological Association, 2006.

Merriam, Sharan B., and Associates. *Qualitative Research in Practice: Examples for Discussion and Analysis.* San Francisco: Jossey-Bass, 2002.

Parks, Sharon Daloz. *Big Questions, Worthy Dreams: Mentoring Young Adults in Their Search for Meaning, Purpose, and Faith.* Rev. 10th anniv. ed. San Francisco: Jossey-Bass, 2011.

Patton, Michael Quinn. *Qualitative Research and Evaluation Methods.* 3rd ed. Thousand Oaks, CA: Sage, 2002.

Powell, Kara, Jake Mulder, and Brad Griffin. *Growing Young: Six Essential Strategies to Help Young People Discover and Love Your Church.* Grand Rapids: Baker Books, 2016.

Rosenberg, Morris, and B. Claire McCullough. "Mattering: Inferred Significance to Parents and Mental Health among Adolescents." *Research in Community & Mental Health* 2 (1981): 163–83.

Schlossberg, Nancy K. *Counseling Adults in Transition.* New York: Springer, 1984.

———. "Marginality and Mattering: Key Issues." Pages 5–15 in *Designing Campus Activities to Foster a Sense of Community.* Edited by Dennis C. Roberts. San Francisco: Jossey-Bass, 1989.

Schlossberg, Nancy K., Ann Q. Lynch, and Arthur W. Chickering. *Improving Higher Education Environments for Adults: Responsive Programs and Services from Entry to Departure.* San Francisco: Jossey-Bass, 1991.

Seversen, Beth. *Not Done Yet: Reaching and Keeping Unchurched Emerging Adults.* Downers Grove, IL: InterVarsity Press, 2020.

Smith, Christian, and Patricia Snell. *Souls in Transition: The Religious and Spiritual Lives of Emerging Adults*. Oxford: Oxford University Press, 2009.

Thomas, Sandra P. "Editorial: What Is Mattering and How Does It Relate to Mental Health?" *Issues in Mental Health Nursing* 32 (2011): 485.

Turner, Victor. "Liminality and Communitas." Pages 47–54 in *Sociology of Religion: A Reader*. Edited by Susanne C. Monahan, William A. Mirola, and Michael O. Emerson. Upper Saddle River, NJ: Prentice-Hall, 2001.

5

· · · · ·

Living a Better Story in Emerging Adulthood

David Setran

· · · · ·

*We need stories like we need food and water; we're built for narrative,
nourished by stories, not just as distractions or diversions or
entertainments but because we constitute our world narratively. It is
from stories that we receive our "character," and those stories in turn
becomes part of our background, the horizons of which we constitute
our world and engage in action. I cannot answer the question, what
do I love? without (at least implicitly) answering the question,
what story do I believe? We tell ourselves stories in order to live.*

—James K. A. Smith, *Imagining the Kingdom*

After our third or fourth meeting, Daniel looked at me with
growing concern in his eyes. We had been spending time discussing the broad story line of the Bible, focusing on the creation,

the fall, God's plan to redeem a people for his glory, and our ultimate hope of a new heavens and new earth. Daniel appeared to be tracking with the arc of the story, but as he began to consider its meaning and consequences, he grew quiet and pensive. "If this is true," he began, "if this really is the 'story of the whole world,' then it means everything and everyone is part of it." "Exactly," I responded. "It explains where we have been, where we are, and where we are going." After a short pause and a long sigh, Daniel added, "It also means that I have been living out the wrong story, one that isn't going to get me anywhere. The happily-ever-after here is nothing more than another dead end. It means I have to write a new story, a better one."

EMERGING ADULTS AND
SPIRITUAL IDENTITY

In his groundbreaking research on individuals between the ages of eighteen and twenty-four, sociologist Christian Smith suggests that there is often a disconnect between emerging adults' stated beliefs and their actual life commitments and priorities. He summarizes his observations as follows:

> Most emerging adults have religious beliefs. They believe in God. They probably believe in an afterlife. They may even believe in Jesus. But those religious ideas are for the most part abstract agreements that have been mentally checked off and filed away. They are not what emerging adults organize their lives around. They do not particularly drive the majority's priorities, commitments, values, and goals. These have much more to do with jobs, friends, fun, and financial security. ... Religious beliefs are cognitive assents, not life drivers.[1]

Smith's findings point to a troubling reality with regard to missional formation. The Christian faith for many emerging adults consists of mental affirmations that are compartmentalized from the rest of life experience. The Christian story has little to do with the shaping of their life stories. While the narrative in its broad outline may be "believed" in a cognitive sense, it does not represent the core of their personal and social identities. Worldview, it seems, does not always shape way of life.

While the reasons for such a disconnect are many and varied, philosopher Nicholas Wolterstorff offers a helpful way to frame the conversation. He notes that people take part in three kinds of learning as they develop. "Cognitive" learning represents the intellectual acquisition of information in which the individual learns "about" some topic or theme. "Ability" learning represents a growing capability or competence in a particular area, learning "how to" do something. A third form of learning, "tendency learning," speaks not to the increase in knowledge or ability but to a growing inclination or disposition to live in a certain kind of way. Unlike cognitive beliefs and abilities, Wolterstorff suggests, tendencies "are grounded in desires, wishes, commitments, values, and the like."[2] Emerging adults can know about prayer (cognitive learning) and know how to pray (ability learning), but tendency learning will only be present if they have an inclination to pray and if prayer becomes the natural inclination of the soul in the circumstances of life. They can know about the plight of the poor and know how to attend to their needs, but tendency learning would imply a settled disposition to act with compassion. It is this kind of tendency learning—really, the formation of virtue—that emerging adults seem to be lacking as we look at the larger impact of faith on their lives.

As ministers and teachers, we often assume that cognitive learning and ability learning will automatically produce tendency learning. We believe that if we teach emerging adults the right

Christian content and abilities, they will develop the tendencies to live as disciples of Jesus. Of course, one cannot develop tendencies without the proper cognitive framework and some guidance in "how" to follow Christ and engage in mission. If we are to believe Scripture itself, however, this will rarely be enough to guarantee the formation of settled tendencies—priorities, commitments, values, and goals. In Ezekiel 33:30-33 (NIV), we see an example of cognitive and ability learning that clearly does not transform the tendencies of the people:

> As for you, son of man, your people are talking together about you by the walls and at the doors of the houses, saying to each other, "Come and hear the message that has come from the Lord." My people come to you, as they usually do, and sit before you to hear your words, but they do not put them into practice. Their mouths speak of love, but their hearts are greedy for unjust gain. Indeed, to them you are nothing more than one who sings love songs with a beautiful voice and plays an instrument well, for they hear your words but do not put them into practice.[3]

Though the people appear to listen and learn from Ezekiel, and even seem pleased to "affirm" what they are hearing, they do not live into this reality. While they speak of love, their hearts are greedy for unjust gain. Similar to what we read in Isaiah 29:13, "These people come near to me with their mouth and honor me with their lips, but their hearts are far from me" (NIV).

This speaks to the reality that emerging adults' tendencies are connected to what the Bible calls their "hearts," the center of thinking, feeling, and willing within the human person. As James K. A. Smith reminds us, at our core we are not just "thinkers" or "believers" but "lovers," people whose hearts have default orientations toward some vision of the good life, some source of worship, some "kingdom."[4] Humans were made to worship, and so our loves cannot be turned off. They can of course, be skewed. This is why sin in Scripture is so often compared to idolatry—the improper worship of created things over the Creator—and adultery—the betrayal of one's first love in favor of false lovers. These ultimate loves, like arrows pointing from the heart, direct our thoughts, feelings, and willpower in ways we often fail to recognize. No matter what one may profess to be true, the heart's "loves" determine the shape of life. As Proverbs 27:19 says, "As water reflects the face, so one's life reflects the heart (NIV). While we often ask emerging adults the questions, "What do you know?" (cognitive) and "What can you do?" (ability), one of the key questions we should be asking is, "What do you love?" (tendency).

EMERGING ADULTHOOD AND THE CONSTRUCTION OF STORIES

It is critical that we think of the development of loves in terms of stories. As the opening quote of this chapter indicates, the question, "What do I love?" is inevitably connected to the question, "What story do I believe?" Emerging adults see themselves as characters in certain stories and therefore end up striving for whatever happy ending to which those stories point. Emerging adulthood is actually a key developmental moment in the formation of life stories. Narrative-identity theorists label late adolescence and the twenties as the time in which individuals begin constructing their stories in more purposeful ways. Rather than simply serving as "actors" (infancy and early childhood) who are consumed with present action or "agents" (middle and later childhood) who begin rudimentary dreaming and goal setting, late adolescents and emerging adults develop as "authors," people who synthesize their past, present, and future experiences into a coherent story.[5] That story is ideally marked by causal coherence (a sense of how earlier life experiences shape present and future ones) and thematic coherence (a sense of how all of one's life experiences are linked together to create the "themes" of one's life).[6]

Important here, however, is that emerging adults develop a certain story not only through self-reflection but by borrowing from the stories they see around them. James K. A. Smith puts it this way:

> We are acting out a script, improvising in an unfold-
> ing drama, taking on a character in a story that has
> captivated us at a level we might not even be aware
> of. We come to see ourselves in a certain way, not
> by introspection or reflection, but because we have
> absorbed a narrative that now functions as the back-
> ground drama of our existence. ... This is not an
> identity I have chosen; it is more like an orientation
> I have assumed—a model of comportment to the
> world that grows out of my implicit, tacit sense of
> who I am within an overarching story of the world.[7]

Where do these stories come from? Emerging adults are con-structing their own stories, but they are borrowing settings, char-acters, themes, and plot devices from a broad array of sources. Some come from the people they know—friends, family members, teachers, and mentors. Others come from cultural figures—actors, sports figures, musicians, and pop stars. Emerging adults can look at such figures and internalize a sense that they want to emulate the life story possessed by these individuals. Sometimes life scripts are borrowed from fictional sources such as books, movies, TV shows, songs, and social media.[8] In addition, certain story types tend to be highlighted in particular cultural contexts. Americans, for example, tend to be fond of redemption narratives that show how someone went from rags to riches or from adversity to tri-umph. They also appreciate stories that demonstrate how people resist group conformity in order to find their own independent and unique path.[9]

So emerging adults live in a world of rival stories, stories that compete with the larger Christian story for their loyalty and allegiance. The biblical narrative reveals a missional God who invites human beings to frequently participate in furthering his plans and purposes. It is a story that speaks to the world's beginning (creation and fall), middle (redemption through Christ's atoning work, gospel spread and impact), and eschatological hope (a future new heavens and new earth). Yet all around there are competing stories that tell different stories of sin, redemption, and future hope. Marketing may present sin as some personal deficiency, redemption as a product that will fulfill personal needs, and future hope as a "good life" achieved through material gain. Certain movies or novels might portray sin as a lack of romance, salvation through the ideal prince or princess, and future hope as the literal "happily ever after" with this person of your dreams. As emerging adults live in the world, they are inundated with such stories, each of which provides a different vision of what a "good life story" should look like. If these are the stories they are living within—if this is what they love—then they will live for these things, no matter what they profess.

One of the challenges for Christian emerging adults is that false stories can get woven together with the Christian story to create unhelpful hybrids. These syncretistic stories then modify the radical nature of the gospel's missional narrative, generally distorting it by removing its unfavorable elements and substituting a new and more palatable ending. For example, the "Christian American dream" story might blend elements of the prosperity gospel with the biblical narrative to describe a story of increasing success, comfort, and affluence as people devote themselves to the Lord. The "Christian romantic dream" story might portray a life in which God will give emerging adults their ideal soulmate if they honor him with the lives and sexuality. The problem in both cases is that Christ becomes not their ultimate love, but rather a tool by which they can gain what they really love: success or marital ecstasy. It also means that those who don't achieve this—the poor, the suffering, the single, and those dealing with same-sex attraction—are locked out of the "happily ever after" these stories portray.

Our goal as ministers of the gospel, therefore, is to help emerging adults begin authoring their own individual stories within and in light of the larger biblical story. In this way, they will be able to (1) interpret their own stories and the events of their lives in light of the themes and narrative structure of the biblical narrative; (2) consider their own lives as characters in this missional plot, helping to bring its themes to fruition; (3) recognize that God himself is the chief actor in their stories; and (4) live their lives with a hope-filled longing for the future—the final ending (telos) of the biblical plot. When this occurs, they will begin to bring their small "kingdoms" into submission to the larger kingdom of God, allowing his kingdom to "come" in their prayers and in their lives.[10]

LIVING THE STORY IN
EMERGING ADULTHOOD

Yet how does this happen? How does this missional story become woven into the very fabric of emerging adults' lives? If cognitive learning does not always produce tendency learning, this will require more than just "telling" the story, though this teaching role is absolutely critical. Emerging adults need to know the outline of the biblical story line, hearing it told with passion and with creativity. But we also need to recognize that this missional story is formed within them through "liturgies" that can continually deepen their identity within and allegiance to that story: practicing the story, plagiarizing the story, and proclaiming the story. I have chosen to describe these with words all starting with the letter p, but they largely reflect three of the categories (ritual, relationships, and rhetoric) defined by Lewis Rambo as the "matrix of transformation" associated with religious conversion.[11] It is my hope that these will provide a grid through which contemporary ministers might consider their own ministry frameworks with emerging adults.

PRACTICING THE STORY

First, it is critical that emerging adults are called into spaces where they can practice the missional story, entering into liturgical rhythms that allow the story to be inculcated within them at a deep level. James K. A. Smith notes, "Liturgies are compressed, repeated, performed narratives that, over time, conscript us into the story they 'tell' by showing, by performing. ... And insofar as we are immersed bodily in these microperformances, we are, over time, incorporated into a Story that then becomes the script that we implicitly act out." In other words, liturgical practices come "loaded with a Story about who and whose we are," and through these rituals emerging adults are immersed within the story at a bodily level.[12] In the context of the local church, this immersion happens week after week and so serves to counteract the false stories that compete for emerging adults' allegiance. If they do not participate in practices that embed the Christian story in their hearts and minds, they stand little chance against the popular stories and cultural slogans around them.

This liturgical counter-formation can happen both through personal spiritual disciplines and through the liturgical practices of the church. Disciplines of abstinence—practices such as fasting, solitude, silence, secrecy, and frugality—can provide experiential "tests" of the stories that dominate emerging adults' lives. As they do without certain things in their lives—food, fellowship, approval, or material possessions—they can begin to see how much rival stories control them. In addition, these disciplines open up spaces for the disciplines of engagement (practices such as study, worship, celebration, service, prayer, fellowship, and confession) that can reconnect them to the story of the kingdom.[13] Within the story told within most Western, industrialized cultures, the "good life" of the twenties is characterized by things such as freedom, autonomy, competence, independence, and fun. The disciplines of engagement weave a different story into the emerging adult heart. They inculcate a story marked by dependence on God, interdependence with others, and giving up one's freedom in loving service to others. The story they tell is that the good life is a cruciform life of costly discipleship in which strength comes from weakness and in which individuals lose their lives to find them.

All of this actually highlights why regular participation in a local church is so important for emerging adult formation. Weekly engagement with Scripture, prayer, confession, and worship brings the missional story before emerging adults on a regular basis. Baptism reminds them that their story goes beyond the elevation of their earthly family to encompass the larger family of God. They remember that they share this story with others to whom they are related not by blood, but by the fact that they are sinners saved by grace. Communion reminds them that the cross is the center of their story and that their own story is one of dying and rising with him. This also raises an important point for ministers.[14] We must recognize that the practices we include in our ministries are shaping people's loves. Whenever we are leading or discipling, we are not only teaching through what we directly communicate but also through the practices and environments we set up and through our own practices and example. So be aware of the way you structure activities, the things you use as rewards, even the visual aids and artwork you display in your ministry spaces. What kinds of loves will those generate in people's lives as they repeatedly engage in them?

PLAGIARIZING THE STORY

As mentioned previously, emerging adults often develop their own stories with reference to the stories of those around them—friends and family members, mentors, and celebrities of various kinds. As much as they want to be seen as the authors of their own stories, they borrow themes and plot devices from others they respect, hoping to live into similar stories of the good life. This acknowledges something the research itself confirms—that stories are always "plagiarized" from others. While it is obviously helpful to tell the gospel story, emerging adults also need to see that story lived out in the lives of people around them. Some of this, of course, can come by reading biographies and stories from church history. Such stories can infuse their spiritual imaginations with models worthy of emulation. In addition, however, emerging adults need opportunities to engage with those who are living for the bigger story of the kingdom. They need mentors.

Research points to the fact that emerging adults are often devoid of mentoring relationships with older adults. While parent-child relationships do often improve in emerging adulthood when compared to adolescence, these relationships tend to be "renegotiated to selectively keep parents in the dark or at a distance about many of the important things going on in emerging adults' lives."[15] Furthermore, emerging adults often fail to develop mentoring relationships with nonparental adults. David Kinnaman has suggested that many emerging adults have no adult friends other than their parents.[16] Christian Smith, in fact, notes,

> One of the most striking social features of emerging adulthood is how structurally disconnected most emerging adults are from older adults. ... Most of the meaningful, routine relationships that most emerging adults have are with other emerging adults. ... This means that most emerging adults live this crucial decade of life surrounded mostly by their peers—people of the same age and in the same boat—who have no more experience, insight, wisdom, perspective, or balance than they do. It is sociologically a very odd way to help young people come of age, to learn how to be responsible, capable, mature adults.[17]

At the very time of life that emerging adults need to see vibrant depictions of adult lives marked by Christian maturity and missional engagement, they lack any kind of structural connection to individuals who might serve in these roles. They thus find themselves captive to the peers around them and to the pervasive influences of social media and the world of entertainment. This is especially dangerous at this time of life. Since adolescents and emerging adults are developing a new capacity for idealism, fostered by rapid brain development at this stage of life, they are cognitively prepared to find exemplars of the "good life" in the people around them. If those people are absent from their lives, or if they can only find such models within the world of celebrity culture, their idealism is apt to turn quite rapidly to cynicism.[18] Why should they believe a story of devoted Christian missional adulthood is possible if they do not see any examples of this lived out in front of them?

Mentors can serve a variety of critical functions in emerging adults' lives. They ask helpful questions that can open emerging adults up to think differently about their stories. Much like Paul with Timothy, they serve as models of the biblical story through which emerging adults can see "my teaching, my way of life, my purpose, faith, patience, love, endurance, persecutions, sufferings" (2 Tim 3:10-11). When many within their spheres of school or work do not pursue lives of kingdom purpose, mentors can serve as a "plausibility structure," helping emerging adults believe that the story of the kingdom is real and powerful.[19] They can help emerging adults develop what Albert Bandura calls "self-efficacy," the belief that they are capable, in God's strength, to enter into contexts that require concrete action.[20] While many emerging adults struggle with what Thomas Aquinas calls "pusillanimity,"[21] the tendency to shrink back when new opportunities present themselves, mentors can give them mastery experiences (helping them develop confidence through competence), social modeling (serving as models of important action), and social persuasion (assuring emerging adults that they are capable of completing important tasks). In a society where adulthood is often despised and delayed, mentors can provide pictures of adult missional living that invite emerging adults into a compelling story.

PROCLAIMING THE STORY

Those writing about emerging adult narrative identity have recognized that identity around a story is actually fostered by telling that story to others. If others affirm the story, it is increasingly likely that the story will be incorporated into the individual's emerging sense of self. As one narrative theorist put it, "Storytelling is a major way we develop and maintain a self-concept. A narratively induced self change happens through the incremental tellings of situated stories to multiple audiences and in multiple contexts."[22] As stories are told, in other words, they are also deepened and solidified. Over time, this becomes an important aspect of emerging adult identity construction.

For Christian emerging adults, it is important that this includes the telling of both the larger story line of the Bible and the telling of their own God-infused missional narratives. Christian Smith has indicated that many teens and emerging adults are not able to articulate even the most basic outlines of the Christian story, struggling to articulate these themes even as they can wax eloquent about the story lines embedded in popular culture. Churches and other ministries can provide more opportunities for emerging adults to teach the story to children and youth. In such settings, they can gain practice telling the story and rehearsing its outline, solidifying these plot points in their own hearts and minds. Many churches keep emerging adults in passive learning modes in which they are constantly receiving teaching. While this is obviously important, churches also need to provide them with spaces in which they can begin to articulate the basic outlines of the faith to others. This is not just a way to fill ministry slots, but a tool for equipping these emerging adults with identity-shaping opportunities to own the story for themselves.

In addition, they can provide more opportunities for the practice of testimony. While this is more common in some ethnic and racial traditions than others, testimony offers a powerful opportunity for emerging adults to speak their stories in light of the larger kingdom story.[23] As these ideas are validated and affirmed by others, these personal stories will gain a deeper hold on their identities. The very process of constructing and then verbalizing a personal testimony helps emerging adults understand who they are and whose they are. This process helps them generate both causal and thematic coherence in their lives, providing space to see God as the central actor in their stories. This process can help them to re-narrate their lives in terms of divine action, enabling them to "transform mere chronology into sacred story, mere biography into spiritual autobiography."[24] As an added benefit, hearing the testimonies of others will both confirm and expand their sense of the impact of the biblical story on the emerging adult life.

CONCLUSION

Ultimately, the goal of identifying with the Christian story is to help emerging adults to live this story, to participate in God's larger missional story. If they begin to see themselves as characters in this story, to recognize more and more that this is the ultimate story of the good life they find themselves within, they will be able shape their priorities, commitments, and values around this narrative. This means that they will look back to see the hand of God in their past experiences, recognizing that their lives have been shaped by a God who is "hiddenly at work in all our working."[25] It also means they will be able to look ahead to see their future secure through Christ's atoning work. And in the present, it will enable them to view their own vocations as a means of participating in God's kingdom story. As James Fowler puts it,

> To be in vocation means to make creative contributions to the ongoing unfolding of the drama, in accordance with the vision and denouement intended by the playwright. To be in vocation means to develop the talents and gifts one has been given for the sake, and within the constraints, of enriching and moving the whole drama-dance toward the climactic fulfillment envisioned by the script. ... The challenge and invitation that the Christian community has to offer late adolescents is that of shaping their young adult dream in terms of vocation.[26]

As emerging adults begin to view their lives as contributing to the larger plot of God's story, they can direct their emerging gifts and passions—their vocational power—to participating in God's redemptive action in the world. And all of this can be done for the glory of the divine Author, both of their lives and of the world's master narrative. A better story indeed.

QUESTIONS FOR DIALOGUE

1. Based on the idea of tendency learning, what do you sense emerging adults in your context are loving as you watch their lives playing out? Use pseudonyms if you share stories to illustrate your point.

2. What do you find most compelling or interesting about narrative identity theory and the role stories play in the formation process?

3. What are the most potent "rival stories" that emerging adults you know are wrestling with that seem to be hindering their missional formation?

4. What are creative ways you can help them practice, plagiarize, and proclaim God's missional story in their lives?

BIBLIOGRAPHY

Anderson, Keith, and Randy Reese. *Spiritual Mentoring: A Guide for Seeking and Giving Direction*. Downers Grove, IL: InterVarsity Press, 1999.

Bandura, Albert. "Self-Efficacy: Toward a Unifying Theory of Behavioral Change." *Psychological Review* 84, no. 2 (1977): 191–215.

Berger, Peter, and Thomas Luckmann. *The Social Construction of Reality: A Treatise in the Sociology of Knowledge*. New York: Anchor Books, 1967.

Buechner, Frederick. *The Sacred Journey*. San Francisco: HarperSanFrancisco, 1982.

DeYoung, Rebecca K. *Glittering Vices: A New Look at the Seven Deadly Sins and Their Remedies*. Grand Rapids: Brazos, 2009.

Drury, Amanda Hontz. *Saying Is Believing: The Necessity of Testimony in Adolescent Spiritual Development*. Downers Grove, IL: IVP Academic, 2015.

Fowler, James W. *Becoming Adult, Becoming Christian: Adult Development and Christian Faith*. San Francisco: Jossey-Bass, 1999.

Kinnaman, David, and Aly Hawkins. *You Lost Me: Why Young Christians Are Leaving the Church ... and Rethinking Faith*. Grand Rapids: Baker Books, 2011.

McAdams, Dan P. "The Problem of Narrative Coherence." *Journal of Constructivist Psychology* 19, no. 2 (2006a): 115–16.

———. "The Psychological Self as Actor, Agent, and Author." *Perspectives on Psychological Science* 8, no. 3 (2013): 272–95.

———. *The Redemptive Self: Stories Americans Live By*. New York: Cambridge University Press, 2006b.

McAdams, Dan P., and Kate C. McLean. "Narrative Identity." *Current Directions in Psychological Science* 22, no. 3 (2013): 236.

McLean, Kate C. "Late Adolescent Identity Development: Narrative Meaning Making and Memory Telling." *Developmental Psychology* 41, no. 4 (2005): 683–69.

McLean, Kate C., and Andrea V. Breen. "Selves in a World of Stories in Emerging Adulthood." Pages 385–400 in *The Oxford Handbook on Emerging Adulthood*. Edited by Jeffrey Jensen Arnett. New York: Oxford University Press, 2016.

Parks, Sharon Daloz. *Big Questions, Worthy Dreams: Mentoring Young Adults in Their Search for Meaning, Purpose, and Faith*. San Francisco: Jossey-Bass, 2000.

Plantinga, Cornelius, Jr. *Engaging God's World: A Christian Vision of Faith, Learning, and Living*. Grand Rapids: Eerdmans, 2002.

Rambo, Lewis R. *Understanding Religious Conversion*. New Haven: Yale University Press, 1993.

Smith, Christian. *Lost in Transition: The Dark Side of Emerging Adulthood*. New York: Oxford University Press, 2011.

Smith, Christian, and Patricia Snell. *Souls in Transition: The Religious and Spiritual Lives of Emerging Adults*. New York: Oxford University Press, 2009.

Smith, James K. A. *Desiring the Kingdom: Worship, Worldview, and Cultural Formation*. Grand Rapids: Baker Academic, 2009.

———. *Imagining the Kingdom: How Worship Works*. Grand Rapids: Baker Academic, 2013.

Volf, Miroslav. *The End of Memory: Remembering Rightly in a Violent World*. Grand Rapids: Eerdmans. (2006).

Willard, Dallas. *The Divine Conspiracy: Rediscovering Our Hidden Life with God*. New York: HarperCollins, 1998.

Wolterstorff, Nicholas. *Educating for Responsible Action*. Grand Rapids: Eerdmans, 1980.

6

. . . . .

Developing Emerging Missional Leaders: No Greater Joy

Deborah A. Colwill

. . . . .

Ministry flows out of being.

—J. R. Clinton

A lex, a twenty-year-old sophomore in college, started a non-profit sports ministry for children in the downtown area of a large city. The ministry launched successfully and grew quickly. With close friends alongside, Alex enjoyed leading the effort to give kids a safe place to gather and have fun. During this exciting time, Alex seized every waking moment to grow the ministry. By contrast, four years later, Alex now feels the weight of managing a growing organization. The early simple structure with Alex at the center of all the activity no longer works. Too many things are falling through the cracks. Volunteers and parents are frustrated with Alex's lack of follow through. The need for change is clear and present; yet, in reflecting on the current situation Alex said, "I feel discouraged and overwhelmed by all the pressure I am under and I don't know what to do."

This true story illustrates some of the joys and challenges of being an emerging missional leader. Alex could be greatly helped by interacting with a wise leader developer during this season. If Alex reached out to you as a leader developer or mentor, what would you say or do? With this question in mind, the focus of this chapter is to explore the development of emerging missional leaders from the perspective of Christian leader developers who walk alongside these young leaders to the glory of God. The chapter will briefly explore some of the theoretical background in terms of core development basics that could be helpful with emerging missional leaders, followed by a few practical applications and a brief conclusion.

THEORETICAL BACKGROUND

Emerging leaders are those who desire to grow in their ability to lead but are relatively new to the experience of leading. Broadly speaking, the goal of "leader development is the expansion of a person's capacity to be effective in leadership roles and processes."[1] Leader development efforts commonly focus on leadership skills and competencies.[2] Yet, skills and competencies cannot be the sole focus of leader development; one must also consider the broader human development of the individual.[3] For instance, growing in character is also crucial for the development of leaders. Sean Hannah and Bruce Avolio succinctly state, "Character and competence are the raw building blocks of effective and sustainable leadership."[4] Bernard Bass and Ruth Bass observe that character "is grounded in core values such as integrity, trust, truth, and human dignity, that shape the leader's vision, ethics, moral literacy, and excellence."[5] In sum, growth in character and competence will likely expand an individual's capacity to lead.

Moreover, scholars distinguish between "leader development" and "leadership development."[6] Leader development focuses on developing individual leaders, whereas leadership development is "the growth of a collective's capacity to produce direction, alignment, and commitment."[7] In other words, the development of leaders should have both intrapersonal and interpersonal aspects.[8] It is leadership development, then, that focuses on the collective interpersonal capacities of a team or organization. Therefore, learning to develop collaborative connections with colleagues is another important aspect of the development of leaders. In the subsections below, we will briefly look at each of these core components of the development of emerging leaders—competence, character, and connections. All three are essential in the missional formation process of emerging leaders.

DEVELOPING COMPETENCE

Competencies are the on-the-ground essential skills that are learned through practice. Peter Northouse describes three categories of leadership skills: administrative, interpersonal, and conceptual. Administrative skills include "managing people, managing resources, and showing technical competence." Interpersonal skills involve "being socially perceptive, showing emotional intelligence, and managing interpersonal conflict." Conceptual skills include "problem solving, strategic planning, and creating visions."[9]

Most would agree that leader competencies are best learned through intentional on-the-ground experience.[10] Moreover, increasing the variety of experiences is particularly important for emerging missional leader development. Varying the experience base of leaders opens up the possibility for the individual to stretch and strengthen their existing skills, as well as gain the opportunity to discover latent abilities or gifts.

One way to increase variety of experience is through "development-in-place" opportunities.[11] These opportunities are specifically designed to provide "challenges to current work and non-work pursuits in ways that broaden the individual's portfolio of leadership experiences."[12] To pursue development-in-place experiences, leaders need to first identify the leadership challenges that could potentially benefit their development. Leadership challenges could include taking on unfamiliar responsibilities, exploring new directions, increasing one's scope and scale of responsibility, attempting to influence without authority, or working across cultures.[13] Other examples include "being granted the opportunity to shadow or be exposed to senior role models."[14]

After identifying which leadership challenges are most appropriate for the emerging leader's growth, the mentor and emerging leader need to "generate ideas about where to find places to locate the leadership challenge experiences."[15] Three possible strategic locations for development-in-place assignments are "reshaping the job, taking on temporary assignments, and seeking challenges outside the workplace."[16] Finally, throughout the development-in-place process emerging leaders will benefit along the way from asking others for ideas and feedback.

While increasing the variety of leadership experience is key for emerging missional leaders, they should also continue the sustained practice of everyday essential skills that need ongoing development. Continued practice is crucial to the growth and retention of any worthwhile skill. If leader developers recognize, identify, and name the strengths they see in emerging leaders, this may reassure and motivate these young leaders toward the daily hard work required in skill development. Furthermore, encouraging emerging leaders to actively reflect on their own experience is also important for their growth. For instance, with the support of a wise mentor, reflecting on hardships, mistakes, and failures can prompt fruitful growth in which emerging leaders learn valuable lessons from their experience "about themselves and how to be more effective as leaders in organizations."[17] On the other hand, "thriving can occur with or without necessarily encountering significant, sustained hardship or challenge, such as when one is challenged with a new opportunity such as a promotion or new project assignment."[18] Experience, practice, and reflection on experience are key to growth.

One caution to keep in mind: supervisors who have emerging leaders that report to them often use a performance-oriented lens to guide younger leaders. And, as a result, supervisors may focus too heavily on growing and leveraging the skills and competence of younger leaders in order to get things done, as opposed to having the development of the emerging leader as their first priority. Providing coaching or training on skill development is necessary but not sufficient. Competence alone will not make a wise and faithful leader. Therefore, we turn next to emerging leader character development.

DEVELOPING CHARACTER

Trustworthy character is foundational to being a good leader. Bernard and Ruth Bass state, "The character of a leader involves his or her ethical and moral beliefs, intentions, and behavior."[19] Additionally, Hannah and Avolio assert, "Character is a (if not *the*) critical component of leadership."[20] Trustworthy character is formed in a leader over their lifetime.

As Christians we recognize that the Holy Spirit transforms our character as we grow in Christ. The fruit of the Spirit is a visible sign that Christlike character is being formed in us. Galatians 5:22–23 tells us, "The fruit of the Spirit is love, joy, peace, patience, kindness, goodness, faithfulness, gentleness and self-control" (NIV). The fruit of the Spirit is expressed through us in our relationships. Over time, as we mature in Christ, we see more and more evidence that the Spirit is transforming us. It is not surprising, then, that Jesus says, "I am the vine; you are the branches. Those who abide in me and I in them bear much fruit; because apart from me you can do nothing" (John 15:5 NRSV). This passage exhorts us to nurture our relationship and connection with Christ the Vine, and when we abide in Christ and he abides in us, then he will bear fruit through us.

Character formation is vitally important for the emerging missional leader. During this early season of a leader's experience, God deliberately focuses on developing Christlike character. This intentional focus flows from the loving heart of God. Jesus wants the emerging missional leader to abide in him and be transformed. J. Robert Clinton asserts, "His approach is to work in you, and then through you." Trustworthy character provides the foundation with which to exercise God-honoring leadership. In other words, "mature ministry flows from a mature person."[21]

However, since Christlike character development does not develop overnight, we need to be patient with one another in our ongoing growth. If Christians genuinely hold a humble learning posture before God, then they are more likely to respond well and cooperate with God's character-development work in their lives. Furthermore, we need a caring community for support and encouragement to keep going when times are challenging. This is especially true for emerging leaders. Emerging missional leaders often face challenges and hardships that feel overwhelming, as illustrated in the opening story about Alex. As such, the developmental value of challenging hardships and setbacks can be deepened by drawing near to God through prayer, reflection, and immersion in his word. Moreover, if a trustworthy leader developer or mentor is alongside, then the emerging leader can process what is going on with their mentor, who will hopefully listen carefully, ask discerning questions, pray with them, and give wise feedback.

On the contrary, if a Christian pursues a pattern of primarily trusting their own skills, competencies, talents, or gifts to accomplish their goals, and if they consistently ignore their relationship with Christ and disregard God's character-building processes in them, then in essence they are learning to operate on their own apart from God. In the long term, an ongoing pattern of trusting competence and neglecting God will have a negative impact. Sadly, this performance-driven orientation usually ends up hurting the leader and those around them.

Emerging missional leaders are in the early stages of ministry, and as such, they are forming patterns and habits that they will carry throughout their lives. As mentioned above, it is short-sighted for those who supervise them to focus too heavily on skill development at the expense of character development. Whether intended or not, if a supervisor reinforces and rewards the "doing" of ministry, then the "being" of the individual is neglected. What you feed grows. Rather, the supervisor also needs to reinforce and support the vital need for young leaders to grow in their relationship with God and cooperate with God's character formation in their lives.

Coming full circle, the development of leadership skills is important; however, emerging missional leaders need to be fully aware and reminded that God desires for them (as a main priority) to be transformed to be like Jesus. John 15 underscores that bearing fruit is Christ's responsibility, and he invites us into his ministry. Clinton observes, "A mature, successful ministry flows from one who has both ministry skills and character that has been mellowed, developed, and ripened by God's maturity processing. Character formation is fundamental. Ministry flows out of being."[22] Therefore, we all need to intentionally cooperate with God's development processes of maturing us and to nurture our relationship with God as our source of life, joy, and hope.

Individual leader development involving growth in competence and character is an essential focus for an emerging missional leader. In addition to focusing on individual development, these emerging leaders also need to grow in their ability to develop connections with colleagues. We now turn to briefly exploring developing connections.

DEVELOPING CONNECTIONS

A healthy organizational culture with strong relational dynamics provides fertile soil for emerging leaders to grow. Leadership is a relational endeavor; consequently, emerging leaders need to grow in their capacity to develop connections. Four types of connections are explored below: positive relationships, wise mentors, leadership role models, and collaboration partners.

Nurturing positive relationships will help emerging leaders cultivate connections in their organizations. More specifically, Scott DeRue and Kristina M. Workman say, "A positive relationship is one in which there is a true sense of mutuality and relatedness, such that people experience mutual giving and receiving, caring, and safety in challenging times."[23] In a "thriving organization," leaders are charged with nurturing positive relationships at work by expressing "compassion, trust, respect, and gratitude."[24] Spreitzer and colleagues note, "When people have positive relationships with others at work, they will be more likely to take the needs of those colleagues into account as they are doing their own work."[25] In short, emerging leaders need exposure to and involvement in positive relationships for ongoing mutual support and encouragement.

Likewise, according to Clinton, "The emergent leader who has a wise mentor early on in those first ministry steps is fortunate. God's guidance through a mentor can be life changing. It can speed up the development process and set patterns that will last a lifetime."[26] Wise mentors provide emerging missional leaders a safe place to process what they are learning. For example, a common developmental challenge for emerging leaders is growing in discernment about whom to trust and whose example to follow. Wise mentors can guide emerging leaders in understanding why trustworthy character is essential for a leader and in discerning what trustworthy character looks like in real life.[27] For instance, emerging leaders need to grow in recognizing when the fruit of the Spirit is being displayed and understanding what true humility looks like, as well as recognizing when immature, untrustworthy leader behavior is being exhibited. The company that we keep matters. Scripture warns, "Do not be misled: 'Bad company corrupts good character' " (1 Cor 15:33 NIV). The leaders we choose to follow closely will have an effect on our character. James Kouzes and Barry Posner put it this way, "People become the leaders they observe. If you want to become an exemplary leader, you have to watch and study exemplary leaders."[28]

While using discernment, emerging leaders should develop connections with trustworthy, experienced leaders. They will benefit greatly from interacting with and following the example of leaders who cultivate a work environment characterized by love, trust, and mutual respect. Observing how trustworthy role models intentionally listen to colleagues, handle conflict, navigate times of crisis, communicate vision, or make critical decisions provides substantive learning for a young leader. Kouzes and Posner state, "Experienced leaders are not only role models. They are also necessary connections to information, resources, and of course, other people."[29] Networking with trustworthy experienced leaders can lead to all kinds of open doors for learning and growth.

Collaboration partners are another connection that emerging leaders need to develop. Broadly speaking, collaboration means to act together to create something. It means working together with common purpose to achieve positive outcomes.[30] The synergy experienced in creating something with others is a gift, but collaboration can be interpersonally challenging as well. Susan Komives and Wendy Wagner write, "Collaboration implies mutually beneficial goals, engaged participants, shared responsibility, and self-aware individuals." In addition, "Collaboration means learning to nurture relationships in which influence and good ideas come inclusively from all directions. Collaborative groups benefit from these diverse perspectives."[31] Moreover, Spreitzer and colleagues say, "When individuals relate heedfully, they act in ways that demonstrate that they understand how their own jobs fit with the jobs of others to accomplish the goals of the system."[32]

Emerging missional leaders need to develop connections through positive relationships, wise mentors, leadership role models, and collaboration partners. We have briefly looked at three core components of the development of these emerging leaders: competence, character, and connections. We will now consider some practical applications.

PRACTICAL APPLICATIONS

If you are a Christian leader, you are called to be a leader developer.[33] However, it takes time, energy, and patience to walk alongside an emerging leader. Honestly, most jobs do not specifically reward efforts to develop leaders.[34] So, for many of us, developing emerging leaders is above and beyond what our day job entails. Therefore, we need to examine our expectations and unpack the expectations of emerging leaders we might agree to mentor. With these introductory thoughts in mind, as leader developers or mentors, what are some practical things we can do?

Jesus asks us to cooperate with his developmental processes in the life of the emerging leader. As mentioned above, John 15 underscores that bearing fruit is Christ's responsibility, and he invites us into his ministry. Therefore, a place to begin is to prayerfully ask God for discernment about whom to mentor and how to mentor. Each emerging leader is unique, and we need to get to know them well by listening to what is important to them, observing them in various settings, and asking insightful questions.

LISTENING

Taking the time to listen well and understand the nuanced meaning of what an emerging missional leader is saying treats them with dignity and shows them respect. When an emerging leader shares important matters and has a sense of feeling truly heard, then deep listening has happened. Listening requires deliberate focused attention on what another is saying, discipline to remain quiet while another is speaking, and asking follow-up questions that draw out the full meaning of the emerging leader.[35] Even so, William Isaacs says, "Perhaps the simplest and most potent practice for listening is simply to be still. By being still in ourselves, quieting the inner chatter of our minds, we can open up to a way of being present and listening that cuts through everything."[36] With a peaceful, still posture, we are fully awake and ready to hear an emerging leader's story, their hopes, their disappointments, their fears, and so on. Listening involves reflecting back what you heard, which reassures the emerging leader that they have been heard.

OBSERVING

Listening and observing are inseparable. Deep listening includes attending to nonverbal communication. If a person says, "I'm fine," and slams the door, what is going on? Mentors need to observe whether there is congruence or incongruence with what is being said and the nonverbal cues, as well as watching for observable patterns in speech and behavior. Also look for observable growth in character. Affirming the evidence of their character growth reinforces it. Likewise, pay attention to an emerging leader's strengths and notice the weak side of their strengths. For example, a missional leader who is action oriented may do a great job of getting things done, but also may move so quickly that they miss important details. Tuck away the observations you make and pray for openings to discuss them and ask the leader to reflect.

ASKING

As you are getting to know an emerging leader, asking for "public" information is a good way of building rapport. For example, asking them to describe their current job and interests they have outside work, asking about whom they consider to be a great leader and why, or asking them to tell you about a high-point experience they have had while working on a team. The goal is to use the opportunity to understand how they see themselves and how they understand leadership. As your mutual trust deepens with an emerging leader, ask them to share their reflections on their experience. Someone once said, "Experience itself is not a teacher; it is reflection on experience that helps us learn." Along these lines, the fruit from your listening and observing provides substance for asking insightful, open-ended questions. Draw out their learning on skill development and character growth. Other questions could include: Who are you gleaning feedback from? How are you stretching yourself? Where do you feel underchallenged or over-challenged? The goal is to help the emerging leader become a voracious learner. Or, in other words, "It's important that every day you take stock of what you've learned. You have to make learning leadership a daily habit."[37]

CONCLUSION

Leader development is a lifetime process.[38] As such, leader developers need to stay connected to Christ the Vine. The development of emerging missional leaders is Christ's ministry, and he invites us to join him in that ministry. As such, we need to prayerfully cooperate with his work in their lives. The work of the Spirit through us is what bears much fruit—lasting fruit. Stephen Seamands asserts that the ministry we have entered is the ministry of Jesus Christ the Son, to the glory of God the Father, through the power of the Holy Spirit, for the sake of the church and the world.[39] The Holy Spirit acts as a powerful conduit through the life of a leader developer, who then models abiding in Christ, being a healthy branch, and intentionally drawing near to God. The modeling, mentoring, coaching, and leading of emerging missional leaders speaks volumes to them because they watch our example closely. Leader developers need to provide an honest, growing, passionate life example of following Christ. What a humbling privilege: no greater joy.

QUESTIONS FOR DIALOGUE

1. Who are the emerging leaders in your context whom you sense God would like you to start investing in more intentionally?

2. What different types of experiences are needed for each of these emerging leaders to develop greater competency as a leader? What needs to happen to open doors to those experiences?

3. In your context, what types of mentorship would best foster emerging leaders' development in "doing" and "being" so they grow both in competency and in Christian character?

4. Who are the best people to connect emerging leaders with at this foundational season in their life to ensure they have good exemplars, collaborators, and others who can support their development?

BIBLIOGRAPHY

Bass, Bernard M., and Ruth Bass. *The Bass Handbook of Leadership: Theory, Research, and Managerial Applications.* 4th ed. New York: Free Press, 2008.

Cameron, Kim S., and Gretchen M. Spreitzer, eds. *The Oxford Handbook of Positive Organizational Scholarship.* Repr. ed. New York: Oxford University Press, 2013.

Clinton, Robert. *The Making of a Leader: Recognizing the Lessons and Stages of Leadership Development.* Rev. ed. Colorado Springs: NavPress, 2012.

Colwill, Deborah A. *Conflict, Power, and Organizational Change.* New York: Routledge, 2021.

Day, David V., and Lisa Dragoni. "Leadership Development: An Outcome-Oriented Review Based on Time and Levels of

Analyses." *Annual Review of Organizational Psychology and Organizational Behavior* 2 (2015): 133–56.

Day, David V., John W. Fleenor, Leanne E. Atwater, Rachel E. Sturm, and Rob A. McKee. "Advances in Leader and Leadership Development: A Review of 25 Years of Research and Theory." *The Leadership Quarterly* 25, no. 1 (2014): 63–82.

DeRue, D. Scott, and Kristina M. Workman. "Toward a Positive and Dynamic Theory of Leadership Development." Pages 784–97 in *The Oxford Handbook of Positive Organizational Scholarship*. Edited by Kim S. Cameron and Gretchen M. Spreitzer. New York: Oxford University Press, 2013.

Hannah, Sean T., and Bruce J. Avolio. "The Locus of Leader Character." *The Leadership Quarterly* 22, no. 5 (2011): 979–83.

Isaacs, William. *Dialogue: The Art of Thinking Together*. New York: Currency, 1999.

Komives, Susan R., and Wendy Wagner. *Leadership for a Better World: Understanding the Social Change Model of Leadership Development*. 2nd ed. San Francisco: Jossey-Bass, 2017.

Kouzes, James M., and Barry Z. Posner. *Learning Leadership: The Five Fundamentals of Becoming an Exemplary Leader*. Hoboken, NJ: Wiley, 2016.

McCauley, Cynthia D. "Identifying Development-in-Place Opportunities." Pages 21–24 in *Experience-Driven Leader Development: Models, Tools, Best Practices, and Advice for On-the-Job Development*, 3rd ed. Edited by Cynthia D. McCauley, D. Scott DeRue, Paul R. Yost, and Sylvester Taylor. San Francisco: Jossey-Bass, 2013.

McCauley, Cynthia D., D. Scott DeRue, Paul R. Yost, and Sylvester Taylor. *Experience-Driven Leader Development: Models, Tools, Best Practices, and Advice for On-the-Job Development*. 3rd ed. San Francisco: Jossey-Bass, 2013.

Northouse, Peter G. *Introduction to Leadership: Concepts and Practice*. 5th ed. Los Angeles: Sage, 2021.

Peterson, Christopher, and Martin Seligman. *Character Strengths and Virtues: A Handbook and Classification*. New York: American Psychological Association/Oxford University Press, 2004.

Quinn, Robert E., and Gretchen M. Spreitzer. "The Road to Empowerment: Seven Questions Every Leader Should Consider." *Organizational Dynamics* 26 (October 199.): 37–48.

Seamands, Stephen. *Ministry in the Image of God: The Trinitarian Shape of Christian Service*. Downers Grove, IL: IVP Books, 2005.

Spreitzer, Gretchen. "Leadership Development Lessons from Positive Organizational Studies." *Organizational Dynamics* 35, no. 4 (2006): 305–15.

Spreitzer, Gretchen, Kathleen Sutcliffe, Jane Dutton, Scott Sonenshein, and Adam M. Grant. "A Socially Embedded Model of Thriving at Work." *Organization Science* 16, no. 5 (2005): 537–49.

Van Velsor, Ellen, Cynthia McCauley, and Marian Ruderman. *The Center for Creative Leadership Handbook of Leadership Development*. 3rd ed. San Francisco: Jossey-Bass, 2010.

Additional Missional Formation Practices

• • • • •

I will instruct you and teach you in the way you should go;
I will counsel you with my loving eye on you.

—Psalm 32:8 NIV

If any of you lacks wisdom, you should ask God, who gives
generously to all without finding fault, and it will be given to you.

—James 1:5 NIV

Missional imagination is a catalytic space where the Holy Spirit works through people to spawn fruitful innovations that move forward God's purposes in the world. Sometimes something wholly new arises. Other times there are new spins on old traditions that God uses in powerful ways. This section shares some innovations being used to facilitate emerging adults formation for mission. The first shares research from a national study; the next three came out of a church, a Christian university, and a seminary, respectively; the last was developed at a public university. Each of the practitioners and educators shares honestly about what they are learning through these formative practices.

The hope is these practices will inspire you to think of innovative approaches that will work in your context. Seldom does one size fit all, but often there are principles and concepts that can be applicable and transferrable more broadly. Thankfully we have the most creative Being, our Almighty God, who invites us to come and ask for advice, insight, and guidance about how to shape new types of learning interventions that will facilitate missional growth and development. We also have the thoughts, opinions, and insights of emerging adults, whose voices are essential for shaping these innovations as well.

7

· · · · ·

How Churches Reach and Develop Emerging Adults

Rick Richardson

· · · · ·

[S]o we, though many, are one body in Christ, and individually members one of another.

—Romans 12:5 ESV

Kevin leads a small church, and the congregation feels like an extended family. People get together for whole-church events and meals often. Now and again small groups meet, but mostly gatherings are for the whole extended family. People who attend the church love the small family feel and would hate to try to become larger or employ any kind of seeker-oriented strategy to grow. People in Kevin's church feel like seeker-oriented churches are shallow. They see those type of churches as being an inch deep and a mile wide, not really doing discipleship, and having superficial and intrusive views of evangelism that have turned them off. The emerging adults in Kevin's church are not interested in the showy and glitzy services that larger, high-tech churches seem to offer. They want authentic sharing about real struggles and weaknesses, and sometimes Kevin, who is a boomer, does not feel comfortable with their level of transparency and vulnerability. When it comes to outreach, although Kevin has a huge heart for his church to reach out, very few people in his congregation share that heart. They would never say so, because who's going to speak publicly against reaching people who don't know Jesus? But that's the reality. Kevin is not sure what to do.

Bill faces a different situation. He leads a large church. It has a wide variety of programs for many types of people in different stages of life. It has men's ministry and women's ministry, Sunday school for retired people, Sunday school for people who especially support missions, and Sunday school for young families. It does a great job with premarital counseling and has a highly developed small-group system. But Bill does not feel like his large church is reaching very many people and helping them come to Christ. He also sees high school seniors graduating and drifting away from the church. Single emerging adults are a huge hole in his church's demographic.

Bill's church has tried various outreach programs and events. It may have seen a win or two, a season of some conversions, but it always seems to fall back into default mode. Most of the people in the church are focused inward, toward the programs of the church that have been designed for Christians. Bill wants that to change, but has no idea how. Not that Bill hasn't tried. He has an evangelism series every year and encourages his people to invite friends, but hardly anybody does. And a few years back, Bill tried to transition the church toward becoming a more seeker-oriented and younger church. He stopped trying when worship wars broke out in his church over the relative mix of hymns and contemporary songs. What's more, a number of his leaders were very concerned that by orienting toward seekers, the church would lose an emphasis on discipleship. And in the six months of trying, though they got a couple new young families, their population of emerging adults didn't grow at all, so Bill let that vision go.

DESIGNING RESEARCH THAT COULD HELP CHURCHES

Can you relate to any of the struggles that Kevin and Bill are facing? Have you ever felt stuck in your ability to reach out to emerging adults? Do you want change? Do you want to see your church grow younger and turn outward? These are the types of questions that drove us to conduct research that could help churches better understand what is needed to turn the tide and change the trajectory of their congregations.

The Wheaton College Billy Graham Center partnered with Lifeway Research to randomly survey online two thousand unchurched people from across the country. Every ethnicity and every region from urban, suburban, and rural communities were included. Of the two thousand unchurched people, 466 were emerging adults aged eighteen to thirty-two. They too represented a broad cross-section of the country.

Next we conducted a phone survey of forty-five hundred Protestant churches. We followed up with sixty pastors and sixty previously unchurched people. Participants who took part in these more in-depth interviews were from congregations that were at the top 10 percent of the sample when it came to church growth through conversions. Of the sixty previously unchurched people, nearly half were emerging adults. This research gave us tremendous data and insight.

OUR RESEARCH FINDINGS

Through this we learned that 90 percent of the churches in America were either plateaued, declining, or growing primarily at the expense of other churches through transfers.[1] As a result, 90 percent of churches in America are primarily playing a zero-sum game. This chapter is about the other 10 percent. It focuses on what we learned about emerging adults, both unchurched emerging adults and emerging adults who were previously unchurched but are now attending congregations. We defined unchurched people as those who had not visited a church in at least the last six months except for special events such as a wedding, funeral, or Christmas service.

This 10 percent of churches in America grows primarily by reaching new people, helping people come to Christ and begin to follow Christ, and making disciples who make disciples. We refer to this 10 percent as "conversion communities."[2] Changed lives and people coming to Christ are a regular experience in those churches, and 10 percent of their regular attenders have come to Christ and stayed in the church in the last year. The really good news is we found these conversion communities in urban, suburban, *and* rural contexts, among small, midsize, and larger churches, and of diverse ethnicities and racial backgrounds. My conclusion based on this broad research and my experience working with a wide variety of churches is this: whatever your context, size, and ethnicity, you too can become a conversion community. And you too can grow younger.

TEN PREDICTIVE FACTORS

What are these churches doing that you could do? We found ten predictive factors that characterized conversion communities.[3] I have put in bold font the factors that were especially important for reaching and retaining emerging adults. As you read, consider which of the factors are in place in your church. Where is your church strong? What do you need to strengthen or put in place?

1. **Church invites, includes, and involves the unchurched**

2. Leader regularly teaches a next-steps class

3. Leader regularly attends evangelism training (e.g., missional pastor cohorts)

4. Leader regularly and personally invites people to Christ

5. Church puts its money where its mouth is, into outreach

6. **People (not just the pastors or professionals) are reaching out and sharing their faith**

7. **Leader translates the regular message to unchurched people and their lives**

8. **Church ministry engages the community**

9. Church culture attracts transfers as well as unchurched people

10. **Leader blocks out time in the calendar to personally reach out and share faith**

I also want you to notice five key things that stand out and are critically important to know and apply, especially as it relates to emerging adults:

- These are predictive characteristics. When you find predictive factors in research, you have found pure gold. We found these through regression analysis, where every factor but one is controlled to discover the impact that factor has. So, you can take these predictive factors to the bank!

- Regarding point 10, that the leader intentionally reaches out and shares faith, and actually blocks out time in the calendar to do so: The leader models the intentionality that he or she hopes others will imitate. For the churches reaching emerging adults, the senior leader intentionally spends significant time reaching emerging adults, building relationships, and being available to them.

- But even more important than what the leader does is that others catch and imitate the leader's behaviors. They don't just sit back and cheer them on. They emulate their leaders and reach out and share their faith. The critical issue as it relates to emerging adult ministry here is that churches growing younger are multiplying ministry *through relational networks of emerging adults* who have caught the senior leader's passion for witness and for reaching other emerging adults.

- These churches engage their communities and both share the gospel and serve the needs of the community. They proclaim *and* they demonstrate the good news and its results. If they only do one or the other, they are not nearly as effective in reaching people. For emerging adults, this social dimension of ministry is of paramount importance. Interestingly, it is not that emerging adults are necessarily engaging in justice or compassion ministry. Most aren't. But they are joining churches that do and are not drawn to churches that don't.

- Notice the first predictive characteristic! There is no silver bullet, but there is, if you will, a secret sauce that flavors effective outreach: Churches that are reaching people today are deeply hospitable to unchurched people. Unchurched people who visit know that they are expected, wanted, included, and able to contribute something to the life of the community. Emerging adults long for community. They live in a world where virtual connection is often stronger than connection through actual, real-time, bodily presence. Though they long for connection, they are often not strong at cultivating in-person community for themselves, but rather often relate through sound bites and through offering self-curated physical images. Emerging adults are encouraged in that way to build a brand, an image, a persona, more than real-time presence in person with people in ways that build authentic, transparent, and substantive community. Churches that provide points of connection, real hospitality, and significant amounts of time for just hanging out and being together are the churches that are effectively reaching and developing emerging adults.

BECOMING A CONVERSION COMMUNITY

To help capture these ten factors, as well as some of the data from our interviews of previously unchurched people, I have simplified the process for churches. I was able to group the factors and additional interview data into three main characteristics of our top 10 percent conversion communities, represented by the following equation:[4]

The Path to Becoming a Conversion Community

| Missional | Missional | Missional | Conversion |
| Imagination | Leaders | Congregation | Community |

Our research has given churches a path to pursue for the long haul. Churches successfully pursuing this simple equation or path *are getting better at* growing through reaching unchurched people, and they are having a greater impact on their community. When they apply this process to reaching and developing emerging adults, they have seen great success. Let me unpack this equation: missional imagination plus missional leaders plus a missional congregation leads to becoming a conversion community. By *missional* I mean: (1) oriented on the needs, concerns, and contexts of those outside the church, (2) offering compassionate service and advocacy, and (3) bold verbal witness to Jesus.

Missional imagination describes the vision and love people have for Jesus and the mission of Jesus. When you attend these churches, there is an excitement about faith and a passion for Jesus that is winsome and contagious. There is also a strong heartbeat for people who do not know Jesus yet. In addition, there is a vision and imagination about the receptivity of people in the culture, and especially of emerging adults. One of the surprising results from our survey of unchurched emerging adults is that although many drift away from church during these years, they also express greater receptivity to faith and to congregations than any other generational cohort. Here are just a few examples.

1. Unchurched emerging adults expect to be attending church in the future at a higher rate than any other generational cohort: 33 percent of unchurched Americans expect to attend church regularly in the future with 39 percent of emerging adults expect to attend church regularly in the future.[5]

2. When asked about whether finding their ultimate purpose is a priority for them, 63 percent of unchurched emerging adults agree or strongly agree, compared to 54 percent for the other generational cohorts.

3. Unchurched emerging adults are more open to Christian friends talking about their faith than any other generational cohort: 81 percent say it's fine, compared to 75 percent among other generations.

4. Unchurched emerging adults are more attracted to churches that show multiple races working together and churches that stand against injustice than other generations, by several percentage points.

5. Unchurched emerging adults are more interested in attending community-service projects sponsored by a church, recovery groups sponsored by a church, and small groups for the spiritually curious sponsored by

a church, by five to seven percentage points for each type of activity.

The news is not all good, as you might expect from other research that has been done. Unchurched emerging adults are also most likely to:

1. Feel that the Christian faith is not for people like themselves (26 percent of unchurched emerging adults told us this, compared to 17 percent in all the other generations).

2. Feel the Christian faith is against things they support (19 percent of unchurched emerging adults versus 9 percent for all other generations).

3. Feel the church is good for society (31 percent of unchurched emerging adults versus 42 percent for all other generations).

Though the picture is mixed, there is much more good news than bad in terms of emerging adult receptivity to Christian faith. What is also clear is that emerging adults in general are more polarized than the other generations. But again, the percentage of receptive emerging adults is higher than for any other generation. That is very good news and needs to be heard far and wide. The church has too often lost hope that there is a harvest among unchurched emerging adults. We desperately need a reenergizing of missional imagination. The fuel for lighting that fire is in Scripture and all around us—in the receptivity of millions of unchurched emerging adults to Christian churches and the Christian faith.

The second factor in the equation for conversion communities is a church having missional leaders. Missional leaders are leaders in the church who model personal outreach, concern, and compassion for the needs of people around them. They build friendships, initiate spiritual conversations, share their faith when they have opportunity, and invite people into Christian community when the time is right. They also meet and serve the needs of others who are hurting, challenged, or marginalized. But missional leaders not only model personal evangelism and compassion; they also model integrating an evangelistic concern into the ministries they lead. They do this by encouraging their leaders to personally reach out, and also by helping the ministries they lead to become more hospitable to irreligious people.

Conversion communities not only have missional leaders. They also have invested time in developing a missional congregation. They have missional practices that characterize the congregation as a whole. Together they create an entire congregational culture that engages with people and needs outside the church, inviting people into the church, and extending spectacular hospitality when they visit. Such congregations have a DNA of extension, invitation, and hospitality. Whether you visit the weekly worship service, a regular ministry of the church such as the ministry for high school students or kids, or a compassion outreach of the church into the community, this engaged, invitational, and hospitable culture marks everything the congregation does.

ILLUSTRATING THE JOURNEY

So how do you develop missional leaders and a missional congregation that is effectively reaching and developing emerging adults? Answering this question is one of the huge passions for us at the Wheaton College Billy Graham Center. It is why I wrote *You Found Me* and why we lead cohorts with hundreds of pastors across the country.[6] Let me share a couple examples that will illustrate key steps you could take.

HILL COUNTRY BIBLE CHURCH

Hill Country Bible Church in Austin, Texas, is a great example of a church that has developed that missional leader part of the equation. Hill Country is a remarkable church that has had a significant impact in Austin, including among emerging adults. They have planted dozens of churches and also are a multisite campus. They have helped the churches across the whole city organize to reach people in Austin. And yet with all their impact, Tim Hawks, the lead pastor, was deeply unsatisfied with their impact in evangelism.

They were not a conversion community, but had tried many ways of moving in that direction. They knew they needed to mobilize and release their people but they just weren't sure how. Tim and his outreach influence leader, Chuck Barber, joined a pastor cohort, and in the last couple of years they have seen incredible progress. What did they do? First, Tim as lead pastor began to model personal evangelism other people could imitate in more intentional and focused ways. Pastors have a lot of ways they reach out that only pastors are able to pursue: funerals, baptisms, weddings, preaching on Sundays, meeting people at church, and so on. But none of their people can imitate those ways of reaching out. If pastors want people to imitate them, which is the only way evangelism ever gets caught, they need to pursue opportunities for reaching out in their neighborhoods and communities that their people can reproduce.

I have been amazed at how much more vibrant in personal outreach senior pastors become with just a little encouragement from their friends, or in our case, other pastors in the cohort. No matter how much pastors value personal evangelism and witness, it is so easy for that value to get lost in the midst of a very busy and demanding leadership life and the huge task of running a church. Tim felt like mission drift had set in for him. So, he recommitted in his efforts to build bridges in his neighborhood and walk around in his everyday life with more awareness about how God might be at work in the unchurched people around him.

And don't miss this: churches that are effectively reaching and developing emerging adults have senior pastors that are prioritizing emerging adults in their personal outreach. In her book *Not Done Yet: Reaching and Keeping Emerging Adults*, Beth Seversen notes that churches reaching emerging adults have pastors who intentionally interact with and spend time reaching emerging adults.[7] For example, many have text strings with emerging adults they have begun to reach out to and then mentor.

Back to Tim and Hill Country Bible Church. Tim then recruited Chuck to help him take that kind of missional lifestyle to the whole congregation. Chuck was in charge of small groups at the time, but also had a huge heart for outreach. He really wanted to see every congregant become engaged in reaching and blessing irreligious people in all of their spheres of influence. Together Tim and Chuck shared this vision with the leadership team at Hill Country Bible Church and started to add several missing pieces to actually make it happen. Every thirty days, Tim and Chuck started asking people to talk about their life of witness. They asked the leaders to talk about whether their passion level for unchurched people was high or low by giving their outreach passion a temperature number between one and ten. Then people were asked to share stories of spiritual conversations they were having with unchurched people.

You might think that this kind of accountability for personal witness would be uncomfortable for people. It may be a little at first, but it has now become the highlight of their leadership meetings. And without this kind of inspiring, loving, direct accountability, people don't change. By providing a little inspiration, accountability, and instruction about how to have spiritual conversations, and planning so that outreach could become more intentional, Tim and Chuck are seeing results. They have begun to see their whole leadership culture shift, and they are seeing an impact. In the last year, seventeen of their key leaders have led fifty-one people to Christ personally. This change represents radical forward progress. This church had the heart and desire, but it just didn't have the path. It is now finding the path, and God is blessing.

CONSTANCE EVANGELICAL FREE CHURCH

On the missional community side of the equation, I think of Constance Evangelical Free Church just north of Minneapolis. Randy Discher, the lead pastor, and Sean McDowell, the outreach leader, have partnered to make five key missional practices part of the whole congregation. We call them the BLESS practices. They are rooted in God's promise to Abraham that God would fulfill his mission by blessing Abraham and then by blessing all the nations of the earth *through* Abraham. The five missional practices are

1. Begin with prayer: for *and* with unchurched people.

2. Listen: to people and their spiritual stories.

3. Eat: develop the relationship through sharing food and drink.

4. Serve: meet needs of others, and ask for help from them.

5. Share: your faith story and the story of Jesus.[8]

Anyone can pursue these practices wherever they live, work, study, or play. And these practices make evangelism doable and motivating for the everyday people in our churches. Constance Evangelical Free Church has wholeheartedly pursued these practices, motivating and equipping all their people and reaching out as a whole church into the community. When they started on this path, it was a huge prayer of faith for them to trust God to lead fifty people to Christ through their congregation. Now after shifting their whole church culture, this church as seen 272 people come to Christ in the last year, most of whom have stuck and are growing in Christ with the congregation. With fifteen hundred in weekly attendance, the church has now become a conversion community and has committed to pursuing this path for the long haul.

Emerging adults long for community and connection. They need to belong before they believe. And since they are in a stage of exploring their identity, emerging adults need to try on Christian identity before they can fully embrace it. As Seversen says, they need not only to belong before they believe, but even need to begin to behave like a Christian before they believe.[9] This stage of life is a period of experimentation. Churches that are reaching and developing emerging adults have figured out ways to invite emerging adults into community and connection with other emerging adults, but also into contexts where they can serve and give *before they commit fully to Christ.*

One approach to understand the process of conversion is to understand the ways sociologists have explored how commitment to organizations works. Seversen unpacks this process.[10] Sociologists measure three main dimensions of allegiance to a group or organization: belief, belonging, and behavior. In the past, many Christians have thought about the conversion process as flowing from belief to belonging, and only then to behavior. People became committed to Christ in a one-on-one encounter where a Christian shared the gospel or through an event designed to preach the gospel, such as a Billy Graham evangelistic event, church evangelistic service, or a concert. Then people joined a local church, or at least were strongly encouraged to do so. Then through that local church they were discipled into behaving out of their Christian identity.

Today for emerging adults who are trying on Christian identity, belonging happens first. They start getting involved in a Christian community where they can explore Christian identity with people who do not judge them or expect them to be something they are not. They are given space, freedom, and affirmation to explore and search. They belong before they believe. If your congregation has no entry points of connection where emerging adults can feel like they belong before they believe, your church will not likely grow younger. But the second step is the biggest surprise. Churches reaching and developing emerging adults also encourage emerging adults to contribute, to invest, to volunteer and help, before they have come to full commitment to Christ. They behave before they believe. They behave on their way to belief and commitment. Then finally, as they try on Christian identity and find it fits, they fully embrace Christ and commit.

Churches and church leaders need discernment regarding how emerging adults who have not yet fully committed their lives to Christ can actually serve others in the church. But one of Seversen's stories illustrates it well. While catching up with an old friend at a church she was visiting, Beth was very curious to know how this friend had found his way into a church. He had not been open or receptive when Beth had known him several years before. He was carrying two coffee urns and explained he only had a minute because he needed to get the coffee to his Sunday morning Bible study community. Beth asked him how long he had been attending the church. His response: this was his second Sunday. He had visited the Sunday before, and already the leader had asked him to help with hospitality for the community.

So many roles can be offered to people on their way toward finding God. They can help hosts with meetings, contact people who are unchurched, host a picnic or a sports outing, contribute through a service or compassion ministry with people who are hurting or marginalized, and so many other ways. Church leaders just need to reflect on how the team they lead could involve unchurched people who are visiting for the first time in a meaningful way. It is possible to find ways that unchurched people can contribute while still maintaining and safeguarding the spiritual vitality and integrity of ministries.

Seversen identifies five key components of ministries that reach and mentor emerging adults:

1. *Initiate* relationships, friendships, and connections with emerging adults.

2. *Invite* emerging adults to events and experiences in which they can begin friendships and conversations with Christian emerging adults.

3. *Include* emerging adults in a community to which they can belong before they believe.

4. *Involve* emerging adults in opportunities to serve, help, and contribute to the life and mission of the community (e.g., by helping in a service project).

5. *Invest* in developing unchurched emerging adults spiritually, for commitment to Christ and for leadership opportunities in the future.[11]

One powerful dimension of this process is that as emerging adults move toward faith in Christ, they get very enthusiastic about their church and turn around and invite many more family members, friends, and other emerging adults. Previously unchurched people are always the best inviters, as they still have many friends who do not follow Jesus yet. What's more, this developmental process not only helps them come to Christ, but it also develops them toward being strong followers of Jesus and witnesses to Jesus when they do commit.

FINAL THOUGHTS

I could tell you so many stories about churches becoming conversion communities and more effectively reaching and developing emerging adults. I think of a Hispanic Pentecostal Assembly of God congregation in Boston that has become a conversion community over these last few years. Or a larger African American Baptist congregation near Washington, DC, that has helped *all* of their many leaders embrace and model witness to Jesus. Or a small Methodist church in Portland, Oregon, that has engaged its community and seen conversion growth in powerful ways. And so many more.

We have seen this kind of change in every size church, of every ethnicity, in every context—urban, suburban, and rural. Based on our research that has identified best practices, and then applying them through pastor cohorts in hundreds of churches, I have become convinced that every one of our churches can become a conversion community. And all churches can grow younger as they become conversion communities.

As you trust and seek God, seek those who don't know Christ, and pursue the conversion community equation by developing missional leaders and missional congregational practices, you too can see your church transform. There is no silver bullet, but there is path and a process for changing the DNA of your congregation. If you want to become a conversion community and grow, you can!

QUESTIONS FOR DIALOGUE

1. What patterns are you seeing in your church or denomination regarding growth? Are you declining, plateauing, growing because Christians are coming from other churches, or growing by reaching the unchurched and dechurched?

2. Which of the ten predictive factors are present in your church or ministry context, and which need to be developed further or added?

3. What in this research surprises you? What encourages you?

4. How can you equip emerging adults whom you know to share their faith in ways that feel natural to them and will bear fruit in their relational networks?

BIBLIOGRAPHY

Barna, George, and David Kinnaman, eds. *Churchless: Understanding Today's Unchurched and How to Connect with Them.* Austin, TX: Barna Group, 2014.

Barna Group. "What Non-Christians Want from Faith Conversations." 2019. https://www.barna.com/research/non-christians-faith-conversations.

Coffman, Curt, and Kathie Sorensen. *Culture Eats Strategy for Lunch: The Secret of Extraordinary Results, Igniting the Passion Within.* Denver: Liang Addison, 2013.

Dean, Kenda Creasy. *Almost Christian: What the Faith of Our Teenagers Is Telling the American Church.* New York: Oxford University Press, 2010.

Drescher, Elizabeth. *Choosing Our Religion: The Spiritual Lives of America's Nones.* Oxford: Oxford University Press, 2016.

Everts, Don, and Doug Schaupp. *I Once Was Lost: What Postmodern Skeptics Taught Us about Their Path to Jesus.* Downers Grove, IL: IVP Books, 2008.

Everts, Don, Doug Schaupp, and Val Gordon. *Breaking the Huddle: How Your Community Can Grow Its Witness.* Downers Grove, IL: IVP Books, 2016.

Ferguson, Dave, and Jon Ferguson. *B.L.E.S.S.: Five Everyday Ways to Love Your Neighbor.* Washington, DC: Salem Books, 2021.

Finke, Roger, and Rodney Stark. *The Churching of America, 1776–2005: Winners and Losers in Our Religious Economy.* New Brunswick, NJ: Rutgers University Press, 2005.

Kinnaman, David, and Aly Hawkins. *You Lost Me: Why Young Christians Are Leaving Church … and Rethinking Faith.* Grand Rapids: Baker Books, 2011.

Niebuhr, H. Richard. *The Social Sources of Denominationalism.* New York: Henry Holt, 1929.

Pathak, Jay, and Dave Runyon. *The Art of Neighboring: Building Genuine Relationships Right Outside Your Door.* Grand Rapids: Baker Books, 2012.

Pew Research. "America's Changing Religious Landscape: Christians Decline Sharply, Unaffiliated and Other Faiths Continue to Grow." 2015. http://www.pewforum.org/2015/05/12/americas-changing-religious-landscape/.

Pohl, Christine D. *Making Room: Recovering Hospitality as a Christian Tradition*. Grand Rapids: Eerdmans, 1999.

Powell, Kara, Jake Mulder, and Brad Griffin. *Growing Young: Six Essential Strategies to Help Young People Discover and Love Your Church*. Grand Rapids: Baker Books, 2016.

Rainer, Thom S. *Surprising Insights from the Unchurched and Proven Ways to Reach Them*. Grand Rapids: Zondervan, 2008.

Richardson, Rick. *Evangelism Outside the Box: New Ways to Help People Experience the Good News*. Downers Grove, IL: IVP Books, 2000.

———. *Re-imagining Evangelism: Inviting Friends on a Spiritual Journey*. Downers Grove, IL: InterVarsity Press, 2006.

———. *You Found Me: New Research on How Unchurched Nones, Millennials, and Irreligious Are Surprisingly Open to Christian Faith*. Downers Grove, IL: InterVarsity Press, 2019.

Seversen, Beth. *Not Done Yet: Reaching and Keeping Unchurched Emerging Adults*. Downers Grove, IL: InterVarsity Press, 2020.

Seversen, Beth, and Rick Richardson. "Emerging Adults and the Future of Evangelism." *Witness* 28 (2014).

Smith, Christian. *American Evangelicalism: Embattled and Thriving*. Chicago: University of Chicago Press, 1998.

———. "Theorizing Religious Effects among American Adolescents." *Journal for the Scientific Study of Religion* 42, no. 1 (2003): 17–30.

Smith, Christian, and Melinda Lundquist Denton. *Soul Searching: The Religious and Spiritual Lives of American Teenagers*. New York: Oxford University Press, 2005.

Stanley, Andy. "Double-Barrel Preaching." Accessed January 27, 2021. https://store.northpoint.org/pages/double-barrel-preaching.

Stetzer, Ed, Richie Stanley, and Jason Hayes. *Lost and Found: The Younger Churched and the Churches That Reach Them.* Nashville: B&H, 2009.

Wuthnow, Robert. *After the Baby Boomers: How Twenty- and Thirty-Somethings Are Shaping the Future of American Religion.* Princeton: Princeton University Press, 2007.

8

. . . . .

Singing Together Missionally

Kevin Turner

. . . . .

*For just as the body is one and has many members, and all the
members of the body, though many, are one body, so it is with Christ.*

—1 Corinthians 12:12, NRSV

Schola has changed my view of the church and
ministry. It has empowered me and given me hope
that we can reach beyond the church walls and
truly be in ministry with the world. Schola not
only reaches an underserved demographic in the
church of young adults, but also goes out into the
community to reach those who are intimidated by
walking through the church doors. Schola is this
eclectic group of people with varying faith backgrounds who seek to reach out in grace and love to
the world. It reminded me that God can use anyone

and speaks to the importance of being ecumenical. Schola speaks to the human need and desire for community in a time and culture where we are more isolated than we have ever been. Schola has taught me the importance of evangelism. (I use this term in an attempt to reclaim its positive attributes while shedding its negative connotations.) Being a part of Schola has inspired me and will impact my ministry going forward.

This is the response of a twenty-six-year-old woman when asked to describe her experience with an experimental choir formed for people who had graduated from high school but were not typically involved in the music ministry at Davidson United Methodist Church. My attempt in creating this choir was to reengage them into the worship life of our church.

MISTAKEN INITIAL ASSUMPTIONS

My initial desire was to create a worship choir that would extend the youth choir experience, and my hope was that these choir members would feel comfortable engaging with the older adult Chancel Choir. I learned, throughout this process of creating an emerging adult choir, that my own initial desires and assumptions were not as important as the desires and hopes of the members of the choir. My ecclesiological vision of a worship choir prioritized strong, centralized leadership. I envisioned a model of ecclesial leadership where I would create an identity for the group, and the members would simply sign up.

What I learned in ministry with millennials and Generation Z was their need for the group to reflect their own communal ecclesiology. This group of singers valued a decentralized, multivalent leadership model. I needed to value community over more traditional markers of success. I also learned the group would only engage if they could determine their own identity. They chose their name, Schola, and the locations in which they would sing. I learned to create space for participants to determine how they best wanted to establish their own community that reflected their own passions for social justice. I believe the lessons learned in our process of beginning an emerging adult choir are not simply anecdotes from a case study. I believe that what the emerging adults taught me transcends the ministry of music and may provide lessons for the church at large.

DEFINING THE ISSUE

David Kinnaman begins his book *You Lost Me* by defining a problem of "dropouts"—young adults leaving the church following their teen years. He lays out the realities of this new generation: "Teen church engagement remains robust, but many of the enthusiastic teens so common in North American churches are not growing up to be faithful young adult disciples of Christ."[1] We certainly have witnessed this trend at Davidson United Methodist Church. Our youth music ministry attendance and participation eclipse those of the youth group in our congregation. We continue to offer many musical opportunities for youth: middle school handbells, middle school choir, senior high handbells, senior high choir, a youth praise band, and, in some years, participation in our compline choir.

However, despite all the participation in the music ministry during teen years, we have a great disparity in participation in our music ministry by twenty-somethings. Kinnaman provides us with stark facts in his discovery process: teens are among the most active religious Americans, but twenty-somethings are among the most religiously inactive.[2] Pew Research shows similar trends.[3] Many emerging adults were reared with a worldview of moral therapeutic deism and later became lost in the transition to adulthood.[4] Yet, it is within this moral ambiguity that church leaders find a new mission field. How do we present the message of Christ as something distinctive on which emerging and young adults can base their entire lives?

DEVELOPING A NEW APPROACH

We had invited these young adults to join our Chancel Choir, which is made up of older adults and younger parents. However, we had not been able to integrate them into the life of our choir. Over time I realized they would never integrate back into the life of the church through our Chancel Choir, a group consisting largely of people who range in age from thirty-five to eighty. At least, they would not integrate in the ways I expected, and I realized that other strategies would be needed. From that realization a new approach emerged.

DIALOGUE ABOUT WHY
CHURCH EXISTS

At Davidson United Methodist Church, we chose to not employ entertainment approaches to entice emerging adults to attend church. Rather, the approach I sought out models what Doug Gay says about the church, "Among other things, the Christian Church is an ongoing conversation with God and with one another about how to live for, with, and in God in our own places and times."[5] My initial strategy was developing an ad hoc choir of emerging adults to lead the Good Friday worship service. As we gathered for our first rehearsal, everyone had their own ideas and dreams about how the new group would develop. However, as we moved through that first cycle of rehearsals and performances, we found the emerging adults were craving something more than musical excellence. They were looking for a community that would pro-vide guidance for applying their developing adult faith to their personal lives.

Jeffrey Arnett's work, which seems to transcend the sacred and secular research, has led me to draw on the term "emerging adult" to describe our new ministry.[6] It generally refers to the ages of eighteen through twenty-nine; however, a few members of our emerging adult community have turned thirty over the course of our journey together. Arnett points out this group defies historical markers of adulthood (e.g., marriage, parenthood), and there is a lack of a rites of passage for these emerging adults. When some graduated high school, our church gave them a Bible. At the end of their final summer choir pilgrimage, seniors in high school each received a "send-off," where they heard words of encouragement from their peers, and they were afforded time to impart their wisdom to those who were younger. While a college graduation can function in this way, not all emerging adults are following the traditional routes to adulthood through a four-year degree.

This group of emerging adults did not have an ability to articulate their sense of ecclesiology, and this term was never used as we formed our community. Instead, we wrestled with the question, "Why does the church exist?" An anonymous answer from our group said the church is "a way for God's love to interact with the world, a place for all to be welcome (or at least it should be) and experience grace and love, and a place to meet people where they are and they can feel supported." As I developed the new ensemble, I realized emerging adults were envisioning a church that would be missional in its proclamation of God's love. Further group discussion revealed that their vision of a church that could "meet people where they are" was reflective of the possibilities of relationships and physical locations outside the walls of the church.

Through the ministry of music, they began encountering an approach to ecclesiology that was different from their teenage church. This new way of being in community needed to match their new life experiences out in the real world. What these emerging adults wanted to experience was an ecclesiology that would be rooted in the walls of the church but would bear fruit into our local community.[7] It was this service choir that was the genesis of our new choir.

BELONGING, BEHAVING, BELIEVING

Through the experience I began learning that a choir could address the sociological needs of emerging adults. The work of Diana Butler Bass assisted me as I began the ensemble in defining the issues of identity and instability challenging emerging adults. In her book *Christianity after Religion*, Bass maintains that belief, behavior, and belonging are three essential components of most religious faiths.[8] Bass observes that churches always emphasize these words in the order: belief, behavior, and belonging. In other words, new people are encouraged to believe according to an established community's beliefs and behave like the community's cultural societal norms.

Only after these first two conditions are met can a new person to the faith belong to typical congregations. But Bass maintains that Jesus worked these concepts in the reverse order. He invited the disciples to belong, which led to a different manner of behaving. Soon after they were assimilated and their behaviors changed, the disciples were believing differently than they did before they met Jesus. From the very beginning of our emerging adult choral fellowship, I wanted our community of service and song to emphasize belonging first.

The initial rehearsal of the new ensemble included Methodists, Episcopalians, Presbyterians, agnostics, and atheists. In some cases, these categories overlapped as some participants who grew up in a faith tradition now considered themselves agnostic or atheist. In this first rehearsal, no one was asked to sign up to be a Methodist or even a Christian. In fact, I stated that this new ensemble would not require regular Sunday worship attendance. This new ensemble was not created to be a place where emerging adults had to believe. Instead I explained that I wanted to establish a place where they could simply belong.

Richard Dunn and Jana Sundene tell us that emerging adults long for mentors who can help them navigate the delayed transition into traditional adulthood.[9] I met with just about every person in the group at a coffee shop near the church at least once during the formation of the community. In a world that is uncertain, our emerging adults needed the certainty of relationships to feel connected to the church.

At the outset of our endeavor, the emerging adults seemed to be a monolithic group. However, as they grew together, they learned how different their experiences were. Some were passionate about LGBTQ+ issues, while others held more traditional views regarding sexuality. Participants who were closer in age to thirty tended to roll their eyes in jest as those who were just beginning college spoke of how busy their lives were. I realized that this emerging adult choral fellowship was not a homogenous group at all, and I determined this diversity could be an asset.

The presence of emerging adults who were approaching thirty had an impact on the younger participants. This mentorship across age differences is crucial, as Setran and Kiesling say, for keeping emerging adults engaged in the life of the church. They explain that emerging adults "need to hear the testimonies of those who have seen God's hand at work in both good and hard times, witnessing to God's faithfulness over the long haul. ... Emerging adults can, by observation, begin to visualize life trajectories that lead to righteousness and peace and those that lead to quiet desperation."[10]

A PARTICIPATORY MODEL

In the ten-mile vicinity of Davidson United Methodist Church, one can find at least three megachurches that follow a multicampus model. These churches also employ worship leadership in their praise bands. Unlike the mainline churches with services employing praise bands, these multisite megachurches do allow emerging adults to be in leadership. However, in many of these churches only the most professional and polished musicians are afforded the opportunity to express themselves as worship leaders. Some of our more affluent local churches who have choral-based music ministries also employ paid singers in their choirs, which mirrors the approach of these megachurches.

In short, some large churches around Davidson approach leading music in what can be termed as exclusive rather than a more populist and inclusive approach where everyone can express their God-given creativity. A selective approach to music ministry, whether in a praise band setting or a more traditional choral-based program, may exclude those who are less capable from the transformative dimension of participating in a community of those praising God. However, I believe God can rework all the imperfections of our voices to make beautiful praise.

SPIRITUAL AND MISSIONAL
FORMATION

The nature of Schola made it difficult for the community to cease rehearsing. After our first Good Friday service, the Schola Cantorum clamored to know, "What's next?" We went on a short hiatus for the summer, and we started in earnest again in September of that year. In that first rehearsal of the fall, the leaders of group wanted to be more proactive in the development of the philosophy and spirit of our ensemble. During a break in singing, they split into different groups led by peers. Each leader asked their group to share what singing in a choral ensemble meant to them. In addition, each group shared social or spiritual issues of significance to them. The topics arising from these discussions included advocacy for different groups of people, as well as developing their faith.

Through group discussions, retreats, and community worship, the Schola community began developing an ecclesiology, which they determined should focus on justice. Out of these conversations the ensemble decided that they wanted to leave the walls of the church and engage the community in issues they felt the community cared about. Schola was creating an identity focused on exploring the nexus of faith and social issues, helping each other navigate the social complexities of their life stage, allowing music to spark conversations of God's involvement in their lives, and engaging with each other through table fellowship following rehearsals.

PRAYER OF THE CHILDREN

For example, one small group contained three female schoolteachers who were theologically and politically disparate. When one of these young women shared her fear of school shootings, the other two agreed quickly. The group discussion yielded a shared passion for common-sense approaches to gun control. Those who had been youth choir members at Davidson recalled singing a piece dealing with senseless violence in our world. "Prayer of the Children" was written by Kurt Bestor (b. 1958) during the Yugoslavian wars of the late twentieth century.[11] The participants of Schola asked whether we could sing this piece again. It seemed the lyrics—"Angry guns preach a gospel full of hate"—resonated differently with these emerging adults now that they were older. Those who requested the piece had matured in life, and their time in the classroom had sharpened their sense of the tragedy of gun violence.

WHERE WOULD JESUS BE?

Our relational sense of justice becomes stunted when we are only around people like us. Schola Cantorum needed to go outside the church to look for healing, redemption, and justice. The ensemble began singing in a wide variety of places. Following a service at the Crafty Beer Guys, the manager of the establishment appeared at my side. She said, "We've had a start-up church meeting here on Sunday mornings for a couple of years. That group just quit meeting, and we would love for you to come back. People here tonight were really into it." As the smell of beer, cigarettes, and diesel exhaust permeated the air, I remembered Pope Francis's words that in order to be successful shepherds, we have to "smell like the sheep."[12] I realized we need to be in the midst of the sheep in order to achieve transformation.

SHARING THEIR FAITH

It may be puzzling that we began this community with a Good Friday service remembering Christ's crucifixion. However, participants of our emerging adult group at Davidson did not shrink from the language of the cross. On the contrary, the community seemed to relish the opportunity to sing for such a powerful day in the life of the church. The repertoire acknowledged the cross and reflected the different theories of atonement.

Also, in order to prepare Schola to share their faith outside the walls, our rehearsals became less like a traditional choir rehearsal and more like a Sunday school class or youth fellowship meeting. We divided into smaller groups to allow opportunities for more reserved individuals to feel it was a safe space to share. We wrestled with simple questions first: "Why do you come here?" and "What does it mean to sing about God?" After a few cycles of these questions, we moved to more detailed questions such as, "Who or what do you wish the church prayed for?"

Schola Cantorum had begun to move from being an insular affinity group inside the church toward being a community that shared the love of Christ in the broader community. By leaving the walls of the church to meet people such as a woman who felt the church had nothing to offer her anymore, Schola experienced what it was like to share their faith and dream of justice with others. The new experience of sharing faith outside the walls of the church had turned Schola into what Pope Francis calls an evangelizing community experience of the power of the Father's infinite mercy.[13]

REFLECTING ON THIS NEW
RITE OF PASSAGE

The participants defined their desire to be a community of faith and service. In the process of creating Schola, I learned about my own biases and predilection to function in an old paradigm of top-down leadership. The fruit of Schola's efforts was so much sweeter, though, when we viewed success through a different lens. Finding an identity and community through singing was what we achieved. This reorientation helped our participants to find a spiritual identity. As we created this ecclesial community focused on singing and social justice, I realized that the emerging adults were experiencing a shift in their own expectations. Schola participants experienced a rite of passage from their preconceived notions of what a choir could be to a community of faith that sings together. Their liminal time together allowed them to value sharing faith together with Christ at the center.

IMPLICATIONS FOR LOCAL CHURCHES

I found our choral engagements with emerging adults were yielding solid results; yet conversation among staff colleagues regarding an emerging adult community often included the question, "Why a choir?" According to some of my colleagues, the idea of a choir seemed to be contrary to news articles most people read online that lament the loss of emerging adults in church life. However, I believe we had such strong involvement because music carries a deep connection to the primitive human brain, and therefore, music can more easily convey a sense of the divine than words alone. Music, which is present in both sacred and secular rituals, forms community. Consequently, what follows are a few insights for congregations who might be considering an approach like this.

First the work of Schola encouraged leaders in the church to ask a different question regarding emerging adults' engagement in the life of the church. Too often, church leaders try to appeal to emerging adults by proposing ideas *for* the emerging adults. Instead, the experiences with Schola should exhort leaders to ask what we can do *with* emerging adults. In starting Schola, I initiated the experience by asking the former question, what we could do for these adults. Indeed, I do believe asking this question was valid. However, my work with emerging adults leads me to believe engaging in work with them will ultimately help reassimilate these children of God into the church.

Second, we must take the advice of Setran and Kiesling seriously.[14] We must commit to the hard work required by both sides of the generation gap to achieve real fellowship.[15] If we were starting Schola again, I would work harder at bridging this generational gap. Older adults would be encouraged to not only listen to the faith stories of our emerging adults, but also work intently to share power earlier in the start-up process with those in the younger ages. I would spend time with emerging adults encouraging them to listen to the older adults' guidance, and I would encourage more faithful interactions with both groups. Mentoring and active listening would be at the heart of Schola. These ideas of mentoring and active listening should not be foreign for those in church leadership. We already participate in these activities when we are guiding youth groups for teenagers. The work of Schola indicates we should continue mentoring relationships with emerging adults as they navigate their rites of passage into adulthood.

Third, church leaders often consider functional adults to be able to plan Sunday school lessons for their class without much training on how to lead a Sunday school class. The work of Schola underscores a need to assist teenagers as they transit the rite of passage from high school to adulthood in order to help them develop a new sense of *communitas*. That is to say, they need to experience a sense of community that occurs from experiencing liminality together. I agree with Robert Wuthnow's charge to church leaders to continue a support system for emerging adults after high school. As he writes, "We cannot hope to be a strong society if we invest resources in young people until they are eighteen or twenty and then turn them out to find their way entirely on their own."[16]

Fourth, the efforts to nurture Schola were investments in the lives of emerging adults through music. But I believe this is a model can apply to many local churches. Work with emerging adults does not have to take the form of a choir. Collaboration can take many forms, such as art, service, sports, and other interests and hobbies that groups of emerging adults share.

FINAL THOUGHTS

How can ministry leaders in the twenty-first century provide guidance for those who are at the leading edge of the church's next generation? How might emerging adults become contributors to congregations where they are given space to offer and plan for themselves rather than passively acquiesce to traditional church structures where a strict, top-down leadership style dominates? Hopefully this case study provides some insights that can help other congregations.

In their most recent service at a local coffee shop, Schola arrived early to set up equipment. Two young emerging adult women said, "I'd like to be a part of a church like this." The challenges and trends mentioned by Pew and other researchers are real, yet participating in a missional music ministry beyond the walls of the church has made me hopeful for the future of the church.

QUESTIONS FOR DIALOGUE

1. What assumptions are you bringing into your relationships with emerging adults, and how will you determine whether they are helping or hindering your efforts?

2. What are creative options for initiating genuine dialogue with emerging adults about forming a new type of ministry, or expanding an existing one, that would be meaningful to them and to their friends?

3. In what ways do your perceptions of leadership need to change so emerging adults have a greater sense of ownership and agency in that new or expanded endeavor?

4. How might emerging adults share their faith in ways that are relevant and genuine as they participate together in *communitas*?

BIBLIOGRAPHY

Arnett, Jeffrey Jensen. "Emerging Adulthood: A Theory of Development from the Late Teens through the Twenties." *American Psychologist* 55, no. 5 (2000): 469–80.

———. *Emerging Adulthood: The Winding Road from the Late Teens through the Twenties.* 2nd ed. New York: Oxford University Press, 2015.

Bass, Diana Butler. *Christianity after Religion: The End of Church and the Birth of a New Spiritual Awakening.* New York: HarperCollins, 2012.

Bestor, Kurt. "Prayer of the Children: The Story behind the Song." Accessed December 14, 2019. http://www.kurtbestor.com/story-behind-prayer-of-the-children.

Dunn, Richard R. and Jana L. Sundene. *Shaping the Journey of Emerging Adults: Life-giving Rhythms for Spiritual Transformation*. Downers Grove, IL: InterVarsity Press, 2012.

Emba, Christine. "Why Millennials Are Skipping Church and Not Going Back." *Washington Post*, October 27, 2019. https://www.washingtonpost.com/opinions/why-millennials-are-skipping-church-and-not-going-back/2019/10/27/0d35b972-f777-11e9-8cf0-4cc99f74d127_story.html.

Gay, Doug. *Remixing the Church: The Five Moves of Emerging Ecclesiology*. Norwich, UK: SCM Press, 2011.

Harper, Brad, and Paul Louis Metzger. *Exploring Ecclesiology: An Evangelical Introduction*. Grand Rapids: Brazos, 2009.

Kimball, Dan. *They Like Jesus but Not the Church: Insights from Emerging Generations*. Grand Rapids: Zondervan, 2009.

Kinnaman, David. *You Lost Me: Why Young Christians Are Leaving Church ... and Rethinking Faith*. Grand Rapids: Baker Books, 2011.

Mitchell, J. Matt, Elizabeth Bjorling Poest, and Benjamin D. Espinoza. "Re-engaging Emerging Adults in Ecclesial Life through Christian Practices." *The Journal of Youth Ministry* 15, no. 1 (Fall 2016): 34–57.

Pew Research Center. "U.S. Decline of Christianity Continues at a Rapid Pace: Update on America's Changing Religious Landscape." 2019. https://www.pewforum.org/2019/10/17/in-u-s-decline-of-christianity-continues-at-rapid-pace/.

Pope Francis. *The Joy of the Gospel: Evangelii Gaudium*. Vatican City: United States Conference of Catholic Bishops, 2013.

Setran, David P. and Chris A. Kiesling. *Spiritual Formation in Emerging Adulthood: A Practical Theology for College and Young Adult Ministry*. Grand Rapids, MI: Baker Academic, 2013.

Smith, Christian. *American Evangelicalism: Embattled and Thriving*. Chicago: University of Chicago Press, 1998.

Smith, Christian, and Melinda Lundquist Denton. *Soul Searching: The Religious and Spiritual Lives of American Teenagers*. Oxford: Oxford University Press, 2005.

Smith, Christian, and Patricia Snell. *Souls in Transition: The Religious and Spiritual Lives of Emerging Adults*. Oxford: Oxford University Press, 2009.

Turner, Kevin. "The World Is About to Turn: Imagining a New Ecclesiology for Emerging Adults through Missional Music Ministry." PhD diss., Southern Methodist University, 2020.

Wuthnow, Robert. *After the Baby Boomers: How Twenty- and Thirty-Somethings Are Shaping the Future of American Religion*. Princeton: Princeton University Press, 2007.

9

. . . . .

Practicing Racial Reconciliation

Daniel Hartman and Peter Cha

. . . . .

You cannot make your young people grow; that's the Holy Spirit's job.
But you can create a space in which they can grow; that's your job.

—Dann Spader

Mosaic was a space where I was able to taste a little
piece of God's coming kingdom each week. God's
transcendence and immanence, heaven and earth,
righteousness and justice, and love for God and
neighbor danced along a thin line. Mosaic deeply
shaped my imagination of what a reconciling community looks like in this polarized and divided society. In my missional formation, Mosaic taught me
that discipleship is never purely speculative but
sprouts through the weathers of honest conversations, uncomfortable encounters, and regular

fellowship. Mosaic also broadened my scope of missional praxis—it is personal, communal, societal, systemic, and cosmic.

T his comment from an Asian American student embodies the heart of Mosaic Ministries while exemplifying two of its key philosophies—to create space where God can form people and to journey together where we can learn and grow as a community. Both the submission to God's work and the commitment to continue gathering create opportunity for significant life change. Indeed, they provide fertile ground for the formation of emerging and young adults.

Today's twenty-somethings live in a world that is filled with uncertainty, complexity, and despair. Understanding one's place in such a world and imagining one's future without losing hope are the daunting tasks that face each person, especially those individuals of color who make up nearly 44 percent of this age group in the United States.[1] How might a Christian community develop a biblically informed approach to assist these emerging and young adults with their task of identity formation in today's world? In this chapter, we will describe how, beginning in 2010, Mosaic Ministries at Trinity Evangelical Divinity School developed a unique learning community for these students—an intentionally multiracial community that sought to assist with their identity, spiritual, and missional formation.

INSIGHTS GATHERED FROM
PREVIOUS RESEARCH STUDIES

According to a recent research study, emerging and young adults today wrestle with three fundamental questions: *Who am I?*, *Where do I belong?*, and *What difference do I make?*[2] These questions point to three interrelated and significant challenges for them: the formation of identity, finding their place and role in community, and developing a sense of purpose.

Unlike previous generations, for whom their identity was greatly influenced or guided by their families, cultural traditions, and societal expectations, today many face the daunting task of constructing their sense of self alone, reflexively negotiating with various voices around them as they seek to shape their own authentic identity.[3] Further, because of social media, this process of identity construction takes place in a context where each person is saturated with competing, and often contradicting, voices and perspectives that come from near and far, making it even more challenging for individuals to form their sense of authentic self.[4]

For nonwhite emerging and young adults, the persistence of structural and systemic injustice and the frequency of experiencing racial prejudice add additional obstacles and pitfalls. Their sense of self and dignity are constantly questioned and assaulted, causing many to experience deep racial trauma and even racial self-hatred.[5] Given that nonwhite individuals make up nearly a half of this age group in the US population, it is essential that Christian communities attend to the intercultural and multiracial dimensions of their identity formation process.

Scholars who study the process of identity formation note that belonging to a safe and affirming community is a great asset.[6] It is not coincidence, then, that many emerging and young adults who are asking "Who am I?" are also seeking to belong to churches that are primarily characterized as "welcoming, accepting, authentic, hospitable, and caring"—churches that have the "warmth cluster."[7] More than any programs or styles of worship, emerging and young adults look for a community where they can safely explore different ideas and perspectives as they develop their own voice, perspectives, beliefs, and identity. For nonwhite emerging and young adults, finding such a faith community is essential.

A Christian community, whether it is a local church or a Christian university, is uniquely equipped to be such a community, a community where members from various backgrounds should have an equal sense of belonging, purpose, and identity. The apostle Paul reminds us that Christ's death on the cross reconciled us with God *and* with one another (Eph 2:11–18 NIV). Therefore, Paul concludes, there are to be no "aliens" and "strangers" among Christians but only "one new humanity" (v. 15). This blessed unity, however, does not erase diversity but rather creates a new "unity-in-diversity," both now and in the future (Rev 7:9).

But how might we experience a slice of this unity-in-diversity in today's broken world? According to Miroslav Volf, when an individual becomes a new follower of Jesus, the indwelling of the Holy Spirit empowers that person to embrace others in a way that begins to transform one's identity.[8] As the result of one's lifelong journey of discipleship, then, the person not only becomes more like Christ our Lord but also becomes what Volf calls the "Catholic Personality"; that is, a person who beautifully embodies the richness of different cultures while maintaining certain aspects of their own culture. In short, a transformative, multicultural, Spirit-led faith community that is rich in diversity has the potential to raise up many effective kingdom leaders.

In such a kingdom community, individual members experience a transformative process not only for forming their identity but also their sense of vocation, a deep and sustained missional purpose. Many studies indicate that emerging and young adults yearn to identify a cause or calling that is bigger than they are.[9] This desire is even more common for those from minority communities whose lives and identity were deeply impacted by various forms of racial injustice.[10] Their passion for social justice has been powerfully expressed through numerous protest movements. It is not a coincidence, then, that many recent studies indicate churches that attract many young adults are those that are actively involved in community-service programs and justice-oriented initiatives.[11] Indeed, today's emerging and young adults are formed by and for such communities.

How, then, might a Christian community create a space where emerging adults can explore and form their identities? As mentioned earlier, today's emerging and young adults are looking for faith communities that are characterized by warmth. However, they are looking for a warmth that isn't just an "add-on but in their church's very DNA."[12] To put it differently, many are looking for a church that has a congregational culture that prioritizes warmth, a culture that has been built over a period of time as it put into use and practice a certain set of values and artifacts.[13] An institutional culture, in turn, powerfully shapes individuals. An ethnographic study of US seminaries concludes that it is the school's educational culture that has the most influence on students' formation.[14] Given these social realities, any Christian community that aims to serve and work with emerging and young adults needs to pay attention to its culture, intentionally shaping it and reshaping it so that all its members, regardless of their backgrounds, might feel affirmed and flourish.

A CASE STUDY

Trinity Evangelical Divinity School (TEDS) is a broadly evangelical seminary with approximately twelve hundred students from around the world. Located in Deerfield, Illinois, its purpose is "to serve the church of the Living God by equipping servants for the work of the gospel of Christ worldwide."[15] The school welcomes and equips students from many denominational backgrounds and increasingly from many ethnic and racial backgrounds.

Mosaic Ministries started at Trinity and expanded off campus, across racial and socioeconomic boundaries, to the neighboring communities of North Chicago and Waukegan. While Deerfield is a wealthy and predominantly white community, North Chicago and Waukegan are racially diverse and have experienced economic challenges due to postindustrial decline. Mosaic responded to this particular cultural and social context, endeavoring to serve these communities while simultaneously equipping young adults in their spiritual formation journey.

Through that process, Mosaic developed four distinct yet overlapping ministries. Trinity is home to the Mosaic cohort and Mosaic Gathering, while Mosaic House Ministries and Mosaic Initiative reside in North Chicago and Waukegan, respectively. The Mosaic cohort is an intentionally multiracial learning community to support student identity, spiritual, and missional formation. The Mosaic Gathering is a weekly meeting that draws students, staff, faculty, and local pastors and focuses on current events and issues (e.g., mass incarceration, immigration, racialization). Mosaic House Ministries is an intentional living community where residents practice prayer, discipleship, hospitality, and fellowship with a missional focus. The Mosaic Initiative serves as an innovation hub to twelve partnering congregations, focused on developing ministries with and for emerging and young adults. In all, Mosaic convenes sacred spaces for the development of emerging and young adults within and between the seminary, churches, and local communities.

OUR FINDINGS

Over the years, we have conducted interviews, focus groups, and surveys to assess Mosaic Ministries, along with countless hours of participant observation. Our findings have been consistent with prominent themes discussed in the literature survey. We have organized and present key findings through the following theological and formational framework, and have identified several practices that nourish young adult development.

A THEOLOGICAL FRAMEWORK FOR HOLISTIC FORMATION

In Mosaic Ministries, we focus on forming ambassadors for Christ in God's mission. The biblical framework of reconciliation assists with this formation. Reconciliation with God in Christ (2 Cor 5:17–21) provides the foundation for three key formational movements: reconciliation with self, with others, and with all things. Each of these interconnected movements intersects with certain felt needs of emerging and young adults—reconciliation with self (identity), with others (community), and with all things (purpose). This distinctly Christian vision informs Mosaic Ministries.

We have observed that *reconciliation with God* is foundational for orienting emerging and young adults in their yearnings. Without this anchoring in Christ, many drift toward popular methods or theories to understand themselves and their desires for change in society. As such, reconciliation with God shapes all aspects of the following reconciliation movements (with self, others, and all things).

We hear many painful stories of how society, and even the church, devalues people in their embodied personhood. Many Mosaic students come to Trinity with wounds and questions about how their sense of self, including race/ethnicity, gender, and culture, intersects with their identity in Christ. *Reconciliation with self* becomes a healing journey toward wholeness. Significantly, this work is often facilitated by a loving community.

God's *reconciliation with others* creates this community. Though often difficult, this journey helps reflect God's intent for humanity—unified and loving through the work of Christ. As students progress together in Mosaic, authentic and unlikely friendships develop, along with ministry partnerships. Further yet, their identity expands toward a broader kingdom citizenship.

Last, God's *reconciling all things* gives ultimate hope with which to live in our broken and fragmented world. The world's brokenness exposes "gaps" between what is and what ought to be.[16] Different students see different gaps. In the context of community, students discern a sense of purpose for how they will participate in God's reconciling work of closing the gap toward salvation, justice, and renewal. As a Latino student described, "It is a community of leaders on the journey toward reconciliation and theological formation where I felt safe to be myself, explore ideas, and experience Christ's love through his people. I cannot imagine going through TEDS without my Mosaic family."

CREATING SACRED SPACES

Space matters—physically, spiritually, culturally, and imaginatively. Where we gather, how we arrange the room, and what artifacts we include all contribute to the formation experience. For example, in contrast to a lecture where students sit in rows, the Mosaic Gathering cultivates conversational learning through round-table discussions. We provide a simple meal for students to enjoy around their table. Culturally diverse music plays in the background. Warm hugs abound. The room is bright and colorful. Moreover, we pray in the space beforehand, asking God to create an atmosphere of hospitality and transformation. We ask that God's space, heaven, would meet ours on earth. Therefore, prayer is a priority in all of the ministries. Emerging and young adults regularly share how these sacred spaces shape them, citing something intangible about the experience.

Essentially, we try to create a new culture in Mosaic—one that is friendly to the formation of emerging and young adults. New language and metaphors support this process. For example, we often employ the gift of stories, the discipline of lament, creative dislocation, practices of unlearning as well as learning, and reconciliation as a journey with God.[17] This language makes room for certain practices that strengthen the formation of identity, belonging, and purpose. Furthermore, we place a high value on the arts—music, painting, poetry, and dance. These cultural expressions help us experience the breadth and depth of emotions in ministries of reconciliation.

In addition to physical and cultural spaces, we create broader spaces between communities that exhibit God's heart and nurture imagination for ministry. For instance, our partnerships between Trinity and Waukegan generate new networks as well as new spaces of communion. In many ways, the habits of mind that are cultivated in cross-cultural and cross-community partnerships assist in forming emerging and young adults for faithful ministry in today's world. Irina illustrated this when she explained that Mosaic provided a "safe space to process difficult things. I appreciated the difficult topics that Mosaic did not shy away from addressing, and the safe space they created that allowed students to wrestle with those topics and process them together. It helped me see the power of dialoguing and to allow different voices and opinions in the conversation and not be threatened by people different than me. It has broadened my perspective on understanding what the church is."

DEVELOPING IDENTITY: STORY AND VOICE

Acknowledging the complex, intersectional, and changing nature of identity, Mosaic creates space for emerging and young adults to learn who they are in Christ. We practice sharing and receiving stories to facilitate greater understanding of oneself, others, and God. These experiences are often deeply healing and redemptive, not only for the one who shares but for the whole community. This process, perhaps more than any other, helps students journey toward what we referenced as a "Catholic Personality" or kingdom leader. Patrick Shin explains it this way: "What Mosaic offered for me through its cohort fellowship was an intentional space to be exposed to different stories, learn from various perspectives, and it gave me opportunities to explore and understand my own voice. Mosaic allowed me to both reimagine and reframe how I integrated my faith, culture, and life experiences in a way that allowed me to lead more authentically while thinking through issues more critically."

Beyond one's individual identity, Mosaic helps cultivate a communal sense of identity. For instance, one of our table values in Mosaic Gathering is, "Be authentically you; become the 'new we.'"

While validating their identity formation, we also point to the bigger picture of belonging in Christ and to one another. Our "we" expands to include all who have called on the name of the Lord for salvation, including, at times, those who have hurt us.[18] This inclusion is important for multiracial communities and demonstrates real unity in diversity. As such, developing one's identity, personally and collectively, is bound up with an authentic sense of community.

BELONGING IN COMMUNITY: VULNERABILITY, LISTENING, AND FOOD

Three key practices, among others, nurture a sense of community in Mosaic. First, emerging and young adults value vulnerability and desire to practice it. They want to be known and to know others. In a space where leaders and peers demonstrate vulnerability, we have consistently seen how students embrace a culture of "being real." Though vulnerability requires risk, when stewarded well, it often results in a feeling of communal safety (e.g., "I'm not alone" or "I feel understood").

Second, one of the most consistent take-aways cited by emerging and young adults in Mosaic is learning to listen. We emphasize this practice immediately to new members by introducing lessons from improvisation. In many ways, to improvise, one must cultivate listening skills in order to build toward a new future together. This translates to listening to God and doing his will in ministry. We also highlight this practice in our Mosaic Gathering, where we frequently discuss controversial topics. Here, the exercise of listening cultivates empathy. Around tables, we encourage deep listening and, in turn, speaking to serve the community. These values are particularly important for students of color, who often tire of explaining or defending their experiences.

For example a Latina student explained that the people in Mosaic "reminded me that I belong and that I am needed in the kingdom of God even when I might not always feel like that in my context. It modeled learning from one another and incarnational listening, which are two tools that I've found vital as I find myself in different situations and trying to adapt to new realities. There is beauty in shared pain, and the best we can do as shepherds is to create spaces where people can process in community."

Third, we deeply value food and eating together. Not only does this practice nourish our physical well-being, but food comes with stories—stories of family, culture, and tradition. Eating together turns to sharing life together. In many ways, this practice makes room for those listed previously. Perhaps it is no surprise, then, that, for Christians, the table remains crucial for community.

DISCERNING PURPOSE: AGENCY, EMPOWERMENT, AND MENTORSHIP

We build Mosaic Ministries along with those who are participating in it. As a result, emerging and young adults have real ownership and agency to contribute to God's work in meaningful ways. Mosaic is not a program, but a community on a journey together. People involved in Mosaic appreciate being a part of "something bigger" and something that is growing (especially when it is growing because of them).

In this community, Mosaic leaders invite students to lead in various capacities on and off campus. An intentional and meaningful invitation, combined with caring support systems, empowers students to exercise their giftings in significant ways. Regular mentorship, then, helps cultivate their leadership journey and sense of purpose. We have observed many who discern and discover their life direction—from church planting, to doctoral studies, to community development.

All of these practices can be summarized through the words of one young man who said,

> Discipleship entails the invitation of God's Spirit to reconcile our brokenness to God and our complex

relationships with others. The Holy Ghost equipped me as a disciple to reconcile my story with God and with others via Mosaic Ministries. Taking after the gospel pattern of our leaders, Mosaic was (and still is!) a family that created space for me to live into the journey of holistic reconciliation in Jesus! Throughout my studies in the intercultural studies program, I was grateful for God's wisdom in helping me understand that the church is missional because we are "sent" by God. Yet, Mosaic ministries gave me the biblical framework of holistic reconciliation (i.e., with God and neighbor) as a "means" and an "end" of the church's sentness. Now, before engaging missionally in my community as a pastor, I tend to ask: Who/what needs to be reconciled to God? What people groups need to be reconciled to one another? How can we address these matters with the gospel/ missional living? I have Mosaic Ministries to thank for this effective missional practice!

IMPLICATIONS AND APPLICATIONS

In the past several years, many people from Christian universities, seminaries, and parachurch groups have visited Mosaic Ministries to observe how we have created a unique space of formation on our campus. Often, our conversations with these colleagues end with a discussion about starting something similar on their campuses. In this context, we offer the following suggestions.

1. Pray for a clear vision that will shape and moti-vate your ministry. This vision must be compelling enough to shape (a) your ministry's identity (and that of your individual members), (b) the group's culture and the dynamics of its members' intercultural/racial

relationships, and (c) the clear missional calling on and off the campus. For Mosaic Ministries, this gospel vision is reconciliation: "Reconciled to be reconcilers!" Over the past ten years, this clear gospel mandate has shaped who we are, what we do on campus, and how we engage our broken world.

2. As you recruit a growing number of potential partners and collaborators to launch a new ministry for emerging or young adults, deepen your understanding of and commitment to the central vision God has given you. Mosaic leaders spent much of the first three years studying what biblical reconciliation means and looks like in today's broken world. At the same time, begin to identify group values that are biblical and relevant to your group's vision. These values will gradually shape the culture of your ministry— as long as you intentionally practice them by using certain artifacts that express those values. At Mosaic Ministries, as mentioned above, we decided to practice the value of listening (to God and to one another), a value that is often overlooked in most academic settings (where lecturing/preaching are prized activities) but is critical when our aim is to learn how to grow as agents of reconciliation. In order to practice this key value, we decided early on that learning and formation would be facilitated mostly through conversations, not through lectures. Thus, all our meetings take place around tables, learning to engage in generative conversations, by listening to understand (not necessarily to speak).

3. Mosaic Ministries offers not only a unique space but also a unique experience of time. The Mosaic program is not a formal course that lasts a semester.

Rather, it is a learning community in which many emerging and young adults participate throughout their years at Trinity (2–4 years). This journey experience is a critical component of Mosaic Ministries since both the process of reconciliation and of identity formation take time. After observing our ministry, some visiting teams returned to their campus and launched different types of initiatives, ranging from weekend retreats to occasional lecture series on reconciliation. However, these efforts did not seem to produce lasting results. Over the years, Mosaic Ministries has enjoyed a level of fruitfulness in its ministries because it embraced the practice of *both* "learning community" and "learning journey" across time, thus contextualizing our Lord's approach to discipleship in today's seminary context.

CONCLUSION

One student spoke of her experience this way:

> Mosaic means family, community, and a safe space. Mosaic is a place to learn, grow, stretch, and challenge norms collectively accepted within the church that don't align with the gospel's call for racial reconciliation. It's a place of welcoming acceptance where those who have historically been marginalized, categorized as "other," or have been minorities are intentionally prioritized. As an African American woman in a mostly white male–dominated major, Mosaic has been a place to feel seen, heard, loved, and completely valued. Mosaic has taught me how to further love all God's people despite the fact that it can sometimes be hard to love. The pilgrimage I

took through Mosaic has fundamentally changed
me in many ways. I believe God used this ministry to
take me to a different level of faith and willingness
to be bold for the sake of the gospel and God's glory.

As we reflect on the past ten years, we clearly see God's hand in
forming emerging and young adults through the holistic and biblical framework of reconciliation. We have sought to offer reflections on key practices that have supported this process, and we
have shared practical applications for starting such communities
elsewhere. Ultimately, though, God is the author of these stories.
It is our prayer that the Holy Spirit will inspire the creation and
development of many more communities that form emerging and
young adults for long-term missional faithfulness.

QUESTIONS FOR DIALOGUE

1. What are qualities emerging adults in your context
   believe form the foundation for a safe and affirming
   community?

2. What types of questions and challenges are emerging
   adults in your context facing?

3. What theological framework would enable them
   to effectively address their biggest questions and
   challenges?

4. What types of partners might be well suited to help
   you build and sustain this type of community?

BIBLIOGRAPHY

Carroll, Jackson W., et al. *Being There: Culture and Formation in Two Theological Schools*. New York: Oxford University Press, 1997.

Cha, Peter. "Constructing New Intergenerational Ties, Cultures, and Identities among Korean American Christians: A Congregational Case Study." In *This Side of Heaven: Race, Ethnicity, and Christian Faith*. Edited by Robert Priest and Alvaro Nieves. New York: Oxford University Press, 2006.

Frey, William F. "The Millennial Generation: A Demographic Bridge to America's Diverse Future." Brookings Institute, January 2018. https://www.brookings.edu/research/millenials/.

Gergen, Kenneth. *Relational Being*. Rev. ed. New York: Oxford University Press, 2011.

———. *The Saturated Self: Dilemmas of Identity in Contemporary Life*. Rev. ed. New York: Basic Books, 2000.

Giddens, Anthony. *Modernity and Self-Identity: Self and Society in the Late Modern Age*. Stanford: Stanford University Press, 1991.

Katongole, Emmanuel, and Chris Rice. *Reconciling All Things: A Christian Vision for Justice, Peace, and Healing*. Resources for Reconciliation. Downers Grove, IL: IVP Books, 2008.

Park, Kyeyoung. "'I Really Do Feel I'm 1.5': The Construction of Self and Community by Young Korean Americans." *Amerasia Journal* 25, no. 1 (1999): 139–64.

Parks, Sharon Daloz. Big Questions, *Worthy Dreams: Mentoring Young Adults in Their Search for Meaning, Purpose, and Faith*. Rev. 10th anniversary ed. San Francisco: Jossey-Bass, 2011.

Powell, Kara, Jake Mulder, and Brad Griffin. *Growing Young: Six Essential Strategies to Help Young People Discover and Love Your Church*. Grand Rapids: Baker Books, 2016.

Richardson, Rick. *You Found Me: New Research on How Unchurched Nones, Millennials, and Irreligious Are Surprisingly Open to Christian Faith.* Downers Grove, IL: InterVarsity Press, 2019.

Ross, Ticola Caldwell. "Exploring the Relationships between Youth Activism, Developmental Assets, and Sociopolitical Consciousness in Emerging Adulthood." PhD diss., North Carolina State University, 2015.

Rowe, Sheila. *Healing Racial Trauma: The Road to Resilience.* Downers Grove, IL: IVP Books, 2020.

Schein, Edgar H. *Organizational Culture and Leadership.* Rev. 4th ed. San Francisco: Jossey-Bass, 2010.

Seversen, Beth. *Not Done Yet: Reaching and Keeping Unchurched Emerging Adults.* Downers Grove, IL: InterVarsity Press, 2020.

Trinity International University. "About Trinity Evangelical Divinity School (TEDS)." Accessed September 20, 2020. https://www.tiu.edu/divinity/about-teds/.

Turkle, Sherry. *Reclaiming Conversation.* New York: Penguin Books, 2015.

Volf, Miroslav. *Exclusion and Embrace: A Theological Exploration of Identity, Otherness, and Reconciliation.* Nashville: Abingdon, 1996.

10

. . . . .

Partners in Mission: Service-Learning Trips as Tools for Growth

Kplang'at Cheruiyot Bii and Jennifer L. Collins

. . . . .

Barnabas wanted to take John, also called Mark, with them, but Paul did not think it wise to take him, because he had deserted them in Pamphylia.

—Acts 15:37–38 NIV

Get Mark and bring him with you, because he is helpful to me in my ministry.

—2 Timothy 4:11 NIV

A Taylor University service-learning course traveled to an overcrowded refugee camp where thousands of Muslim refugees endured unusually harsh winter conditions. Rain-soaked tents collapsed under the weight of additional rain, along with unprecedented snow and ice, and families suffered greatly from cold and further displacement. Stressed camp staff worked at 110 percent capacity with little rest in the chaotic and desperate situation. The enthusiastic Taylor group jumped in for three weeks of intense service, giving their all to help in every way the staff directed. When the team returned, the students had been deeply affected by their exposure to severe suffering.

One participant, Thomas,[1] said that after the trip he entered into a "difficult, angry dialogue with God," which became a springboard for profound spiritual growth. The trip "thrust me into an entirely different way of approaching God as still God, but not necessarily as just a loving Father who wanted all of my wildest dreams to come true." Thomas learned to trust God in the midst of trauma and within his limitations in ways not possible through secondhand news reports. He came to see God "as an ocean I didn't know had as much depth as it does and discovered a newness in him." He grew in empathy and in walking alongside those experiencing hardship, and returned to the camp for three months after completing his degree. Later Thomas co-led a similar trip involving ethno-tourism in Muslim villages and serving the communities. Thomas has since embarked on a two-year term with a well-known agency to serve at the original camp.

A BIBLICAL PRECEDENT FOR GROWTH

Many Christian emerging adults are eager to serve others and please God. Their generation "is committed to those around them and motivated by making a difference." They are caring and compassionate and "recognize that societal issues are much larger than just themselves." For example, one study revealed that 61 percent of college students are concerned about poverty, and 56 percent about racism and sexism.[2] Pew found that among Gen Z, "most see the country's growing racial and ethnic diversity as a good thing," and that "roughly two thirds think blacks are treated less fairly than whites in this country ... compared with about half of Gen Xers and Boomers."[3]

Trends show that Gen Z has a redemptive outlook and wants everyone to be respected, no matter who they are.[4] But like youthful Mark in Acts 15, enthusiastic Gen Z believers may not be ready to *effectively* engage in God's mission. How can we nurture mission formation through service and help them grow as Mark did? Later in Scripture we find that the young deserter and cause of a sharp disagreement became Paul's beloved helper near the end of the great missionary's life (2 Tim 4:11). Mark also became Peter's close associate (1 Pet 5:13) and a Gospel author.

How did Barnabas's mentoring of and belief in Mark on a trip to Cyprus (Acts 15:39) contribute to Mark's transformation? While we don't have scriptural details to answer that question, we can be encouraged that ill-equipped and even immature emerging and young adults can develop into mature kingdom servants who significantly contribute to God's mission.

THE ROLE OF SERVICE-LEARNING TRIPS

Based on extensive research of outcomes in students who participated in international service-learning, we believe high quality service-learning and short-term mission experiences can play an important role in emerging adult mission formation. According to Tim Elmore and Andrew McPeak, many of today's young people are empowered through technology without wisdom gained through hands-on experience. Due to our culture's safety orientation and parental overprotection, many are underexposed to real-world involvement where something important is at stake. However, often they are overexposed to mature information far earlier than they are emotionally ready to process and act on it. These emerging adults need "high-stakes experiences that challenge and prepare them for adulthood, all surrounded by conversations to help them process those experiences and mature."[5]

Engaging emerging adults in high-stakes service, such as mission trips in under-resourced communities or among Muslims, is not without risk. Yet, many missionaries and global leaders willingly assume that risk and invite emerging adults to serve in their contexts on service-learning and short-term mission projects. Just as the African saying that it takes a whole village to raise up a child resonates with many, so too the people who organize and lead these trips, those who host them, and peers all have important parts to play in fostering growth.

A service program at Taylor University has been part of the village involved in forming emerging adults for mission. It has achieved documented success in harnessing youthful passion and transforming it into effective outreach and lasting change among students. This chapter will describe key factors in the program's goals, principles, and design for cultivating positive, long-term growth in today's students. We believe these elements are transferrable to other ministries looking to nurture emerging adult development through intercultural service.

TAYLOR'S LIGHTHOUSE PROGRAM

Taylor University's Lighthouse program began in the fall of 1971 when Dr. Ruth Ann Breuninger prepared students for a ministry project in Nassau, Bahamas, in January 1972. The resulting trip counted as the capstone course for seniors majoring in Christian Education and studying vocational ministry. The group conducted seminars for church leaders on ministry principles through partnership with a Bahamian ministry leader. The program remained the capstone experience for Christian Education majors until 1978, when the university moved it to the campus ministries office, added the fall preparation course, and opened it to other majors. Since 1972 more than 2,700 students have participated in 187 projects in

36 countries; currently 80–100 students serve annually in high-impact service-learning experiences outside the classroom.

Former Lighthouse director Jennifer Collins researched short-term mission and wrote about its strengths and weaknesses in *Overcoming the World Missions Crisis*. She joined with others to develop best practices in short-term mission based on input gathered from hundreds of mission leaders, and in 2003 she helped start the organization Standards of Excellence in Short-Term Mission. The Lighthouse program's philosophy is to strive for short-term mission best practices such as God centeredness, empowering partnerships, qualified leaders, robust preparation, and intentional debriefing/follow-through while also drawing from service-learning principles such as frequent reflective activities and serving communities in a *with*, not *for*, approach.

The program has been a hallmark of collaboration between Taylor's student ministries office (Taylor World Outreach) and the academic curriculum, which is an atypical form of collaboration in university settings and contributes to its success. There is a waiting list of potential partners eager to host the well-prepared groups. Some teams have earned credit in specific academic disciplines such as philosophy, environmental science, social work, or communications, while others earn interdisciplinary credit in intercultural service. In a fall preparation course, student groups study the cultural, historical, social, structural, and religious aspects of a host context and examine service-learning and short-term mission best practices. As the class begins, faculty sponsors introduce students to their host leaders and emphasize Taylor's long-term partnership with the host ministry. From start to finish, program leaders and faculty stress a learner narrative and focus on the program as a long-term discipleship process rather than a three-week experience, with emphasis on prayer, Scripture, and journaling.

During Taylor's January term, the teams enroll in a service-learning course and minister abroad under the guidance of host partners and faculty sponsors, who reinforce and expand prefield learning outcomes. During and after the trip, teams are involved in several reflection, debriefing, and follow-up activities with emphasis on internalizing and integrating lessons learned into life at home. While each service project is unique, from witnessing on a university campus alongside local ministry leaders to home stays among Muslim families, every team's goals are the same. They seek to enter other cultures as humble servant-learners and deepen their faith and their understanding of those who serve in the host communities. In these high-stakes experiences, students develop intercultural competency, grow spiritually, gain exposure to and experience in cross-cultural outreach, and put their idealistic passions for God and service into firsthand practice.

As an illustration Thomas, whose story was shared earlier, was asked what helped his mission formation, and he mentioned four things. First, the trip's faculty leaders were key. They had prepared well and led the group effectively, and they were available for support even as they themselves were confronted by the chaotic situation. Second, the team had a debriefing time with host leaders before leaving that helped them process and prepare to return. Third, the course's postfield debriefing structure and informal group gatherings aided greatly. The team community provided space where students could express spiritual and emotional questions and support each other. Fourth, mentoring from caring adults within the larger campus community (a residence hall director and two additional faculty members) allowed him to work through his anger and questions over time. Thomas said he was grateful that people supported him emotionally and spiritually, but also allowed him the freedom to wrestle with questions without offering pat answers.

ENCOURAGING FINDINGS FROM LONGITUDINAL RESEARCH

Many have examined the potential benefits and harmful effects of short-term missions and service-learning trips. There is a wealth of literature available to help practitioners improve outcomes among receivers and participants; several are listed at the end of this chapter. Few, however, have researched the long-term effects of short-term mission and service-learning or have used surveys that evaluate a holistic approach to intercultural competency as described below. Past studies often lacked control groups or tended to focus on a single growth area such as intercultural awareness or spiritual growth.[6]

Taylor University psychology professor Stephen Snyder and a team of student assistants analyzed Taylor's global engagement efforts including Lighthouse, study tours, and semesters abroad from the years 2008 to 2020. Snyder had no direct involvement with any of the programs. The studies utilized the Taylor University Intercultural Inventory (TUII), an instrument developed and tested for reliability by an experienced intercultural research group. The TUII's holistic assessment includes eight dimensions of intercultural growth: knowledge of cultural facts, truths, and values; awareness in perceiving differences among unique cultures; attitudes about different cultures; actions that are appropriate and effective; internal growth; intellectual development; interpersonal relationships; and spiritual growth in relating to a personal God and a spiritual community of a different culture.[7]

After several years of examining outcomes through pre-trip and post-trip TUII surveys and interviews, the research group undertook a longitudinal study of Lighthouse alumni using the Taylor instrument. The alumni had substantially higher perceived intercultural competency and spiritual outcomes than a control group with no significant difference found between alumni two to seven years post-experience and alumni eight to thirteen years post-experience. The longitudinal results show Lighthouse alumni scored higher than control group alumni on seven of the eight intercultural growth scales. This shows long-lasting differences between the two groups and is consistent with two other investigations into the long-term effects of intercultural experience.[8]

When researchers controlled for semester study abroad experiences, they found that Lighthouse alumni who also studied abroad had significantly higher means on all eight scales, and that Lighthouse was especially affecting competency in intercultural knowledge, appropriate and effective intercultural behavior, and spiritual development in relating to God and a spiritual community of a different culture.[9]

Existing literature indicates that preparation, reflection, and debriefing are all essential in contributing to positive growth through intercultural experiences. A lapse in any one of these will decrease growth outcomes. Taylor's longitudinal study affirms these findings as the Lighthouse structure and leaders place rigorous emphasis on these three areas. Programs such as Lighthouse "can significantly improve the long-term perceived growth of intercultural competency in participants if the proper structure of, approach to, and time for preparation, reflection and debriefing occur."[10]

DEEPENING EMERGING ADULTS' BIBLICAL FOUNDATION

Open-minded, compassionate emerging adults are oriented toward social justice and concerned about racism and poverty.[11] They are on track to be the best-educated generation yet and see education as a path to career stability.[12] Here, there are opportunities to mentor in biblical foundations for compassion and justice, and on how all knowledge—all that is good, beautiful, and true—has its source in God. Gen Z will appreciate learning about the early church's inclusive, multiethnic, and multiclass character, and they may need to be challenged with the early Christians' uncompromising stance on core truths about Christ, salvation, and ethics.

Promisingly, a Barna study found that "young adults who remain active in the faith are, statistically speaking, just as eager as older Christians to share [their faith]."[13] Barna also found that "when given a chance to imagine themselves serving in specific overseas missionary roles" (business leader, entrepreneur, artist, church trainer), half of Christian young adults say yes, they can see it.[14] Still, many may benefit from a fresh discovery of what makes the gospel of the kingdom good news, that it goes beyond personal salvation, and that sharing it can be a joyful privilege rather than a duty-bound chore. They will especially benefit from studying Bible passages that show how gospel proclamation and social justice are integrated into a seamless whole of good news and good action, such as Luke 4:16-21, 25-27; 9:1-6; 10:8-10; Matthew 4:23; 7:35; 10:5-8; Acts 3; 6:1-7; 1 Peter 2:9-12; and 3:13-17.

Regarding evangelism, word choice matters. Gen Z has been exposed to stereotypes of insensitive evangelism and mission association with colonialism. Barna discovered that young adults prefer phrases such as "sharing faith" and "making a difference" over "convert," "winning souls," "making disciples," and "evangelism."[15] It's helpful to emphasize that God is the one who brings conversion and growth, and to expose young adults to biblical wording connected to mission that has less cultural baggage.

POSITIVE OUTCOMES CONTINUE

Current postfield evaluations and ongoing Taylor University Intercultural Inventory research demonstrate that significant group and individual transformations continue among Gen Z students. For example, current Lighthouse Director Kplang'at Cheruiyot Bii found that as students reflected on what they learned from the Lighthouse experience in 2020, a majority indicated a shift from "me" focus during the prefield application phase to "he and we" focus postfield. Another shift was from "What can I do?" to "What is God doing, and how can I join with him and others to be part of what he is doing?"

Recent participants also indicated they were challenged to develop reliance on God and to trust in teammates when they realized "I can't do this myself." High-stakes field experiences prompted students to embrace the truth that they don't have to be amazing in everything. The body of Christ (manifested in team support) became a significant safety net in times of hardship and gave students freedom to relax, knowing that God is in control. Participants learned to draw strength and accept support from others in their areas of weakness. Finally, students indicated frequently a shift in their view of failure. Postfield, they showed a desire to see failure as an opportunity to learn at feet of Jesus in his grace and knowledge and in the presence of an encouraging community.

UNDERSTANDING AND RESPONDING TO TRENDS

Mentoring emerging adults toward mission formation begins with understanding them. Leaders and hosts will do well to recognize several trends regarding traits, beliefs, and attitudes they bring into these high-stakes service experiences. Mentoring is often needed in these areas.

NAVIGATING CONFLICTING PRIORITIES

Globally aware Gen Zers navigate a post-Christian, post-truth world even while 78 percent still believe in God.[16] Many perceive the world as dangerous, are risk-averse, and seek security. "They tend to avoid conflict and ask authority figures to solve problems for them."[17] Yet, they are also motivated to bring positive change and intend to pursue career stability with an entrepreneurial spirit.[18] These conflicting priorities may cause internal dissonance and difficulty acting on good intentions. Leaders can encourage emerging adults to trust God, his word, and their interdependent, multigenerational team. They can also affirm and guide entrepreneurial impulses and enact appropriate risk management and training.

It's interesting that tech-savvy Gen Z report at high rates they prefer face-to-face interaction over media-based.[19] Many experts recommend pursuing in-person engagement and then following up with these digital natives by text message.[20] Mentors should seek to stay connected and offer their availability. Gen Z desires humble and genuine leaders who exhibit collaborative mentoring and walk alongside them in personal ways.

GUIDING SELF-DIRECTED LEARNING

With nearly unlimited data available at their connected fingertips, emerging adults have likely experienced student-centered education that accommodated their preferred learning methods.[21] Yet, constant online stimuli of varying quality may lead to confusion, lack of reflection, and difficulty forming deep convictions. For example, young adults may consult tourism websites about a country without realizing such sites are directed toward wealthy tourists, offer superficial summaries, and gloss over systemic realities. It's helpful for leaders and hosts to be attuned to these self-directed learners, provide starting points for study, facilitate information discovery, and guide analysis and application of online material.

Mentors can engage emerging adults' learning style by asking what they think, know, and feel about mission and cultural topics from their own exploration. This is better than leaders overloading them with expertise. Jesus asked the disciples, "Who do you say I am?" (Matt 16:15). He regularly responded to questions with questions. It's essential to follow Jesus's approach and use open-ended questions to demonstrate interest in young adult views and create space for individual and group reflection. It's also vital to facilitate discovery of the *missio Dei* (God's mission)—that God's sending and redemptive nature is the source and center of all human mission effort. Believers have the privilege to respond to his invitation and join the work he is already doing in the world.

WORKING THROUGH CHALLENGING EMOTIONS

Young adults feel performative pressure to appear happy at every turn on social media, which does not pair well with authentic spiritual connection and honesty about personal struggles.[22] It also leads, in part, to increased anxiety, depression, and restlessness.[23] Leaders can provide frequent messages of hope and safe spaces for Gen Z to express spiritual doubts that may be especially pronounced during and after a service experience. Mentors can energize Gen Zers to pursue their identity in Christ and provide confidence that God has gifted them and will help them develop their competency (2 Cor 3:5). Due to inexperience with failure and high-stakes experiences, mentors should assure emerging adults that mistakes are part of life and that when they make them, they can fall on Jesus and God's people to go forward, just as we see with Barnabas and Mark in Acts 15.

FINAL RECOMMENDATIONS

In addition to what has already been shared, a few remaining points are also important to highlight. They provide guidance about how these intercultural service groups help emerging adults grow from a self-focus to trusting others and God more deeply. The roles of accountability, partnerships, and learning outcomes have been significant for their missional formation as well.

LEARNING TO TRUST MORE DEEPLY

Emerging adults who grow up in environments where individualism is nurtured and valued are inclined to desire safe spaces where their perspectives are validated and unchallenged.[24] Left unopposed and without high-stakes risks, these trends of self-focus and inward drive may lead young adults on a path of destructive narcissism rather than missional formation. However, well-structured service projects allow them to immerse themselves into something far greater than their individual capacity and personal accomplishments. These opportunities are important and valuable in helping emerging adults achieve lasting spiritual growth and increased capacity to engage the world as they shift from an individualized focus to trusting others and God more deeply, so they might best live into the many opportunities afforded to their generation.

To optimize their formation, emerging adults benefit from engaging in a group setting where intercultural service experiences and faith challenges are processed and interpreted collectively. Well-structured groups facilitated by spiritually mature and interculturally competent leaders create spaces where their inner drive is challenged by multiple perspectives. As an illustration, students from the most recent Lighthouse cohort indicated in post-trip reflections that working and learning alongside others transformed their perspectives on interdependence and trusting others in challenging circumstances. Leaders and hosts facilitated a significant part of this growth by asking deep questions and guiding them through collective reflection that went beyond personal concerns to group and contextual issues.

Well-structured and well-led service groups provide a space where emerging adults learn to feel safe with each other and with caring adults, and individually open up to new perspectives on God, the world, and other cultures. Through ongoing challenge and support, emerging adults who process service experiences collectively find it meaningful to embrace the team's ethos, energy, and support. They move from self-focus or hyperindividualism to us-focus and interdependence, and ultimately are transformed in how they view the world's brokenness and possibilities. Therefore, to cultivate growth, it is important to think creatively and intentionally about team-building dynamics and quality time together. It's beneficial to carve out regular time on the trip and afterwards for supporting one other and reflecting, and to resist the ever-present temptation to focus mainly on the trip's logistical details.

A group-centered approach to learning and serving also allows emerging adults to surrender their inadequacies to our all-powerful God. Leaders and hosts can cultivate courage, a focus on things greater than self, and dependence on God and others through collective, vulnerable engagement; mutual support;

and consistent prayer, Scripture readings, and devotions. These spiritual disciplines embedded in the team's preparation process, during the trip, and afterwards ground young adults in biblical truths and shape their faith in practical ways as they move from spectators to hands-on servants.

ACCOUNTABILITY, PARTNERS, AND OUTCOMES

Additionally, Gen Z has increasing access to a variety of information sources and experiences fewer limitations when it comes to global travel. This unrestricted access to information and the freedom to explore places, people, and cultures without guidance, accountability, and responsibility may create an illusion of global interconnection and perceived intercultural sophistication that does not match reality. A group-centered approach and well-prepared leaders can provide meaningful accountability regarding how emerging adults view and engage global cultures. Leaders should give careful attention to students' potential false perceptions of global interconnection and intercultural competency.

Accountability is incomplete without the collaboration of valuable host partners, who should be viewed as co-educators. Partners who receive service teams in intercultural contexts shape how they engage in service, the extent of the field immersions, and the quality of cross-cultural interactions and learning. It is vital to build authentic, empowering, long-term partnerships so that hosts can guide emerging adults in humbly submitting to, learning from, and serving alongside local leaders well devoid of a savior mentality. Engaged hosts are a key component of an embodied, multigenerational community experience that will foster missional growth.

Also, university service-learning programs involve formal courses with stated learning outcomes and service goals. Assignments and plans are designed to fulfill those outcomes and goals. This intentionality is transferrable to ministry-based short-term mission projects. Both service-learning and short-term mission best practices recommend deliberate and meaningful preparation, reflection, and follow-through. It is crucial for leaders and host partners to consider carefully together what change they want a service project to cultivate in participants and in host communities, and then purposefully design the pre-field, field, and post-field phases to fulfill intended outcomes. It is vital to foster a learner narrative and long-term view from start to finish and to position service activities within this larger discipleship perspective.

CONCLUSION

"Knowledge is like a garden; if it is not cultivated, it cannot be harvested" (African proverb). Without purposeful and patient cultivation of a garden over time, harmful weeds start to prevail. Just as Barnabas patiently mentored Mark after a ministry failure, leaders can help emerging adults put their idealistic good intentions into high-stakes practice that bears desired fruit long-term. As we and our partners design and implement service opportunities to form young adults for God's mission, we must understand and respond to their generational traits, have patience, and follow established best practices. We can effectively engage emerging adults in service that nurtures their strengths and prunes them where needed. This chapter describes a program that involves a several-month process requiring effort, time, and persistence. We understand that ministry leaders are busy, yet maintaining an intentional investment over time is vital and will bear abundant fruit.

QUESTIONS FOR DIALOGUE

1. What role has a "safety orientation" played in the stories and experiences of emerging adults whom you know? In what way is this the same or different from what people in other generations whom you know experienced?

2. What types of high-stakes service opportunities are already possible for emerging adults in your context, and what new ones could be created?

3. What ideas intrigue you about Taylor's Lighthouse Program that could inform how you work with emerging adults in service-learning or short-term mission projects to better facilitate their missional formation?

4. How do the several trends regarding traits, beliefs, and attitudes that emerging adults are understanding and learning to respond to compare to what you are seeing and learning in your context?

BIBLIOGRAPHY

Annan, Kent. *Slow Kingdom Coming: Practices for Doing Justice, Loving Mercy, and Walking Humbly in the World.* Downers Grove, IL: IVP Books, 2016.

Barna Group. *The Future of Mission: Ten Questions about Global Ministry the Church Must Answer with the Next Generation.* Ventura, CA: Barna Group, 2020.

———. *Spiritual Conversations in the Digital Age.* Ventura, CA: Barna Group, 2018.

Bergler, Thomas E. "Generation Z and Spiritual Maturity." *Christian Education Journal* 17, no. 1 (2020): 75–91.

Blomberg, Fran. "From 'Whatever' to Wherever: Enhancing Faith Formation in Young Adults through Short-Term Missions." Pages 505–30 in *Effective Engagement in Short-Term Missions: Doing It Right!.* Edited by Robert J. Priest. Pasadena, CA: William Carey Library, 2008.

Bringle, Robert G., and Julie A. Hatcher. "Innovative Practices in Service-Learning and Curricular Engagement." *New Directions for Higher Education* 147 (2009): 37–46.

Burrows, Dominique, Stephen J. Snyder, and Andrew Ferro. "Perceived Longitudinal Effects of SLMTs." *Journal of Psychology and Theology* 46, no. 3 (2018): 168–83.

Corbett, Steve, and Brian Fikkert. *Helping without Hurting in Short-Term Missions: Leader's Guide.* Chicago: Moody Press, 2014.

Dearborn, Tim. *Short-Term Missions Workbook: From Mission Tourists to Global Citizens.* Rev. and exp. ed. Downers Grove, IL: IVP Books, 2018.

Elmore, Tim, and Andrew McPeak. *Generation Z Unfiltered: Facing Nine Hidden Challenges of the Most Anxious Population.* Atlanta: Poet Gardner, 2019.

Erlacher, Jolene C. *Daniel Generation: Godly Leadership in an Ungodly Culture.* Southern Pines, NC: Vigil Press, 2018.

Heerwagen, Brian, and Dianne Grudda. *The Next Mile Goer Guide: Practical Short-Term Resource with Emphasis on Post-ministry Follow-Through.* Downers Grove, IL: IVP Books, 2005.

Howell, Brian M. *Short-Term Mission: An Ethnography of Christian Travel Narrative and Experience.* Downers Grove, IL: IVP Academic, 2012.

InterVarsity. "Engaging Gen Z: Urbana 18 Exhibitor Webinar with Jolene Erlacher." Video. 2018. https://urbana.org/engaging-gen-z.

Kinnaman, David. *Faith for Exiles: Five Ways for a New Generation to Follow Jesus in Digital Babylon.* Grand Rapids: Baker Books, 2019.

Lausanne Movement. "Raising Younger Leaders for the Kingdom of God." Video. 2020. https://www.youtube.com/watch?v=OZYTZV9NhXo&list=PLYGxDL2dvuo7PbVIoDuQ5wk4lNvzKG2FJ&index=9&t=0s.

Livermore, David A. *Serving with Eyes Wide Open: Doing Short-Term Missions with Cultural Intelligence.* Updated ed. Grand Rapids: Baker Books, 2012.

Lukianoff, Greg, and Jonathan Haidt. *The Coddling of the American Mind.* New York: Penguin, 2018.

Peterson, Roger. "Missio Dei or 'Missio Me.'" Pages 752–56 in *Perspectives on the World Christian Movement.* Edited by Ralph Winter and Steven Hawthorne. Pasadena, CA: William Carey Library, 2009.

Pew Research Center. "On the Cusp of Adulthood and Facing an Uncertain Future: What We Know about Gen Z So Far." Accessed September 30, 2020. https://www.pewsocialtrends.org/essay/on-the-cusp-of-adulthood-and-facing-an-uncertain-future-what-we-know-about-gen-z-so-far.

Priest, Robert J., ed. *Effective Engagement in Short-Term Missions: Doing It Right!* Pasadena, CA: William Carey Library, 2008.

———. "Short-Term Missions: Case Studies from Peru." Video. 2010. https://www.emsweb.org/resources/teaching-resources/.

Probasco, LiErin. "Giving Time, Not Money: Long-Term Impacts of Short-Term Mission Trips." *Missiology* 41, no. 2 (2013): 202–24.

Richter, Don C. *Mission Trips That Matter: Embodied Faith for the Sake of the World.* Nashville: Upper Room Books, 2008.

Seemiller, Corey, and Meghan Grace. *Generation Z: A Century in the Making.* New York: Routledge, 2019.

———. *Generation Z Goes to College.* San Francisco: Jossey-Bass, 2016.

Standards of Excellence in Short-Term Mission. https://soe.org/resources/.

Twenge, Jean M. *iGen.* New York: Atria Books, 2017.

White, James Emery. *Meet Generation Z: Understanding and Reaching the New Post-Christian World.* Grand Rapids: Baker Books, 2017.

11

· · · · ·

Growing through Philanthropy

Patricia Snell Herzog and Jamie Goodwin

· · · · ·

And I submit that nothing will be done until people of goodwill put their bodies and their souls in motion.

—Martin Luther King

B rad, June, and Amanda were among hundreds of interviewees, and thousands of survey participants, who were striving to make meaning of their lives in the National Study of Youth and Religion. Many of these young people were attempting to make meaning outside the contours of organized religion, essentially working through it alone. For example, Brad described his life as focused on "taking care of number one, what would make me happy, help me get ahead."[1] He held religious beliefs but did not enjoy the "religious scene." Figured into these beliefs was the idea that volunteerism is good, but not a priority. This story, and many other examples like it, highlights that the absence of religious practice is connected to less generous activity.

In another example, June had never volunteered or given money away, though she occasionally cared for her sick mom and grandmother. "People give me money now," she laughed, referring to her difficulty in finding steady work and the recent removal of her young son from her care by child services. June was raised with little religion and could remember going to church only twice in her life. She prayed desperately "to whoever" to get her son back and was working on being grateful. She said, "I try to be positive, to wake up and think: at least I'm alive today ... there's nothing physically wrong with me ... my son's in good health, even though he is not with me."[2] The struggle to regain custody of her son was overwhelming for June, and knowing this context helps to explain why she was understandably focused on herself rather than engaged in giving to others. June's story, and many others like it, further highlights the ways that low engagement is connected with minimal religious practice.

Not all the stories of young people are like Brad and June, however. Distinctly, Amanda was working as a summer counselor at a religious camp. She described her life as "blessed," claiming the biggest challenge for herself and people her age was "deciding who we are, the growing up process of separating from our parents and deciding for ourselves what we want to be and do." Her morality was based off the Bible, the idea of loving God and other people. She believed that everyone had a moral responsibility to give, "It's kind and compassionate, that's what God would do." Amanda plans to tithe someday, but gives away little now because she does not have much to spare.[3] Amanda reveals a countertrend among some young people: experiences surrounding religious practice laid a strong foundation for a life of giving, once resources were available. But what happens when that religious foundation is missing?

INTRODUCTION

These stories illustrate the wide range of experiences that young people face as they grow up. For too many, the road to becoming an adult is deeply confusing and often painful.[4] In the United States, many families are struggling to make ends meet with insecure social and economic supports.[5] This often results in young people receiving fragmented help in making sense of their lives during emerging adulthood: the life stage that many people in their twenties and early thirties are traversing.[6]

Meaning making is a central development task of emerging adulthood, and this process is complex and difficult for many emerging adults today.[7] One possible explanation for rising challenges is that activity participation is key to meaning making, since it structures time and connects young people to others, helping them to venture outside the self.[8] For many in the past, the path of meaning making for emerging adults included regular participation in social activities, such as religious and philanthropic engagement, but for many emerging adults today, such social supports are missing.[9] This is a troubling trend that can negatively impede their formation for mission.

TEACHING PHILANTHROPY

As a response, this chapter addresses how teaching philanthropic attitudes and action can aid emerging adults in developing meaning making.[10] Teaching philanthropy addresses emerging adults as givers, volunteers, activists, promoters, burgeoning practitioners, and also as recipients of philanthropy, while also addressing the crucial role of religion.

PHILANTHROPIC ENGAGEMENT

Philanthropy is a socially constructed process that occurs across multiple social levels: micro, macro, and meso.[11] Individuals enact ways of being generous to others through the actions they do (or do not) take in society. Societies, cultures, and nations embed ways of being, social norms, and taken-for-granted assumptions about what is acceptable to be and do, including what counts as the good. Philanthropic actions occur within organizations and informal social groups, which in turn shape the contours of philanthropic action.

Across these levels, broader orientations to the good shape the ways that individuals engage in supporting other people. Philanthropy is at root a moral action that relies on an imagination for ways the world could be that it is not yet, and a belief in the ability to make the world better.[12] Indeed, philanthropy has a long history of working to promote social justice, and not just by placating pernicious inequalities through handouts or Band-Aids but by engaging transformational changes that confront social and economic injustices.[13] Questions at the center of philanthropy are wrought with ethical quandaries, moral dilemmas, and critical issues.[14] For example: What is the public good?, For whose good?, In what ways?, With what equitable participation?, and For what ends?[15]

PHILANTHROPY'S BEDFELLOW

Religion is philanthropy's bedfellow, as the history of philanthropy is intricately intertwined with the roots of religiosity.[16] Philanthropy is most often understood as the giving of time and money to charitable, social, religious, and environmental causes, and charitable donations of time and money are more common among religiously active people.[17] This "tie that binds" is profound in the United States and also occurs globally.[18] Across diverse religious traditions some refer to this close relationship between philanthropy and religious traditions, and the high intensive of volunteerism by religious congregations, as the "invisible caring hand."[19]

This intertwining requires attention to religiosity within teaching philanthropy. Attending to both can facilitate meaning making. Indeed, many young people today hunger for action, and a sense of agency, in a complex world. Meeting young people where they are can be a powerful way to further engage them into more formal organizations. While the graying of many churches reveals that traditional methods may be ineffective in truly engaging the next generation, teaching young people about philanthropy, and its connections with the big questions of life, is a profound way to ignite the moral imagination and facilitate broader meaning making that facilitates their missional formation process.

A CRITICAL TEACHING FRAMEWORK

In the changing higher-education context, it is important to articulate one's teaching approach.[20] In our classes within the Indiana University School of Philanthropy at IUPUI, we prioritize teaching within what Alan Skelton refers to as a critical pedagogical framework.[21] Critical approaches emphasize social inequalities in the creation, dissemination, and normalization of mainstream knowledge that is codified into common-sense notions, which are taken for granted as valid operating assumptions that are perceived to be value-free and neutral. By positioning higher education as a critical process through which such norms are challenged, student-teacher interactions are centered on diverse and inclusive approaches to knowledge construction that position ideas within theories of social change.

In this framework, the goal of higher education is to aid students in taking greater control of their lives, and in turn acting as an informed citizenry. Civic action resulting from critical education is enacted through decisions that are less based within biased, intuitive senses of good which were developed within small elite social circles. Rather, the transformative teaching process engages students in questioning "common-sense ways of thinking and behaving, leading to new forms of consciousness and ideas for effecting social and political change."[22] This experience may not feel particularly pleasant for all students, especially not those that represent the dominant approaches of highly resourced social segments that benefit from those common-sense notions. Thus, critical teaching could result in a degree of discomfort with the dismantling of dominant approaches and is best measured by criteria for significant learning.

CRITERIA FOR SIGNIFICANT LEARNING

The scholarship on teaching and learning emphasizes the validity of educational taxonomies that define measurable criteria to assess significant student learning. For more than half a century, scholarship has prioritized the taxonomy developed by Benjamin Bloom and revised by Lorin Anderson et al.[23] Bloom's taxonomy emphasizes cognitive dimensions of learning, to: remember, understand, apply, analyze, evaluate, and create knowledge. Extending this taxonomy, Fink added six significant learnings for students: (1) acquisition of foundational knowledge and conceptual ideas; (2) application of knowledge; (3) integration of concepts into a broader set of knowledge; (4) discovery of the human dimensions of learning about self and others; (5) caring by developing new interests, values, and feelings; and (6) learning how to learn by becoming a better student that is self-directed and inquisitive.[24]

GROWING THROUGH PHILANTHROPY

To exemplify this approach, we describe our approaches within two undergraduate courses within the Indiana University School of Philanthropy at IUPUI: Giving and Volunteering in America, and Philanthropy and the Social Sciences.

GIVING AND VOLUNTEERING IN AMERICA

In this course, students are taught that philanthropic studies are an interdisciplinary endeavor rooted in the liberal arts tradition, which "seeks to reflect on its subject as well as see its work carried forward into the world."[25] Since ancient times, philanthropy has been understood as the love of humanity. If we now define philanthropy as voluntary action for the public good, we might operationalize our research as the giving of time, talent, treasure, and influence. Students are introduced into these streams of thought and practice, explore the important role of philanthropy in American life, and gain exposure to the diverse practices of and responses to charity and philanthropy within American culture.

Students also actively and regularly participate in philanthropic activities in the community, then reflect on how such experiences integrate with what they already know and have experienced. In particular, the course prompts students to consider their motives for giving and volunteering and how their motivations reflect or diverge from broader cultural trends. The DEAL reflection model, among others,[26] prompts students to synthesize, deconstruct, then reassemble their philanthropic experiences in the classroom within existing knowledge. Contrary to anecdotes of forced volunteerism, students' favorite aspects of the course are the immersive experiences in the community, as they observe or participate in meaningful philanthropic work. Since the course is taught at a public university, the class text draws on traditions of thought from major religions. From the Christian heritage, it focuses on philanthropic themes of charity and solidarity worldwide.

PHILANTHROPY AND THE SOCIAL SCIENCES

In this course, the goal is to introduce students to analytical approaches that the social sciences bring to the study of philanthropy. The course surveys the role of philanthropy in promoting social justice and civil society, including intersections with important social issues, such as race, class, gender, youth, and religion. In this course, students engage in considering the "forever questions"[27] of philanthropy, such as: What is philanthropy? The answer is often understood as "voluntary action for the public good,"[28] but what is "voluntary," and what is "public good"?

Overall, a central goal of the course is to increase students' evidenced based reasoning by learning how to identify valid sources of data, evaluate the unintended consequences and social justice of philanthropic interventions, and synthesize information about how changing social contexts and technology evolve notions of a good life. Importantly, this approach views philanthropy as a contested concept with many interests and constituents. In this context, religiosity is examined as an important social phenomenon that intersects with philanthropy.

The social-scientific approach to the intersection of philanthropy and religiosity is explained as an examination of how to measure religiosity and what social impacts religiosity has, especially with regard to giving, volunteering, and taking action in social movements. In seeking to move beyond simplistic understandings, religious literacy is developed through attention to issues such as religious pluralism, religious diversity, religiosity as a form of social participation, individual beliefs, importance (or salience) of beliefs, and diversity in terms of social class, gender, race, youth, age, and generation. Evidence garnered from a wide range of disciplines is engaged in pursuing forever questions, such as: What are the causes, manifestations, and consequences of generosity?[29] Religious giving is defined as consisting of two primary forms: (1) giving to support religious organizations, and (2) religious people giving to general charitable, social, and environmental causes.

An example of a class activity attending to the second definition of religious giving comes from an empirical analysis of the types of givers.[30] After reviewing the survey questions that undergird the giver types, students are asked to self-identify by personally answering these survey questions. The giver types include planned givers, habitual givers, selective givers, and impulsive givers. Of these, habitual givers are the most religious, with many of these givers centering their approach around the concept of tithing, and thus intentionally situating their giving on autopilot.

Students are then walked through how to place themselves within the giving typology. Then the results of the analysis are reviewed. Next, students are invited into small group discussions that are designed to elicit responses from a diverse set of giver types around this question: How can philanthropic strategies be tailored to each giver type? This approach empowers each student to speak on behalf of the type they represent, even if (or perhaps especially if) they are the only one in the group of that type.

In this way, even in a public university class setting, students who are religious can engage their faith safely, explaining to others how it helps to explain the meaning behind the evidence. Likewise, non–religiously practicing students can also shed light on other motivations for and approaches to giving. In turn, each learns an appreciation for the diverse ways that religiosity shapes, or not, philanthropic engagement. Plus, in the process of attending to the motivations for their philanthropic activities, many students come to appreciate the ways that their early formative experiences in religious settings continue to shape their moral guideposts. Ultimately, we believe that such approaches aid emerging adults in making meaning of their agency by situating the self in a broader, historical, and social understanding of giving to others.

PRACTICAL APPLICATIONS, BEYOND CLASSROOMS

Based on our experiences as scholars and teachers, we offer the following four practical applications, with implications beyond classrooms, that can aid in the missional formation process. These five recommendations are centralized around this thesis: we believe that practicing generosity can aid emerging adults in making meaning and transforming their lives, and the world, for the better. So, how can we help?

First, we need to understand that, because of the broad range of experiences that young people have during emerging adulthood, their paths of meaning making will be their own. This does not mean that every person's experiences are entirely unique, as indeed there are far too many groupable patterns for that to be the case. Rather, recognizing the diversity of segments within young people helps to personalize their experiences and not commit the prevalent homogeneity error: viewing all young people the same, the pernicious "kids today" idea. Instead, adult mentors can help young people wrestle with the big questions of life and to grapple through the challenges of making meaning in a complex, pluralistic, and fragmented world. This requires us to head straight into the difficult conversations and to accept that deeply engaging means that sometimes people will feel uncomfortable. People cannot figure out how to live a meaningful life by only thinking; they must "get out in the world" to experience themselves in communion with others. It is not simply actions of any kind, but particularly prosocial actions—activities oriented toward benefiting others—that are of greatest importance. Adults interacting with young people in a range of contexts can be companions on their journey to greater meaning.

Second, young people want to be hands-on philanthropists. But honoring this requires a few challenges to the status quo of traditional philanthropy, because emerging adults think about philanthropy differently from, and similarly to, their counterparts from other generations. For example, young people generally have less allegiance to institutions (religious or otherwise), and as a result, they typically do not feel a sense of duty to support them or guilt if they do not. Young people tend to like causes, not formal organizations. As with other areas of their life, young people today are accustomed to a variety of choices. Their philanthropic giving, likewise, is seen as a personal choice, not a social duty. Many were taught to volunteer in school, but often that institutionalized expectation came without any explanations as to why, or reflection about the meaning of the activity, or integration into studies of social change.

Emerging adults do give generously. Seeing this necessitates noticing that many young people are highly motivated by personal networks, compelling causes, and a sense of making a difference.

While young people have received fierce criticism, their approach may provide fresh authenticity to philanthropy and volunteering. Valuing their contributions helps engage young people in authentic relationships that build social trust. Many emerging adults are eager to share what they know and have learned about social change from their own experience and networks. This peer collaboration is especially important for them, and hierarchical approaches are less effective. They see this act of collaboration as a public good in itself—generating not only the solutions to problems, but the capacity for groups to solve problems together. Emerging adults do not want to sit at a distance and give money. They want to be an integral part of the work, with close friendships, where their advice and talent is valued.

Third, in a highly pluralist society, philanthropy and volunteerism may build a bridge for reengagement with religion. Philanthropy and volunteering may provide new insights for emerging adults who have no previous experience with religion. Through authentic experiences and forming relationships, emerging adults may be able to increasingly learn to make meaning of their own lives. We also believe, however, that philanthropic and religious institutions may need to be refreshed by this engagement. In other words, success is not measured by simple numbers of passive, young participants, but rather true engagement necessitates some reconfiguration of the old ways. For example, terms such as social change, social justice, and collaboration resonate more with young people, while words such as philanthropy and volunteering are tied to the institutionalism that they often seek to evade. Many philanthropic practices are less formal, involve kinship networks, and are built on understandings of mutual benefit. Reflection on the wording can improve the vibrancy of an organization and its giving culture.

Fourth, young people who care less about God will give less. Emerging adults affiliate with religious institutions less and less. Though they do not affiliate with organized religion, religious "nones"

often believe in God and an afterlife, pray, and have spiritual conversations much like other generations. They also ask questions
about faith openly. Perhaps, then, emerging adults are interested
in spirituality but are shifting away from the formal engagement
that defined prior generations. One problem with this approach,
however, is that with less God often comes less giving. Rising
levels of nonaffiliation and decline in attendance contribute to
the decrease of giving and involvement in a wide range of causes.
The approaches we offer above are intended to respond to this
problem by reinvigorating a sense of urgency to engage on behalf
of others and to situate that call to action within the historical role
that religious bodies have had in providing a grassroots, community-
located, responsive social safety net. When emerging adults do not
engage with religion, they will most likely not sacrifice themselves
for the good of others. In this context, teaching about philanthropy
is crucial and perhaps more important than ever.

CONCLUSION

We believe that practicing generosity can aid emerging adults in
making meaning and transforming their lives for the better. Even
in the most pluralistic contexts, religion is key to forming emerging adults for this mission and for helping young people make
meaning of their lives. Those who are empowered as agents of
change out of their faith commitment have discovered how the
stories of their spirituality align with their work in the world, and
this brings great joy. It is this type of growth that leads to a generous way of life.

QUESTIONS FOR DIALOGUE

1. How do emerging adults that you know view giving
    and philanthropy?

2. In what ways might you be able to help emerging adults connect philanthropy with the big questions of life in ways that ignite their moral imagination?

3. What aspects of the teaching methods mentioned intrigue you and why?

4. What are ways you can facilitate the bridge-building process by helping emerging adults grow in their faith through philanthropy?

BIBLIOGRAPHY

Anderson, Lorin W., David R. Krathwohl, Peter W. Airasian, Kathleen A. Cruikshank, Richard E. Mayer, Paul R. Pintrich, James Raths, and Merlin C. Wittrock. *A Taxonomy for Learning, Teaching, and Assessing: A Revisions of Bloom's Taxonomy of Educational Objectives*. New York: Longman, 2001.

Arnett, Jeffrey Jensen. *Emerging Adulthood: The Winding Road from the Late Teens through the Twenties*. 2nd ed. New York: Oxford University Press, 2015.

Ash, Sarah L., and Patti H. Clayton. "Generating, Deepening, and Documenting Learning: The Power of Critical Reflection in Applied Learning." *Journal of Applied Learning in Higher Education* 1, no. 1 (2009): 25–48.

Bach, Richard. *The Bridge across Forever: A True Love Story*. New York: William Morrow Paperbacks, 2006.

Barman, Emily. "The Social Bases of Philanthropy." *Annual Review of Sociology* 43, no. 1 (2017): 271–90. https://doi.org/10.1146/annurev-soc-060116-053524.

Barry, Carolyn McNamara, and Mona M. Abo-Zena. *Emerging Adults' Religiousness and Spirituality: Meaning-Making in an Age of Transition.* Oxford: Oxford University Press, 2014.

Bloom, Benjamin S. *Taxonomy of Educational Objectives, Handbook 1: Cognitive Domain.* 2nd ed. New York: Addison-Wesley Longman, 1956.

Burton, Dorian O., and Brian C. B. Barnes. "Shifting Philanthropy from Charity to Justice (SSIR)." Stanford Social Innovation Review (SSIR) (blog). January 3, 2017. https://ssir.org/articles/entry/shifting_philanthropy_from_charity_to_justice.

Chan, Melissa, Kim M. Tsai, and Andrew J. Fuligni. "Changes in Religiosity across the Transition to Young Adulthood." *Journal of Youth and Adolescence* 44 (2014): 1555–66. https://doi.org/10.1007/s10964-014-0157-0.

Cnaan, Ram, and Stephanie C. Boddie. *The Invisible Caring Hand: American Congregations and the Provision of Welfare.* New York: New York University Press, 2002.

Cooper, Marianne. *Cut Adrift: Families in Insecure Times.* Berkeley: University of California Press, 2014.

Dale, Elizabeth J., Genevieve G. Shaker, and Heather A. O'Connor. "Teaching Philanthropy: Developing Critical and Compassionate Approaches to Giving." Pages 165–80 in *Teaching Nonprofit Management.* Edited by Karabi C. Bezboruah and Heather L. Carpenter. Cheltenham, UK: Edward Elgar, 2020.

Drezner, Noah D., Itay Greenspan, Hagai Katz, and Galia Feit. *Philanthropy in Israel 2016: Patterns of Individual Giving.* Tel Aviv: Tel Aviv University, 2016.

Fink, L. Dee. *Creating Significant Learning Experiences: An Integrated Approach to Designing College Courses.* Rev. and updated ed. San Francisco: Jossey-Bass, 2013.

Forbes, Kevin F., and Ernest M. Zampelli. "Volunteerism: The Influences of Social, Religious, and Human Capital."

Nonprofit & Voluntary Sector Quarterly 43, no. 2 (2014):
    227–53. https://doi.org/10.1177/0899764012458542.
Franklin, Jason. "Placing Social Justice Philanthropy in a
    Historical Context: Key Moments from 20th Century
    U.S. Political & Philanthropic History." Bolder
    Giving, Sustainable Agriculture & Food Systems
    Funders (SASF) (blog). 2011. http://www.safsf.org/
    documentsold/2011Forum_BolderGiving_Overview.pdf.
Grönlund, Henrietta, and Anne Birgitta Pessi. "The Influence of
    Religion on Philanthropy across Nations." Pages 558–69
    in *The Palgrave Handbook of Global Philanthropy*. Edited by
    Pamala Wiepking and Femida Handy. London: Palgrave
    Macmillan, 2015.
Gutierrez, Ian A., and Crystal L. Park. "Emerging Adulthood,
    Evolving Worldviews: How Life Events Impact College
    Students' Developing Belief Systems." *Emerging
    Adulthood* 3, no. 2 (2015): 85–97.
Herzog, Patricia Snell. *The Science of Generosity: Causes,
    Manifestations, and Consequences*. Palgrave Studies
    in Altruism, Morality, and Social Solidarity. London:
    Palgrave Macmillan, 2019.
Herzog, Patricia Snell, and Heather Price. *American Generosity:
    Who Gives and Why*. New York: Oxford University Press,
    2016.
Husbands, Chris, and Jo Pearce. "What Makes Great Pedagogy?
    Nine Claims from Research." Theme One. Research and
    Development Network National Themes. Nottingham,
    UK: Department of Education, National College for
    School Leadership, 2012.
Illingworth, Patricia, Thomas Pogge, and Leif Wenar, eds.
    Giving Well: The Ethics of Philanthropy. New York: Oxford
    University Press, 2012.
Khan, Sabith. "New Styles of Community Building and
    Philanthropy by Arab-American Muslims." *Voluntas:*

International Journal of Voluntary & Nonprofit Organizations 27, no. 2 (2016): 941-57. https://doi.org/10.1007/s11266-015-9553-7.

King, David P. "Millennials, Faith and Philanthropy: Who Will Be Transformed?" *Bridge/Work* 1, no. 1 (2016): 2.

Lawford, Heather L., and Heather L. Ramey. "'Now I Know I Can Make a Difference': Generativity and Activity Engagement as Predictors of Meaning Making in Adolescents and Emerging Adults." *Developmental Psychology* 51, no. 10 (2015): 1395-1406.

Mayseless, Ofra, and Einat Keren. "Finding a Meaningful Life as a Developmental Task in Emerging Adulthood: The Domains of Love and Work across Cultures." *Emerging Adulthood* 2, no. 1 (2014): 63-73. https://doi.org/10.1177/2167696813515446.

O'Leary, Matt. "Monitoring and Measuring Teaching Excellence in Higher Education: From Contrived Competition to Collective Collaboration." Pages 75-108 in *Teaching Excellence in Higher Education: Challenges, Changes and the Teaching Excellence Framework*. Edited by Amanda French and Matt O'Leary. Bingley, UK: Emerald, 2017.

Payton, Robert L., and Michael P. Moody. *Understanding Philanthropy: Its Meaning and Mission*. Bloomington: Indiana University Press, 2008.

Perkins, Graham. "The Teaching Excellence Framework (TEF) and Its Impact on Academic Identity Within A Research-Intensive University." *Higher Education Policy; London* 32, no. 2 (2018): 297-319. http://dx.doi.org.proxy.ulib.uits.iu.edu/10.1057/s41307-018-0082-z.

Phillips, Susan, and Steven Rathgeb Smith. "Public Policy for Philanthropy: Catching the Wave or Creating a Backwater." Pages 213-28 in *The Routledge Companion to Philanthropy*. Edited by Tobias Jung, Susan D. Phillips, and Jenny Harrow. Philadelphia: Routledge, 2016.

Ruiter, Stijn, and Nan Dirk De Graaf. "National Context, Religiosity and Volunteering: Results from 53 Countries." *American Sociological Review* 71, no. 2 (2006): 191-210.

Skelton, Alan. *Understanding Teaching Excellence in Higher Education: Toward a Critical Approach.* New York: Routledge, 2005.

Smith, Christian, Kari Christoffersen, Hilary Davidson, and Patricia Snell Herzog. *Lost in Transition: The Dark Side of Emerging Adulthood.* New York: Oxford University Press, 2011.

Smith, Christian, and Patricia Snell. *Souls in Transition: The Religious and Spiritual Lives of Emerging Adults.* New York: Oxford University Press, 2009.

Turner, Richard C. "Philanthropic Studies as a Central and Centering Discipline in the Humanities." *International Journal of the Humanities* 2, no. 3 (2004): 2083-86.

Yen, Steven T., and Ernest M. Zampelli. "What Drives Charitable Donations of Time and Money? The Roles of Political Ideology, Religiosity, and Involvement." *Journal of Behavioral and Experimental Economics* 50 (2014): 58-67. https://doi.org/10.1016/j.socec.2014.01.002.

A Sample of Missional
Formation Contexts

· · · · ·

There is a part for every person to play in God's mission,
and each person's contribution needs to be valued.

T he most difficult aspect of writing a book like this is not being
able to include a larger number of stories about how God
is working with racially and ethnically diverse emerging adults.
Revelation 5:9–10 makes it clear how much God deeply values
people from every tongue, tribe, and nation. Each has been pur-
chased by the blood of the Lamb, and each has a role in God's eternal kingdom. He wants all people to come to know him (2 Pet 3:9),
and Scripture reveals that each person's contribution is needed for
the church to grow to maturity and for it to be fully functioning
in the world (Rom 12; 1 Cor 12).

God's heart and perspective needs to be ours. God desires that
racially and ethnically diverse emerging adults come to faith in
Christ, use their gifts in local congregations, and develop in ways
that enable them to make their greatest missional contributions
in the world. In prior chapters we have tried to integrate the perspectives of emerging adults from a variety of cultural contexts. In
this section we highlight approaches and strategies for facilitating

missional formation in specific cultural contexts. Our hope is that these stories will trigger greater research and broader publishing from diverse racial and ethnic contexts.

12

. . . . .

Latinx Migration and Mission

Marcos Canales and Juan Martinez

. . . . .

Somos una especie en viaje
No tenemos pertenencias sino equipaje
Vamos con el polen en el viento
Estamos vivos porque estamos en movimiento
Nunca estamos quietos, somos trashumantes
Somos padres, hijos, nietos y bisnietos de inmigrantes
Es mas mío lo que sueño que lo que toco
//Yo no soy de aquí
Pero tú tampoco//
De ningún lado del todo
De todos lados un poco.

—Jorge Drexler, "Movimiento"[1]

E ster shared excitedly: "My friend Tami is getting baptized![2] I have been discipling her for the last three months! ¡Qué chévere! ¡Dios es tan bueno!" After migrating from El Salvador, Ester worked in retail while finishing her GED, and then she enrolled in a local community college in Los Angeles to pursue a degree in child development. Tami, a Taiwanese American, grew up in a Buddhist household and had deep curiosity for spiritual things not related to organized religion. Ester and Tami met at a math class, where they were assigned a group project. Their taste in music and passion for trying new foods and hiking deepened their friendship and their conversations. Tami's baptism was a celebration that Ester shared as she was amazed at how the Spirit had brought them together and how much they had learned from each other. Ester is not only leading others to Christ on her campus; she is also *la pastora de jóvenes* (youth pastor) for her parents' church in El Salvador. On a weekly basis, she mentors, disciples, and connects with adolescents in the *departamento* of La Paz, El Salvador; records a brief sermon; maintains communication via WhatsApp with each of the youth group leaders; and provides prayer support for parents.[3]

AGENTS OF GOD'S MISSION

Ester's life and ministry provides one snapshot into how she and others like her can engage as agents of God's work in the world. At the same time, when one considers the multiple and intersecting realities inhabited by Latinx emerging adults in the United States, it must be stated that levels of self-identification, acculturation, and assimilation with and away from the Latinx community occur across a wide spectrum.[4] This is a spectrum that is also affected by the realities of globalization, migration, and the Latina church. In fact, the 2020 U.S. Census reveals that the Latinx community's population reached sixty million people;[5] this community is characterized by a median age of twenty-eight.[6] Therefore, the Latina church must move toward a deeper self-reflection, specifically in terms of her missional imagination with and alongside Latinx youth. How will the Latina church accompany Latinx emerging adults in navigating a society that is apparently receptive of ethnic diversity, inclusivity, and multiculturalism while being historically, systemically, and practically homogeneous, racist, sexist, and nationalist? Further, given the alarmist post-Christian narrative that dominates ecclesial structures and declining white denominations, what kind of initiatives could transnational Latinx emerging adults lead to revitalize or reimagine the witness of the church throughout the Americas and beyond? This requires a shift away from the question, "*¿Qué hacemos con los jóvenes?*"[7] toward "*Dios, ¿qué imaginación misional les has dado a nuestros jóvenes?*"[8] Certainly these questions reorient our attention toward the processes of accompaniment that Latinx emerging adults can and should experience in the midst of congregational life.

This chapter sets out to describe Latinx emerging adults as missional agents in God's kingdom through the gifts of their transnational commitments, polycentric identities, and missional leadership. First, migration and mission are presented as catalyzing forces for the Latina church's missional engagement, especially in light of the transnational realities and imaginations that Latinx emerging adults inhabit. Second, we will name the identity formation processes that shape and inform Latinx emerging adults' self-identification dynamics as inhabiting multiple realities of belonging. Last, we will prioritize the formation of Latinx emerging adults as missional leaders for and beyond the Latina church, and provide practical next steps.

MIGRATION AND MISSION

The United Nations estimated that in 2019 there were 272 million international migrants, accounting for 3.5 percent of the world's population; this number does not take into consideration the approximately 740 million internally displaced people around the world.[9] Migration, when considered as a means of grace, it is an opportunity for movement and encounter that promotes *convivencia* across generations. In other words, migration promotes the cohabitation of multiple narratives, identities, and cultures in mutually transformative relationships. This vision is echoed in the Hebrew Bible's exercise on collective remembrance as a people in movement (Deut 26:5). This exercise shaped Israel's engagement in the world as a people cognizant of Yahweh's sole ownership of the land (Lev 25:23) and attuned to their immigrant neighbors' humanity and need (Lev 19:33-34; 23:22), while at the same time often forgetful of its vocation (Isa 56:3; Ezek 22:29; Jer 7:6; Mic 6:8). Jesus's ministry and teaching embodied this dynamic law of love of God and neighbor (Matt 25; Luke 4), and the early Christian communities needed a similar exhortation as a sojourning, immigrant people dispersed throughout the Roman Empire (Heb 11:13; 1 Pet 2:11; Jas 1:1).

Migration, when considered as a deficit or a threat to a nation-state, turns into an "issue" that needs to be legislated, policed, or ignored for partisan politics and the preservation of cheap labor. The biblical thematic arch previously mentioned is often relativized by racist ideologies (manifest destiny) and violent theologies (doctrine of discovery).[10] In fact, a review of historical occupations by European colonial powers of the southern and western territories of what is now the United States gives witness to the various combinations of conquest, annexation, expansion, interventionist policies (both militaristic and economic), and constant migratory patterns that have interlaced the entire region of the Americas.[11] Even as migration studies across the disciplines account for migration's impact on both the sending and receiving countries,[12] more recent studies revolve around the faith(s) that immigrants embody across borders. Therefore, the Latina community in the United States inhabits this intersection of movement, memory, and meaning both as it finds a deeper generational presence within the social fabric of the United States and continues to be perceived as perpetual foreigners.[13]

Yet, migration has energized Latino *evangélico* witness throughout the United States for decades, and it has allowed for a reimagining of ministry models that engage the Latina church and beyond.[14] Part of this revitalization for missional engagement originates in the transnational commitments that these Latina communities hold across borders. Transnationalism is defined as a set of networks and family systems that transcend the confines of the nation-state and that, due to its relational nature, reshape the agency of migrants and reconstitute spaces of innovation and collaboration. As such, transnationalism expands a sense of belonging for those in the borderlands, and it activates a third space of engagement where resources are distributed for the well-being of communities locally and across the border.

In the United States, Latinx emerging adults have access to transnational networks and relationships, both familial and communal, which allow them to engage as the new missionaries of the twenty-first century. As culture makers and missional catalyzers, these Latinx emerging adults, often bilingual, bicultural, and technologically savvy, are deeply connected to their local US Latina communities and their parents' or their own country of origin. Latinx emerging adults who have an immigration status that allows them to travel back and forth between the United States and Latin America are capable of experiencing the Spirit's movement across borders and traditional Christian mission organizations and practices. Latinx emerging adults who possess alternate documentation, restricted from moving back and forth across the region, are still vital visionaries and financial contributors to missional efforts that seek holistic restoration of entire communities. This is where Latinx emerging adults' identity formation processes are crucial in the discerning of the Spirit's leading across borders—processes that must be informed by polycentric identities.

POLYCENTRIC IDENTITIES

Latinx emerging adults navigate both societal and familial markers of adulthood, which allow for an inhabiting of both a premature and a full participation of adulthood at various developmental stages, creating a "bicultural conception of the transition to adulthood."[15] We believe that polycentric identities allow for self-identification processes that allow one to "negotiate" various cultural markers from within the Latinx community, the dominant culture, and other ethnic groups.[16] In other words, polycentric identities provide at least seven Latinx subcultures that represent how Latinx move through, relate to, or are marginalized by the Latina community.[17] Essential to polycentric identities is also the explicit movement between Latin America and the United States as referential points of cultural, religious, and social wealth. In other words, polycentric identities follow the tracks and pathways forged by Latinx youth in their constant movement for belonging, relationships, and transitions into adulthood. Instituto Fe y Vida has also proposed four "types" of Latinx youth that describe belonging as well as self-determination in the midst of moving to and from the Latina community: immigrant workers, identity seekers, mainstream movers, and gang members.[18]

These categories, when overlapped, present a more composite and multidirectional identity formation processes that truly provide inroads for Latinx youth to name their agency and self-worth in the world. We firmly believe that this framework of "fluid diaspora identities and experiences" serves as an act of resistance against the nationalist, racist, and hegemonic narratives that invisibilize and dehumanize migrants and children of immigrants.[19] The complexities of lived Latina experiences characterized by the encounter between the Latina community and the assimilating culture of the United States must account for the movement across multiple self-identifying terms. Here terms such as "Latinx millennials," "emerging adults," or "jóvenes" can also be used to expand the spectrum and realities of polycentric identities.[20] For example, Elena is an emerging adult who self-identifies as a Latina millennial with a full-time job living with her parents and older siblings—some of whom may have an alternately migratory status. Roberto is a US-born Latino millennial who prefers "emerging adult," since he is establishing his own web design business while working as a bank teller to supplement his family's income. Evelyn is a Latinx emerging adult, DACA recipient, born in Guatemala, living in Los Angeles, pursuing a master's degree in social work, and employed at a local immigration advocacy nonprofit. Tatiana—as a foreign-born Latinx millennial originally from Colombia—keeps close contact with family, friends, and church via WhatsApp and social media as she plans to return to Colombia to set up her own business once she saves enough money.

In fact, these polycentric identities with two active "hubs" in the Two-Thirds World (Latin America and immigrant communities in the United States) uniquely present a missional opportunity that exemplifies God's decentralizing mission also known as a *polycentric missiology*.[21] When God's missional focus shifts from solely places toward people, Latinx emerging adults are central to the flourishing of world Christianity. For Latinx emerging adults a polycentric missiology that takes their agency, transnational commitments, and innovative ministry models seriously can expand their realm of missional imagination. Polycentric identities, when framed around God's polycentric mission, can serve the local Latina church and her leadership in identifying, promoting, and accompanying Latinx emerging adults in their process of leadership formation. We agree with CLADE V's pastoral letter titled "Youth, Actors of Transformation" in confessing the *adult-centered* ministries that have for so long prevented the sharing and embodiment of the kingdom of God to this generation.[22] And we also long for the Latina church to foster the integration of polycentric identities and Christian discipleship for missional formation and leadership.

MIJA/O LEADERSHIP FORMATION

The theological imagination of a reconstituted *familia* creates a space where Latinx emerging adults can integrate polycentric identities and transnational commitments in a way that fosters their missional agency. Latina *evangélica* theologian Zaida Maldonado Perez—in describing the dynamism and communal interrelatedness of the Triune God—points to the motif of a reconstituted *familia* as a rich and subversive imagery for theological and cultural reflection.[23] She states, "From Genesis to Revelation, God invites 'whosoever will' to join this new, subversive *familia*, a reconstituted family, a *hermandad* of equals, called to imitate the life and work of our Triune God."[24] She acknowledges the limitations that a romanticized idea of *familia* may have on Latinas' lived realities in the United States (i.e., intact hierarchical and patriarchal structures), so she uplifts the virtues of a *familia* that, in mirroring the loving, inclusive, and empowering nature of the Trinity, reconfigures a family of solidarity, mutuality, and agency for the kingdom of God. The richness of this imagery serves the Latina church in deepening her self-assessment as to which kind of community it is forming in its current US context.

A reconstituted *familia* has the ability to affirm one's identity as *mija/o*: a profound sense of belongingness and connectivity that serves as a reference point as one navigates polycentric identities in the world.[25] In fact, *mija/o* tethers one to a community while at the same time releases one to be and act as one who does not *olvida de donde vino* ("Forgets where one comes from"). *Mija* and *mijo* are not words reserved exclusively for blood ties; rather, these identifiers connote appreciation, belongingness, connectivity, visibility, and an embrace that collectively shapes one's agency and purpose in the world. The Latina *evangélica* church as a reconstituted *familia* often tends to provide that sense of familial relational connectivity, especially within first-generation immigrant communities, so it is not inappropriate to extend this connection to subsequent generations. Yet, under the presence and equalizing presence of the Spirit (Acts 2), the Latina *evangélica* church's commitment to the missional engagement of Latinx emerging adults must go one step further in promoting a *mija* leadership formation process.

Noemi Vega Quiñones highlights the Synoptic Gospels' account of a nameless bleeding woman as one that resembles the marginality of Latinas in the United States while at the same time emphasizing Jesus's rehumanizing words: *mija*.[26] As Jesus welcomes the woman into a reconstituted *familia*, these words begin a holistic healing process that empowers her for *mija* leadership: where courageous faith, resourcefulness, truth telling, and intergenerational ministry are essential for agency in God's kingdom.[27] *Mija* leadership formation functions as a biblical framework that the Latina church can incorporate as she accompanies, affirms, and sends Latinx emerging adults into the world.

Let us be clear that this formation process is not a retention strategy for Latinx youth in church communities; it is actually a rethinking of youth ministry not as auxiliary or secondary to adult-centered ministries. *Mija* leadership formation processes take seriously the lives, stories, gifts, context, and skills of Latinx emerging adults and see them as essential catalyzers and leaders in God's mission. This posture will also require that the Latina church and her leaders will cease to think that the validity of their leadership formation process is measured only internally—as to what benefits the life and ministry of the congregation inwardly. Rather, *mija* leadership formation processes, within reconstituted *familia* contexts of mutuality, individuation, and healthy attachment, involve the formation of Latinx leaders for the sake of *el barrio* (the "hood") and to the ends of the world. In addition, the bilingualism and transnational commitments present within Latinx emerging adults (and subsequent younger generations) naturally facilitate their adaptability and bridge-building capacity across borders, cultures, and races—a reality that may move them into leadership roles outside the Latina church and into the community, workplace, or other institutions.[28] In Pentecost-like fashion, Latinx emerging adults' bilingualism and biculturality (and multiculturality) are gifts that remind ecclesial leadership in North America that God's mission is multilingual, inclusive, and for the public space; God's missional agents engage the world and its surrounding communities with Christlike solidarity and Spirit-driven border crossing.[29] Elizabeth Tamez Méndez keenly notes that Latinx youth are conversation and ideation partners, cultural translators and insiders, and strategic collaborators uniquely positioned to envision new roads into missional witness and presence in our current context.[30] These new inroads and innovative approaches will probably not be contained in church programs, denominational structures, or missions agencies.

RECOMMENDED RESOURCES

Practically, we would like to suggest some resources that we have used and recommend in the accompaniment and formation of Latinx emerging adults. Holistic mentoring of Latinx emerging adults is rich when it addresses the integration of vocation and discipleship. Pastoral experience has taught us that Latinx emerging adults often face the dichotomy (imposed or taught) between the church (sacred) and el mundo (secular). Holistic mentoring addresses discipleship as lived in lo cotidiano (daily lived experiences) and informing the interconnection between skills, giftings, education, finances, career, and Christian witness and presence in public spaces with the common good in mind. Elizabeth Conde-Frazier has an extremely helpful series of open questions that facilitate holistic mentoring between older and younger Latinx generations aimed at fostering spaces of mutual growth, learning, development, and generative communication.[31]

Latinx emerging adults may also benefit from Latinx leadership frameworks originating from community organizing and the nonprofit world. We recommend Juana Brodas's book *The Power of*

Latino Leadership as a resource that may facilitate a bilingual inter-generational leadership development process within a Latina congregation led primarily by Latinx emerging adults, since the book is published in both English and Spanish.[32] If your current ministry context need revolves around the establishment or repair of relational and collaborative processes between Latina generations, Jennifer Guerra Aldana and I (Marcos) created a bilingual downloadable toolkit for Fuller Youth Institute titled *Understanding and Relating to Latino/a Youth: A Bilingual and Intergenerational Conversation Toolkit*.[33] This toolkit addresses both critical issues in Latina youth ministry and the church while also providing practical next steps to promote a healthier reconstituted *familia* within your church.

Another practical suggestion is to address the intersections of gospel and justice, spirituality and activism, and the church and liberation: intersections richly formed by Latinx and Latin American theology and history. Robert Chao Romero has recently published *Brown Church*, a historical account of five centuries of Latino/a witness, advocacy, and justice-driven initiatives from and for the Latina community in tune with Jesus's *Plan Espiritual de Galilea* (spiritual plan of Galilee).[34] Specifically written for Latinx emerging adults living in the spiritual borderlands of white North American evangelicalism and Latina *evangélica* communities, this book will incite a series of conversations, webinars, reading groups, documentary nights, or experiential border pilgrimages. This book's rich contribution can also extend an invitation for Latinx emerging adults who are artists, filmmakers, musicians, and others to express the lament of current and past injustices[35] confronted with the liberation of the gospel of a God of justice.

Last, we would like to encourage the strengthening of transnational missional initiatives and relationships with Latinx emerging adults. For some this may look like a trip that reconnects them with their parents' country of origin; for others it may jumpstart entrepreneurial visions infused with kingdom-of-God values in their own country of origin. The transnational impact and missional agency that Latinx emerging adults have and will continue to have present further areas of research in the coming years as the changing sociopolitical, religious, and economic landscapes of Latin America and the United States continue to be interwoven.

CONCLUSION

The lens of transnationalism, the richness of polycentric identities, and the *mija* leadership formation processes weave together one possible angle from which integrative formation can take place alongside Latinx emerging adults. We have pointed to migration and mission as intricately connected and as a means of grace that serves as the backdrop for Latinx emerging adults' formation processes both in their commitments and interconnectedness. Put simply, Latinx emerging adults' lived realities and identities across and within nation-states enrich their ability to join God in mission while at the same time resisting and dismantling homogenous, nativist, and racist narratives that continue to marginalize them. The Latina church in the United States has a role to play in the accompaniment, affirming, and sending of Latinx emerging adults as missional leaders and agents for and beyond the Latina community.

QUESTIONS FOR DIALOGUE

1. How is God using Latinx emerging adults as agents of mission in your church or community? If you do not know, whom can you talk with to gain a broader understanding about this? Which of the resources mentioned in the article would be best for you to read or access next?

2. In what ways are Latinx emerging adults sharing their faith with other emerging adults? What can be learned from their approaches?

3. Many Latinx emerging adults are bilingual, bicultural, technologically savvy, and deeply connected to their local US Latina communities and their parents' or their own country of origin. How are these factors, and polycentric identities, shaping their missional imagination?

4. In what ways can the concepts of *mija* leadership and church as a reconstituted *familia* inform new approaches to working with emerging adults?

BIBLIOGRAPHY

Bordas, Juana. *The Power of Latino Leadership: Culture, Inclusion, and Contribution.* A Bk Business Book. San Francisco: Berrett-Koehler, 2013.

Brettell, Caroline, and James Frank Hollifield. *Migration Theory: Talking across Disciplines.* 2nd ed. New York: Routledge, 2008.

Cervantes, Carmen M., and Ken Johnson-Mondragón. *Pastoral Juvenil Hispana, Youth Ministry, and Young Adult Ministry: An Updates Perspective on Three Different Pastoral Realities.* Stockton, CA: Instituto Fe y Vida, 2007.

Canales, Marcos, and Jennifer Guerra Aldana. *Understanding and Relating to Latino/a Youth: A Bilingual and Intergenerational Conversation Toolkit.* Pasadena, CA: Fuller Youth Institute, 2018.

Charles, Mark, and Soong-Chan Rah. *Unsettling Truths: The Ongoing, Dehumanizing Legacy of the Doctrine of Discovery.* Downers Grove, IL: InterVarsity Press, 2019.

CLADE V, Jóvenes. "Youth, Actors for Transformation." Pastoral letter. 2012. https://jovenescladev.files.wordpress. com/2012/07/carta-pastoral-de-la-consulta-de-jovenes-ingles.pdf.

Conde-Frazier, Elizabeth. "Jovenes Latin@s: Children of the Basilea." *Apuntes* 37, no. 2 (2017): 92–103.

Drexler, Jorge. "Movimiento." *Salvavidas de Hielo* [CD]. Warner Music Spain, 2017.

Dyrness, Andrea, and Enrique Sepúlveda III. *Border Thinking: Latinx Youth Decolonizing Citizenship.* Minneapolis: University of Minnesota Press, 2020.

Galambos, Nancy L., and Jeffrey Jensen Arnett, eds. *Exploring Cultural Conceptions of the Transition to Adulthood.* New Directions for Child and Adolescent Development 100. San Francisco: Jossey-Bass, 2003.

García-Johnson, Oscar. *Spirit Outside the Gate: Decolonial Pneumatologies of the American Global South.* Downers Grove, IL: IVP Academic, 2019.

González, Juan. *Harvest of Empire: A History of Latinos in America.* New York: Penguin Books, 2001.

International Organization for Migration and United Nations. "World Migration Report." 2020. https://www.un.org/ sites/un2.un.org/files/wmr_2020.pdf.

Johnson-Mondragón, Ken, and National Study of Youth & Religion (U.S.). *Pathways of Hope and Faith among Hispanic Teens: Pastoral Reflections and Strategies Inspired by the National Study of Youth and Religion.* Pathways and Journeys for a New Generation 5.1. Stockton, CA: Instituto Fe y Vida, 2007.

Kohn, Natalia, Noemi Quiñones Vega, and Kristy Garza Robinson. *Hermanas: Deepening Our Identity and Growing Our Influence.* Downers Grove, IL: InterVarsity Press, 2019.

Lopez, Mark Hugo, Jens Manuel Krogstad, and Antonio Flores. "Key facts about young Latinos, one of the nation's fastest-growing populations." Pew Research Center, September 13, 2018. https://www.pewresearch.org/fact-tank/2018/09/13/key-facts-about-young-latinos/.

Martell-Otero, Loida I., Zaida Maldonado Pérez, and Elizabeth Conde-Frazier. *Latina Evangélicas: A Theological Survey from the Margins*. Eugene, OR: Cascade Books, 2013.

Martínez, Juan Francisco. *The Story of Latino Protestants in the United States*. Grand Rapids: Eerdmans, 2018.

———. *Walk with the People: Latino Ministry in the United States*. Nashville: Abingdon, 2008.

Pew Research Center. "English Proficiency on the Rise among Latinos: US Born Driving Language Changes." May 12, 2015. https://www.pewresearch.org/hispanic/2015/05/12/english-proficiency-on-the-rise-among-latinos/.

Pew Research Center. "About One-in-Four U.S. Hispanics Have Heard of Latinx, but Just 3% Use It." August 11, 2020. https://www.pewresearch.org/hispanic/2020/08/11/about-one-in-four-u-s-hispanics-have-heard-of-latinx-but-just-3-use-it/.

Rodriguez, Daniel A. *A Future for the Latino Church : Models for Multilingual, Multigenerational Hispanic Congregations*. Downers Grove, IL: IVP Academic, 2011.

Romero, Robert Chao. *Brown Church: Five Centuries of Latina/o Social Justice, Theology, and Identity*. Downers Grove, IL: IVP Academic, 2020.

Sensis & Think Now Research. "Hispanic Millennial Project." 2014–2015. http://www.hispanicmillennialproject.com/waves.

Tamez Méndez, Elizabeth. "Rethinking Latino Youth Ministry: Frameworks That Provide Roots and Wings for Our Youth." *Apuntes* 37, no. 2 (2017): 42–91.

U.S. Census Bureau. "65 and Older Population Grows Rapidly as Baby Boomers Age." 2020. https://www.census.gov/

newsroom/press-releases/2020/65-older-population-grows.html.

Yeh, Allen L. *Polycentric Missiology: 21st-Century Mission from Everyone to Everywhere*. Downers Grove, IL: IVP Academic, 2016.

13

. . . . .

Hip-Hop in Missional Formation

Dwight Radcliff

. . . . .

*A hip-hop hermeneutic demands that this total
person is allowed to approach the Scriptures.*[1]

Reflecting on her experience, "the poet" talked about her severe depression and suicide attempts and how hip-hop spoke directly to her soul and her reality. "Through that I found hip-hop music speaking the language, speaking the language of the Bible per se. But not really saying this is Scripture, this is the Bible, this is the Word. But it took me out of a depressed state because I felt like the people from hip-hop at that time understood me. And understood the rawness and the struggle that I was going through."[2] The Bible, which she already had some knowledge of, was actually made alive through hip-hop. She said, "I totally believe that God used the genre of hip-hop to save my life."

WHAT IS HIP-HOP?

Defining hip-hop is a difficult process mainly because it is simultaneously one thing and several things. Hip-hop is a genre of music,
a culture (or subculture), a prophetic voice, a billion-dollar global
industry, a language, a type of poetry, a type of dance, a style of
clothing, a mentality, and more. To further complicate things, hip-
hop is each of these things individually and collectively. A person
can get a myriad of answers as to how hip-hop should be defined
based on the context of a conversation. However, academic integrity and heuristic needs demand that I clearly delineate what it
means when I am discussing the phenomenon in this chapter.

The term hip-hop, for this discussion, refers to the culture
birthed in the ghettos of New York in the 1970s. I reference hip-
hop as an urban culture that seeks to express a lifestyle, attitude,
or theology that rejects the oppression of the dominant culture and
seeks to prioritize Black voices from the margins, along with their
histories, experiences, realities, and perceptions.[3] The primary
language of this culture is musical, poetic, and artistic in nature,
borrowing heavily from traditions rooted in the African diaspora.

WHY IS HIP-HOP IMPORTANT
FOR THIS CONVERSATION?

Like so many people in my demographic, hip-hop was part of my
childhood—it was part of my formative years and was attached
to many of my childhood and adolescent experiences. Like many
others experienced, the church soon condemned this part of my
life. Hip-hop may have been raw, graphic, and, at times, even
ungodly—but it was not godless. Unfortunately, my Pentecostal
(and strict Baptist) upbringing did not agree. I was forced to
choose between hip-hop and the gospel, a false dichotomy com-
municated frequently to teens and emerging adults. It was not
until many years later that I began to realize that I did not have
to accept everything hip-hop offered in order to appreciate it,

engage it, and love it—just as I did not have to accept everything the institution of the church offered in order to appreciate it, engage it, and love it.

As I began to be influenced by the writings of authors such as Cornel West, Michael Eric Dyson, Kelly Brown Douglas, James Cone, and Ralph Watkins, I came to the realization that hip-hop was more than music and clothing—it was a culture. Hip-hop was Black culture. It was part of the Black experience, and to deny hip-hop was to deny part of my own formation and identity. Even more, hip-hop was a culture that was already doing theology, and it was as in need of Christ as any other culture.

To be clear, I am not asserting that hip-hop culture is the only Black experience. Frederick Ware reminds us: "Like religion, Blackness is a malleable category. There is not one but many conceptions of Blackness. Blackness has never been defined definitively, once and for all times."[4] Each generation has pushed the boundaries of the definition of the Black experience in meaningful ways. Hip-hop is not the entirety of the Black experience, but its impact is felt across age, gender, and socioeconomic demographics. However, as part of the Black experience, this voice is often removed from theological discourse as we minister to and with emerging adults.

HOW HIP-HOP CONNECTS
WITH GOD'S MISSION

Hip-hop contains elements of vulgarity, misogyny, homophobia, criminal activity, and idolatry in its vernacular, style, and imagery. Although the same can be said of any culture, this argument has often been used to eliminate any missional necessity in relation to hip-hop culture and to exclude hip-hop culture from hermeneutic and homiletic processes. However, it is also assumed that the work and obligation of the *missio Dei* involve every people group, culture, nation, and identity. As such, all people are worthy of the practical and scholarly attention necessary to engage them with the gospel of Jesus Christ. Further, it should be stated overtly that God is present in hip-hop culture.

Hip-hop is a powerful and prophetic voice against injustice, and a cultural phenomenon in this country (and worldwide). As such, it deserves to be clarified for the missiological audience and then treated with the same attention every culture (or subculture) deserves. The Spirit of God desires to take on every culture, not simply inhabit a dominant one.[5] Further, Efrem Smith and Phil Jackson write, "When one begins to see hip-hop as more than just rap music, as a whole culture, new doors open for evangelism, and we can become learners, observers, and missionaries to those living in hip-hop culture and those influenced by it."[6]

HIP-HOP'S FORMATIVE INFLUENCE

Watkins's focus is on hip-hop socio-theologians and God-talk occurring outside the church and the academy.[7] However, hip-hop has been a formative influence for many who are "inside" and engaging in ministry. For example, in my dissertation research I interviewed several Black preachers across the country. Ninety percent of the preachers who participated in this research acknowledged being formed by and identifying with the culture, even when their denominations placed a separation (at least at some point) between hip-hop culture and the church. Many find themselves at the other end of the spectrum from what organized religious traditions are saying about it. These preachers said things such as: "We are hip-hop." "I am a product of it." "I keep thinking I'm gonna grow out of it. But it doesn't leave me. It won't let me go." "I can't escape it, you know." "But it's life to me. It's a lifestyle. It's a perspective." Their experiences are real, as are the feelings, values, and beliefs accumulated in the culture; and these are not easily disposed of.

One explained, "Well, it's a genre of music in general. But for me, as an artist, it's an outlet. It's a tool used to convey a message, to me. It gets a message through, to me, like nothing else can." Consistently, then, and across the board, all participants in the research reported meaningful ways and levels of being shaped and formed in hip-hop's crucible. The preachers who participated in the study are using hip-hop culture to see Scripture with deep connectivity and to communicate with their audiences while highlighting the continued suffering of the Black experience.

PERSONAL REALITIES RECOGNIZED

Several respondents described the difficulty of growing up in inner-city neighborhoods or ghettos. They spoke about their neighborhoods, the deficiencies of the school systems, and the effects of poverty. They were exposed to certain experiences that have come to typify inner-city living in minority communities. While their experiences were commonplace for them, with the popularization and spread of hip-hop, they found others talking about this reality in the mainstream. When they saw and heard hip-hop, they felt an authenticity that was bred from their own experiences. It was a self-identification. "This is what expresses what we see," one said. Another reported, "Everything that we saw on a daily basis from the time we woke up, even when we were dreaming, I would say to the time we went back to bed—somebody [in hip-hop] had music about all of it." Another said, "I think it was just the mere fact of someone on a bigger scale being able to share [my story] with the world." They found, in hip-hop, a vocal representation of their own experiences. Hip-hop spoke their realities in the same raw language they heard each day. Another said, "Just the stories growing up in the 'hood. And [hip-hop] being able to tell, to voice our story. And it being cohesive. They could relate [to me]." Author Phil Jackson expresses it this way: "Hip-hop brings hope back. Even if it offers no change, it at least gives confirmation that your situation is recognized and identified."[8]

THE INTERPRETIVE TASK

Translating the content of Scripture into the vernacular of a recipient culture is not a new concept in missiology. According to Charles Kraft, God enters humanity's "frame of reference," and "God's basic method is incarnation."[9] Andrew Walls argues that the Christian faith, from its inception, has been heavily "veiled" in the cultural environments of its adherents. Christianity, for Walls, is constantly and consistently indigenized in cultural contexts because it is impossible to separate "an individual from his social relationships and thus from his society."[10]

Walls's contention is that from the incarnation event forward, Christians have been indigenizing the faith to the point that it is often unrecognizable in certain points in history and in certain geographic locations. In another work, Walls makes the express point that Christianity is vernacular in its very nature.[11] At its core it is pliable enough to cross cultural boundaries. He later insists: "Christian faith must go on being translated, must continuously enter into vernacular culture and interact with it, or it withers and fades."[12]

Lamin Sanneh continues Walls's point, holding that "language and culture are essential aspects of Christian transmission."[13] Both Walls and Sanneh push the idea that the nature of Christianity is to engage the idioms and expressions—the vernacular—of a culture. They argue, as does Robert Hood, against the fallacy of a static cultural and linguistic container for the Christian faith.[14] Sanneh, engaging C. S. Lewis's thought, verbalizes it this way: "The divine humility of the incarnation justifies reducing Scripture to the vulgar, unliterary speech of the humdrum world."[15] In the incarnation, Kraft, Walls, and Sanneh see God entering into the cultural conditions of humanity. Not just humanity in general, but a specific cultural context, in a specific geographic region, at a specific time in history. As God entered into the specific culture of humanity, so the *missio Dei* compels Christians today to do the same. Hence, Christianity "renders itself as a translatable religion, compatible with all cultures."[16]

Another respondent shared his story with me, and it illustrates this process well. He said,

> I actually accredit hip-hop for my real conversion to Christianity. ... I was going to church, you know, but I was still getting high and listening to Nas and Jay[-Z]. And you know, whatever. I was going to the clubs and doing everything else everyone else was really doing. But then I grabbed hold of artists like Sho Baraka, Lecrae. You know, some of these guys who embraced the culture of hip-hop, yet they spoke about evangelism and the struggles of, you know, lust and pride. Just real issues that I avoided, but they did it through the art form of hip-hop that spoke to me. No sermon ever spoke to me in that way. They didn't really bring the change in my life. It didn't happen until I heard it in hip-hop form.

A BRIDGE TO SCRIPTURE

A hip-hop hermeneutic invites the totality of the person into the interpretive task. All emotions and experiences are welcomed. Feelings of shame, guilt, sexuality, joy, pleasure, failure, success, love, and pain are not excluded from the interpretive task, nor are they placed in a spiritual hierarchy. This is characteristic of Black preaching and the Black Christian experience in America. Cleophus James LaRue gives four essentials that collide in Black preaching: God, Scriptures, the preacher, and the Black experience.[17] The lived experience of Black people is an "essential," and if we hope to reach and develop emerging adults in a missional formation process, this part of their experience cannot be discounted or ignored. As Henry Mitchell emphasizes, "Another imaginative aspect of Black preaching is the choice of illustrations—gripping modern parallels to the biblical text. In the process of making the point clear, the Black experience is lifted up and celebrated, identity is enhanced, and the hearer enters vicariously into the story, making it his or her own personal story."[18]

While things such as imaginative language are indeed treasured hallmarks of Black preaching, so too is the strict authority of Scripture. Scripture, in Black preaching, is held in the highest regard, and to disregard Scripture is to disregard the very act of preaching. LaRue comments: "Thus, Black preaching is inextricably tied to Scripture. In the eyes of the Black church, a preacher without Scripture is like a doctor without a Black bag."[19] Strong language, graphic imagery, and raw emotions are part of hip-hop. It does not shy away from complicated, profane, sexual, or violent language and topics. But neither do Old Testament books, which contain explicit laments that include genocide, infanticide, sensuality, oppression, and abuse—yet they are affirmed as part of the holy canon.

Returning to the research, several participants mentioned how hip-hop is the lens through which they see the Bible, as narrative after narrative in the Scripture was turned into an interpretation from a hip-hop perspective. For example, one said:

> I see 'hoods. I don't just see stories in Galilee and Bethlehem; I see communities. And I see ghetto stories in the Bible. I see Cain and Abel. When Cain can just kill his brother, and Abel's blood was crying to God from the ground, I think about a lot of men— whether they are in a gang or not, innocent or not— that have spilled their blood, and I see them and hear them. Their blood crying out to God. Because

when that happens, God moves. So, I see 'hood stories in the Bible.

A FORM OF LAMENT

As one respondent explained,

> I think about hip-hop in the form of the laments—the lament psalms and protest psalms. So that's been my focus in regard to hip-hop. Because I've been trying to really help people to understand and get past some of the language in the music. Now some of the language in the music is just because people are not creative enough to make music without cursing. But some of the harshness of the language in hip-hop is valid. ... And it's the same way even in the psalms, and even in some of the lamentations. And how they are structured, and what's being said, and why they're protesting against God. You know—angry and crying and mourning because they are in exile. And theologically, we look at the church being in exile. When we look at the children of Israel being in exile, when you look at communities of color in poverty, being in exile ... that all speaks to the same thing.

He continued by saying,

> So, one, in particular, is a Tupac song, "Cry So Many Tears." And so, when you listen to that song, or even if you look at the lyrics, he's lamenting. It's why he said he's cried so many tears. That's a lament. He's crying; he's mourning because of all of the devastation and the hurt and the violence and death that's happened around him, in his community. And he's crying out in that song. And then another song he

had was, "Is There a Heaven for a G?" It's like he's
asking that question just like the psalmist in 22 said,
"My God, my God, why have you forsaken me?" That's
the same thing that Tupac is saying, in so many
words, in his generation.

Watkins affirms outright the omnipresence of God in hip-hop
and likens hip-hop to the work of Jeremiah.[20] He goes even further
to call much of hip-hop a prophetic lament, just as the research
respondents reported.

IMPLICATIONS FOR THE FUTURE

This chapter and the research that underpins it speak to the
African American church and community context in the United
States. However, many of the themes discussed, and the missiological model itself, have broader implications. Hip-hop is now a
global phenomenon. The imprint of hip-hop can be felt in Ghana's
Gh hip-hop, through K-hip-hop in Korea, or the Palestinian hip-
hop group DAM. Globally, hip-hop is used to explore, discuss, and
work through issues of marginalization, oppression, race, and
politics.[21] Language and imagery are being created globally to
help marginalized communities express and share their experiences. And, as marginalized populations encounter hip-hop in
their own contexts, they too will begin to connect with both local
and global expressions of hip-hop culture. Many emerging adults
will identify with it, be formed by it, and as they come to faith
in Christ, they will look for opportunities to share the gospel to
others through a hip-hop worldview or lens.

CLOSING THOUGHTS

The Black preachers mentioned in this chapter each demonstrate
their own deep formation, their interpretive lens, and the need

to communicate in the language of their audiences. They bring their entire selves to the tasks of preaching and mission, and they deem hip-hop culture as the appropriate vehicle to enhance their communication of Scripture. As one explained, "Whenever we're expressing the gospel, to me, it's more so of being able to understand [the audience's] background, understanding where they come from, understanding the culture that they live in, the experiences that they have today, and then being able to communicate that on the same level." Each saw and spoke about the ability of hip-hop to speak to people, touch hearts, move spirits, and communicate hope and grace. Perhaps this ability is further evidence of God's presence among God's people everywhere. Communicating in the language and vernacular of the people is a missional principle that cannot be ignored or set aside by those who seek to facilitate the spiritual and missional formation of many emerging adults who are influenced by hip-hop. "Culture is a factor that cannot be overlooked" if one hopes to be fruitful in this endeavor.[22]

QUESTIONS FOR DIALOGUE

1. What role does hip-hop play in the lives of emerging adults you know? In what ways do they believe it influences their lives and how they see the world?

2. What bridges and barriers has hip-hop created for them as they interact with churches and ministries?

3. What insights from hip-hop music and culture can your church or ministry build on as you facilitate emerging adults' formation for mission?

4. What forms of lament are available to emerging adults in your context? What would enable you to grow these opportunities or develop them so they are more meaningful and potent?

BIBLIOGRAPHY

Cone, James H., and Gayraud S. Wilmore. *Black Theology: A Documentary History, 1966–1979*. 2nd rev. ed. Vol. 1. Maryknoll, NY: Orbis, 1993a.

Douglas, Kelly Brown. *The Black Christ*. Maryknoll, NY: Orbis, 1994.

———. *Sexuality and the Black Church: A Womanist Perspective*. Maryknoll, NY: Orbis, 1999.

———. *What's Faith Got to Do with It? Black Bodies/Christian Souls*. Kindle ed. Maryknoll, NY: Orbis Books, 2005.

Dyson, Michael Eric. *Between God and Gangsta Rap: Bearing Witness to Black Culture*. New York: Oxford University Press, 1996.

———. *Debating Race: With Michael Eric Dyson*. New York: Basic Civitas, 2007.

———. *Holler If You Hear Me: Searching for Tupac Shakur*. New York: Basic Civitas Books, 2001.

———. "Performance, Protest, and Prophecy in the Culture of Hip Hop." Pages 12–24 in *The Emergency of Black and the Emergence of Rap*. Edited by Jon Michael Spencer. Durham, NC: Duke University Press, 1991.

Hodge, Daniel White. *The Soul of Hip Hop: Rims, Timbs and a Cultural Theology*. Downers Grove, IL: IVP Books, 2010.

Hood, Robert E. *Must God Remain Greek: Afro Cultures and God-Talk*. Minneapolis: Fortress, 1990.

Kraft, Charles H. *Communication Theory for Christian Witness*. Kindle ed. Maryknoll, NY: Orbis Books, 1991.

LaRue, Cleophus James. *The Heart of Black Preaching*. Kindle ed. Louisville, KY: Westminster John Knox, 2000.

———. *I Believe I'll Testify: The Art of African American Preaching*. Louisville, KY: Westminster John Knox, 2011.

Mitchell, Henry H. *Black Preaching: The Recovery of a Powerful Art*. Kindle ed. Nashville: Abingdon, 1990.

Radcliff, Dwight. "The Message: A Hip Hop Hermeneutic As A Missiological Model." PhD diss., Fuller Theological Seminary, 2019.

Sanneh, Lamin O. *Translating the Message: The Missionary Impact on Culture*. Rev ed. Maryknoll, NY: Orbis Books, 2009.

Smith, Efrem, and Phil Jackson. *The Hip-Hop Church: Connecting with the Movement Shaping Our Culture*. Downers Grove, IL: InterVarsity Press, 2005.

Snell, Karen, and Johan Söderman. *Hip-Hop within and without the Academy*. Lanham, MD: Lexington Books, 2014.

Sunquist, Scott W. *Understanding Christian Mission: Participation in Suffering and Glory*. Kindle ed. Grand Rapids: Baker Academic, 2013.

Walls, Andrew F. *The Cross-Cultural Process in Christian History: Studies in the Transmission and Appropriation of Faith*. Kindle ed. Maryknoll, NY: Orbis, 2002.

———. *The Missionary Movement in Christian History: Studies in the Transmission of Faith*. Kindle ed. Maryknoll, NY: Orbis Books, 1996.

———. "The Translation Principle in Christian History." In *Bible Translation and the Spread of the Church: The Last 200 Years*, edited by P. C. Stine. Boston: Brill, 1990.

Ware, Frederick L. "Methodologies in African American Theology." In Oxford Handbook of African American Theology online. 2014. http://www.oxfordhandbooks.com.fuller.idm.oclc.org/view/10.1093/oxfordhb/9780199755653.001.0001/oxfordhb-9780199755653-e-008.

———. *Methodologies of Black Theology*. Eugene, OR: Wipf & Stock, 2002.

Watkins, Ralph. "From Black Theology and Black Power to Afrocentric Theology and Hip Hop Power: An Extension and Socio-Re-theological Conceptualization of Cone's

Theology in Conversation with the Hip Hop Generation."
Black Theology 8, no. 3 (2015): 327–40.

———. *Hip-Hop Redemption: Finding God in the Rhythm and the Rhyme*. Grand Rapids: Baker Academic, 2011.

———. "The Underground: The Living Mural of a Hip-Hop Church." Pages 231–40 in *The Gospel after Christendom: New Voices, New Cultures, New Expressions*, Kindle ed. Edited by Ryan K. Bolger. Grand Rapids: Baker Academic, 2012.

Watkins, Ralph C., and Jason A. Barr. *The Gospel Remix: Reaching the Hip Hop Generation*. Valley Forge, PA: Judson, 2007.

West, Cornel, and Prince. *Dear Mr. Man*. Hidden Beach Records, 2007.

Westbrook, Alonzo. *Hip Hoptionary TM: The Dictionary of Hip Hop Terminology*. New York: Harlem Moon, 2002.

14

· · · · ·

Chinese American
Emerging Adults

Ministries to Non-Christians and Christians

Russell Jeung and Michael Karim

· · · · ·

*College was the whitest racial situation I ever experienced, so
it made it significant to be a minority instead of a majority. I
became really involved in Asian American groups for ethnic pride,
and I was able to identify myself more as Asian American. The
number of people who talk about religion in college is incredibly
low, so people were horrified by the idea of me being curious
about it. It was nice to not have to think about it for a while.*

—Sandra Liu

S andra Liu, a labor attorney, grew up in a fairly religious context within the Asian American community of Houston, Texas.
Her mom, a Christian from Taiwan, thought "it was great" to have

her and her brother exposed to Christian morals, so she sent them to a Chinese Baptist church from third to eighth grade.

Initially, Sandra didn't mind attending because "it was the thing to do, because everyone was at church." There she listened to sermons, attended Sunday school, and loved the great food afterwards at the church luncheons, which were as important a ritual as communion. She said, "You just sit there, then you went to Sunday school and you eat some food and get drunk from that food."

Besides its cultural functions, the church provided an empowering racialized, social network for Sandra. She lived in the South, where she was teased for being Asian American. She observed, "I think definitely [going to church] made my life easier. It was one way I could fit in and not be weird. It was an easy way not to stand out."

As she got older, though, she found that she couldn't agree with the conservative teaching of that church. Sandra shared, "I went to Sunday school, and they started saying things like the woman should be submissive to their husband. I called it stupid and never went back. I then quit for real." Even though she felt the Chinese American church community was authentic, Sandra realized, "It just wasn't worth it. If I didn't want to believe, then it seemed ludicrous to me that I was going to hell. So I couldn't go anymore."

A DIFFERENT STORY

Robert Fong, a first-year university student from the Dallas–Fort Worth area, had a similar upbringing to Sandra's, but he has kept his faith in college. As he was raised in a devout Christian family and participated in the life of a conservative church from childhood through high school, his social network from school and church overlapped. He observed, "My whole life I've been surrounded by Chinese people that are Christian. And I went to a Chinese church. So I think for me it's always just been normal ... to see Asians at church."

When Robert arrived at the University of Texas, he was surprised by the few Asian American students there. He slowly noticed, and then more frequently, the subtle disrespect and gazes that aimed to intimidate or scorn him. Further isolating him, his major had few other minorities.

Robert soon began studying at night with his former high school classmates and others he met from Asian American campus ministries. The latter groups welcomed him, listened to him, and encouraged him regularly. Robert also engaged in the kinds of spiritual conversations he anticipated before arriving on campus. Those discussions in small group Bible studies and the spontaneous prayer that followed reassured Robert about his almost-daily decisions to hold true to his faith.

LOSING OR KEEPING FAITH

Sandra and Robert reflect why and how Chinese Americans lose and keep the Christian faith, and their differences are essential for people who care about missional formation to understand. Now an agnostic, Sandra typifies the majority of Chinese American young adults. Over half of all Chinese Americans, and 63 percent of the Chinese American second generation who were born in the United States, do not affiliate or identify with any religion; they are considered religious "nones." Yet Sandra's religious nonaffiliation isn't based on an antipathy toward the idea of religion or any animosity toward Christians as a community. Instead, she can't embrace exclusive, conservative teachings of the American evangelical church that she finds politically objectionable or intellectually "ludicrous." Further, she no longer needs the ethnic church for social and cultural reasons, as her immigrant mother or Robert might. Consequently, she continues to say "no thanks" when friends invite her to church, since "saying I'm going to hell is not a good way for me to believe in God."

Robert and Chinese Americans who identify themselves as Christian make up a smaller proportion of this ethnic group. Only 31 percent of Chinese Americans describe themselves as Christian, and only 22 percent identify as Protestant.[1] The low numbers of East Asian Americans at his university and in his major, along with the awkward and micro-aggressive behaviors of other students, contributed to Robert's developing awareness of his ethnic identity as a Chinese American. At the same time, Robert has gravitated to other Chinese American Christians in need of racial support, thus creating what is known as the "Asian bubble" that helps him to retain and further his faith.[2]

RESEARCH INSIGHTS THAT HELP
TO EXPLAIN THE DIFFERENCES

This chapter details two key findings about Chinese Americans overall.[3] First, Chinese Americans generally hold to a *liyi* approach toward religious traditions that privileges values and rituals over strict beliefs. Second, the familism of Chinese Americans is an underlying cultural orientation and value system that shapes both Christians and non-Christians. It also describes two critical trends about Chinese American emerging adults who retain their Christian faith.[4] The familism of Chinese American Christian households is reinforced in their ethnic network help to nurture and retain the faith of the second generation. However, their families and congregations rarely address the second generation's racialized experiences, which clearly shape their social relations and identities; this deficiency misses an opportunity to make Christianity more relevant to both Asian American Christians and non-Christians.

FINDING 1: A *LIYI* APPROACH

Ministries working with Chinese and Asian Americans must address the worldview and ethics of this group. From a Western perspective, the concept of "religion" assumes that persons hold to exclusive beliefs and affiliate in distinct churches. When we interviewed Chinese American emerging adults who were not religious, however, these individuals struggled identifying their own clearcut beliefs about what is "true" about the supernatural. Religious nones such as Sandra either hold to a scientific mindset or a postmodern one. For example, she explained why her family could not be certain about spiritual matters: "My [brother's] reasoning is a lot more like my dad's—there needs to be physical evidence that God really exists. But I can't personally fathom the stuff that the church preached. I think partly it was that I couldn't experience how others experienced God." Sandra would argue that what may be true as experienced by Christians is not necessarily true for herself.

Instead of a belief and belonging paradigm based on Western religions, we propose a Chinese indigenous concept, *liyi*, to analyze Chinese Americans' relationship to the supernatural, their ultimate values, and their ethical system. *Li* translates to "ritual propriety." Chinese are less concerned about *believing in* religion than they are concerned about *doing* religion. Proper conduct of rituals, whether formal offerings or informal acts of hospitality and greeting, inculcates moral virtues. *Yi* means "righteousness," especially in regards to one's relationships and responsibilities. Confucianists combined the two words as *liyi* for their foundational concept of "humanity," or what makes humans different from animals or barbarians. Ritual propriety (*li*) was the means by which righteousness (*yi*) could be practically and properly embodied in the concrete, while righteousness (*yi*) was necessary to guide the practices that constituted *li*. By promoting *liyi*, Confucianism established a moral system of rituals and responsibilities that defined who was righteous and virtuous.

This theoretical concept is useful in understanding emerging adults, especially Chinese Americans. For example, although Sandra refrains from affiliating with any belief system, she could easily share about her ultimate values about what was right and how she lives them out in regular practices. She articulated that she practices vegetarianism as an expression of her desire to "give back," which reflects a strong Chinese value of reciprocity: "I think we have to create our own meaning. I'm vegetarian. Around the age of fifteen, sixteen, I had a lot of existential angst, which is common. I felt like I was taking lives so I thought I should give back. So I gave up eating red meat when I was sixteen. I really wanted to figure out a way to do good stuff for the world."

Similarly, Robert and his Christian friends described their own theologies as primarily related to their practices woven into their relationships. In his faith journey to become "a better person," Robert narrates his faith as involving spiritual disciplines enacted with his family and friends. In his understanding of being a Christian, he always spoke of his faith in terms of right relations (*yi*) and in its practices (*li*). His ultimate values, practicing what was right before God and parents (Exod 20:12), finds expression in his relationships and practices of worship and missions. That is, Chinese Americans can better be understood by the virtues they practice devotedly, rather than the truths they claim.

FINDINGS 2: FAMILISM OF CHINESE AMERICANS

In applying a *liyi* heuristic of Chinese Americans, we found that they adhere to familism, "a lived tradition that prioritizes family interdependence and right relationships through the meaningful rituals of being family."[5] Their family history, their love for their family, and their plans for future family are the primary narrative by which they find meaning, purpose and identity.

Sandra, for instance, sees her purpose in life as being a good friend and family member; these relationships (*yi*) give her meaning. Assuming the role of the eldest child, she takes on the responsibility of supporting her parents through regular phone calls to her parents (*li*). She states, "I really try to be a good friend and family member. I think those connections you make are the most meaningful for sure. I'm the older one so I try to call my parents once a week. I try to be really close to them." Although she has a successful career and significant relationships in San Francisco, she would give them up if she had to take care of her parents. This moral responsibility to support one's parents was a common theme among our respondents. Even though Sandra is relatively young and her parents don't necessarily need her financial support, she gives strong consideration to her parents' health and retirement plans. She explained, "My mom is retiring, and we talked a lot about our living situation. Eventually, I want to live close to my parents if they're still in Houston. I definitely feel like if anything should happen, I would be one of the good people responsible for caretaking. I've thought about this pretty often." Indeed, caretaking for parents would help her feel like she's one of the "good people" who are "responsible."

Results from the 2012 Asian American Survey by the Pew Research Center further highlight how second-generation Chinese Americans consider family matters in their priorities and decision-making. When asked about the top goals in their life, Chinese Americans listed "being a good parent" as their foremost answer, with 96.5 percent of the second generation agreeing with that statement. "Having a successful marriage" was second-most common answer (81.8 percent agreeing). Thus, family matters are the highest priority of young Chinese Americans, even when they are starting their careers and could focus on their own lives. In fact, other individual and material pursuits, such as home ownership (62.8 percent) and a high-paying job (49.7 percent) were less valued.[6]

Additionally, Chinese Americans highly consider their parents in important decisions in their lives. More than half of the Chinese American second generation sampled (51 percent) agreed that parents should have some influence over their careers. Our interviewees noted that since their immigrant parents sacrificed so much for their opportunities, they felt indebted to pay back their parents by working hard through their careers and later financially supporting them. Further, one-half of the second generation surveyed said that parents should have influence over their spousal choice. Instead of viewing marriage simply as a relationship between two individuals, Chinese Americans seem to see that marriage involves a relationship between two families. Familism gets reinforced in Chinese American congregations and households.

FINDINGS 3: CONNECTING FAITH IN CARING WAYS

Chinese Americans who retain evangelical Christianity, like Robert and his friends, notably had devout parents who connected their faith to key areas of their children's lives. These areas include their future careers and their sense of mission. Long before moving to campus, Robert had discussions with his parents regarding the selection of his major, its career prospects, and its relationship to his faith. He shared, "You hear about Asian kids' parents [say], 'Be a lawyer, be a doctor, do business, do engineering.' I think for the most part the friends I know, including me, their parents have let them choose what they want to do. They have not placed any pressure on me to do any single kind of profession."

Robert's vision for his future vocation developed through family discussions that followed worship services. He shared, "Our family heard sermons about work. The purpose of work is to show that God is at work within you." In contrast to the "tiger parent" stereotype in which Chinese parents placed high expectations on worldly achievement, his Christian parents instead listened to Robert about his dreams and expected his faith to be made manifest in and through his work.

This encouragement in the faith also included practices to spur Robert's following of Jesus. He recalled his parents encouraging him to take mission trips in the summer with their church teams to serve among the Native peoples in Arizona. They also supported compassion ministries—beyond academic pursuits such as math and science camps—that involved volunteering in English as a second language (ESL) classes and caring for the poor. Robert recalled how a tutoring ministry among refugees he joined was hard, "but it was fun." Oftentimes the families would embark on these ministries together, both to serve and to keep the family together. Robert enjoyed accompanying his parents to visit elderly adult migrants who attended the church-sponsored ESL class. These activities brought his family together in mission.

In his retention of the faith, the emotional nurturance of his parents was as critical as their family activities. Chinese American Christians knew their parents loved them and in return, they loved their parents. Again, in stark contrast to tiger parents, who are known as being emotionally distant, these Christian households were caring and supportive. For instance, Robert disclosed: "Before I went to college, my parents asked me, 'What would you like to do when you grow up?' So, I thought about that a lot. My dad likes to pose the question, 'What is your passion?' He loves to ask me that." The Chinese languages of love included positive affirmation, as well as practices of prayer, support through food and material needs, and family times together. Thus, collaborative decision-making, family practices of service, and nurturing households were prevalent experiences in the life of the Christian Chinese American emerging adults. Missing from this Christian socialization, however, was an understanding of the racial dynamics impacting this group.

FINDING 4: RACIALIZED FRIENDSHIPS,
PRACTICES, AND FAITH

For Robert and his peers on campus, their faith commitment becomes solidified with co-ethnic Chinese Americans, but the racialized dimensions of these relationships went unaddressed. Robert and his Christian friends encountered two types of racialized experiences as students of color at the university that impact their faith commitment. First, they faced regular microaggressions, the "brief, everyday exchanges that send denigrating messages to certain individuals because of their group member-ship."[7] Robert noted,

> I'm the only Asian person in my class. And one of the
> people in my class, I can see him interacting with
> everybody except me. Whenever we talk, he kind
> of diverts [the conversation] away and then starts
> talking to a different person. I can kind of feel that
> it's maybe how I look. I guess it's like they're being
> racist; I just feel judged before they know me.

This dismissal of Robert by white classmates repeated through-out his first year of university, compounded with more slights by others in his class and subtle resistance in welcoming him, gen-erated increasing disappointment regarding his white classmates in his major.

Second, these students lacked Asian American teachings in church. Even on Sunday mornings, the sermons omitted any bib-lical content that affirmed Robert's ethnicity or that of any non-white person. Instead, the faith experiences of whites were to be normative for all, including students of color. Robert observed how he feels the megachurch he attended was "predominately white," in both membership and teaching, but he and his friends continued to go there. Subsequently, they found a disconnect from their racialized experiences on campus with the teachings at church.

Amid this racial and religious dissonance, Robert and his Chinese American peers find solace in maintaining faith practices within their family and ethnic network. Robert and his Christian friends had regular FaceTime calls with their believing parents that included prayer. They kept their attendance at the weekly small group, where praise, the reading aloud of the Bible, a study of short Bible passage, and intercession for each other helped sus-tain and empower their faith. He explained he receives a great deal of emotional satisfaction from his faith community: "It's encouraging for me to be around people who are spiritual who believe in and interact with God."

These faith practices, unsurprisingly, reinforced Robert's social network, which was narrow and small. Robert did not connect with any of the other residents in his dormitory wing. Likewise, other first-year Chinese American students had a limited number of relationships. Even though Robert had plenty of cross-racial interactions in his courses, none developed into close relationships.

The double minority experience of Chinese American Christians, as students of color and as devout evangelicals, results in a strong, reactive solidarity to deal with the cognitive dissonance of being Christians of color. They remain strong in the faith as long as they remain close and enclosed in their co-ethnic, Asian bubble.

IMPLICATIONS

For those who care about emerging adults' formation for mission, these concepts raise a number of significant implications. For instance, not only do Chinese Americans hold to a *liyi* orientation, but most American emerging adults do so currently, too. The United States is now much more like China in that its young people are in religiously pluralistic contexts. Subsequently, they develop postmodern and relativistic sensibilities where ultimate truth claims are difficult to maintain. Further, they also base their identities on their relationships and practices rather than ascribed categories, as evidenced by the growing proportions of those who are spiritual but not religious. Given this paradigmatic shift in how Americans approach religion and religiosity, a focus on people's values and practices offers more insight on their spiritual lives than their beliefs and religious affiliations.

A *liyi* approach to ministry to both Chinese and non-Chinese emerging adults, then, would seek first to introduce and inculcate the values and ways of Jesus. Given the greater concern of Chinese Americans and American emerging adults for authentic

values and relationships, the church needs—first and foremost—
to practice what it preaches and to embody grace, humility, love,
and forgiveness. Jesus is not only the truth, but also the way
and the life.[8] Christians can better introduce Jesus to their non-
Christian friends as they address issues related to environmental
and racial justice.[9] Indeed, concern for the marginalized and for
the environment easily relate to the teachings of Jesus.

In 2020, the Black Lives Matter uprising over the deaths of
George Floyd, Breonna Taylor, Ahmaud Arbery, and others, as
well as the resistance to anti-Asian hate during the Covid-19 pan-
demic, offered Chinese Americans concrete opportunities to join
in racial-justice movements. A Pew Research survey found that
four in ten African Americans and Asian Americans reported that
others acted "uncomfortable" around them since the coronavirus
outbreak.[10] Asian Americans, among all racial groups, faced racial
slurs and feared racial attacks the most. Clearly, Christian ministries need to take into account the heightened racial awareness
of Chinese American emerging adults, both from campus microaggressions and societal animus, and to address these key issues
that impact the daily lives of people of color.

For example, Asian American Christian groups protested in
solidarity with the Black Lives Matter movement. In both Chicago
and the San Francisco Bay Area, Asian American churches and
ministries joined with African American congregations to conduct host "protest processions" that included praise and prayer.
According to Pastor Brian Hui, who helped to coordinate the Bay
Area event, the young Chinese American adults reported back
that the testimonies left them "appreciative and hopeful." These
introductions to the values and ways of Jesus lend themselves to
empowering young adults for both constructive transformation
in the world and developing a tangible, witnessing spirituality for
life among friends in the way of Jesus.

Along with promoting the values and ways of Jesus, the *liyi*
paradigm suggests that faith in Jesus does not necessarily have

to entail clear-cut belief in all absolute truth claims; individuals come to God with a range of questions. Instead, churches must make room for individuals whose faith includes following and obeying Jesus even with doubts—"Help me overcome my unbelief!" (Mark 9:24 NIV). Making room for persons with doubts involves listening well to their questions, as well as what matters most to them. Even if the friendships of the young adults may be largely co-ethnic, these young adults make their way in a world that is increasingly culturally diverse and religiously plural, and it remains fractured by class and race, which generate questions of how to follow Jesus. Those questions will necessarily expect a communal response that does not set aside truth claims, but expects to have an embodied, communal practice of those truth claims.

Questions and doubts about following Jesus in one's social and cultural context should be considered as a sign of a healthy, developing faith journey, even if the person has yet to become a professing follower of Jesus. Having a pastor or lay leader listen well to what matters most to the emerging adult cannot be overemphasized. Such active listening must be primarily about affirming their disclosures and their own subjectivity, and not about straightening out their theology.

Finally, in regards to Chinese American familism, we further propose that ministry with Chinese and Asian Americans welcome and address the role of family. Indeed, ministry leaders must integrate familism when collaborating with Asian American emerging adults, even while incorporating social justice efforts, which may not be supported by families. Rather than driving a wedge between the young adult and their family, affirming their commitment to their family and integrating a collective mindset in following Jesus reduces the dissonance between Chinese Americans' racial experiences and their familism. Any affirmation of the kingdom of God and social change that excludes one's family may not be perceived as good news at all.

CONCLUSION

Those who care about missional formation among Chinese emerging adults can be aided by these insights. Just as a Chinese *liyi* approach toward ministry is culturally appropriate for many American emerging adults, Chinese American familism may be a cultural resource that can offset the hyperindividualism that pervades the United States. Chinese American emerging adults share the same passion and pursuit of personal autonomy, fulfillment, and efficacy as other Americans. What tempers their individualistic behaviors, however, is their family loyalty, collective consciousness, and responsibility to the group. These values can be seen in how Chinese Americans—both Christian and non-Christian—religiously spend time with their families, financially support one another, and communicate regularly. Chinese American congregations demonstrate these values through the sense of interdependence and obligation members have toward the church family. The American church, which currently sees a decline in regular attendance, can learn from this devotion and prioritization of the group over one's individual concern.

QUESTIONS FOR DIALOGUE

1. How do Asian American emerging adults describe their experience in your community? If they are not telling you personally, who would they be willing to tell so you can understand what they are experiencing?

2. In light of the concept *liyi*, which focuses on proper conduct, relationships, and responsibilities, what ways could you begin highlighting in your ministry Christ's actions and relationships, and how Jesus lived out his responsibilities?

3. What responsibility does your ministry have for facilitating and furthering authentic intercultural relationships in your community?

4. How can you make greater space for challenging questions, doubts, and genuine concerns that emerging adults have? What would help difficult questions to be viewed as a normal part of growing as a disciple?

BIBLIOGRAPHY

Alumkal, Antony William. *Asian American Evangelical Churches Race, Ethnicity, and Assimilation in the Second Generation.* New York: LFB Scholarly, 2003.

Chen, Carolyn, and Russell Jeung. *Sustaining Faith Traditions: Race, Ethnicity, and Religion among the Latino and Asian American Second Generation.* New York: New York University Press, 2012.

Eagen, Kevin, Ellen Bara Stolzenberg, Abigail K. Bates, Melissa C. Aragon, Maria Ramirez Suchard, and Cecilia Rios-Aguilar. "The American Freshman: National Norms, 2015." Cooperative Institutional Research Program at the Higher Educational Research Institute at UCLA. 2016. https://www.heri.ucla.edu/monographs/ TheAmericanFreshman2015.pdf.

Jeung, Russell. *At Home in Exile: Meeting Jesus among My Ancestors and Refugee Neighbors.* Grand Rapids: Zondervan, 2016.

Jeung, Russell M., Seanan S. Fong, and Helen Jin Kim. *Family Sacrifices: The Worldviews and Ethics of Chinese Americans.* Oxford: Oxford University Press, 2019.

Karim, Michael Scott. *Keeping the Faith by Second Generation Chinese American Freshmen: A Morphogenetic Analysis of Reflexive Mediation of the Christian Faith over the First Year of University Life*. Fuller Theological Seminary, School of Intercultural Studies. ProQuest Dissertations Publishing, 2020.

Khang, Kathy. *Raise Your Voice: Why We Stay Silent and How to Speak Up*. Downers Grove, IL: InterVarsity Press, 2018.

Kim, Rebecca Y. *God's New Whiz Kids? Korean American Evangelicals on Campus*. New York: New York University Press, 2006.

Lee, Hak Joon, ed. *Intersecting Realities: Race, Identity, and Culture in the Spiritual-Moral Life of Young Asian Americans*. Eugene, OR: Wipf & Stock, 2018.

Louie, Vivian S. *Compelled to Excel: Immigration, Education, and Opportunity among Chinese Americans*. Stanford, CA: Stanford University Press, 2004.

McLaren, Brian D. *More Ready than You Realize: Evangelism as Dance in the Postmodern Matrix*. Grand Rapids: Zondervan, 2002.

Park, Julie J. "I Needed to Get Out of My Korean Bubble: An Ethnographic Account of Korean American Collegians Juggling Diversity in a Religious Context." *AEQ Anthropology & Education Quarterly* 42, no. 3 (2011): 193–212.

———. *Race on Campus : Debunking Myths with Data*. Cambridge: Harvard Education Press, 2018.

Pew Research Center. "Asian Americans: A Mosaic of Faiths." 2012.

———. "The Rise of Asian Americans (Updated Edition, 4/4/2013)." 2013.

Ruiz, Neil G., Juliana Menasce Horowitz, and Christine Tamir. "Many Black, Asian Americans Say They Have Experienced Discrimination amid Coronavirus." Pew Research Center's Social & Demographic Trends Project (blog). July 1, 2020. https://www.pewsocialtrends. org/2020/07/01/many-black-and-asian-americans-say-

they-have-experienced-discrimination-amid-the-covid-
19-outbreak/.
Scandrette, Mark. "The Ninefold Path: Exploring the Way of the
Beatitudes." http://www.markscandrette.com/#new-
page-2.
Sue, D. W., J. Bucceri, A. I. Lin, K. L. Nadal, and G. C. Torino.
"Racial Microaggressions and the Asian American
Experience," *Cultural Diversity & Ethnic Minority
Psychology* 13, no. 1 (2007): 72–81.

15

· · · · ·

How Will We Respond?

*Mary T. Lederleitner, Andrew
MacDonald, and Rick Richardson*

· · · · ·

*Indeed, if an emerging adult is going to be initiated into a
profession, organization, or corporation as it is presently
defined and practiced, a mentor who guides the way is
enough. But if one is going to be initiated into a profession,
organization, or corporation and the societies they serve as
they could become, only a mentoring community will do.*

—Sharon Daloz Parks, Big Questions, Worthy Dreams

As we think about the various examples and fruitful models of
ministry with emerging adults that are highlighted throughout this text, the concept of mentoring communities often underpins them. These potent forms of community share a variety of
essential traits, and we want to unpack those a bit more explicitly,

for we believe emerging adults are heading into a future that will likely look far different than what prior generations have experienced. For example, we are at the dawn of a new age of artificial intelligence. Whole industries that have been commonplace for generations will disappear, and unprecedented opportunities for good and evil will emerge from innovation in that field alone.

In our introductory chapter we discussed how emerging adult formation for mission is now frequently happening in cultures and contexts that undermine Christian discipleship. We believe Christian spiritual formation leads to vibrant followers of Jesus who are engaged in congregations and culture. Through this process emerging adult disciples will then live for Christ, enter into congregational life, and engage in mission in distinctively Christian ways. Because of the significant cultural, sociological, political, technological, bio-tech, and economic changes likely to take place in the near future, formation for mission in emerging adulthood has never been a more pressing need. We therefore want to look at mentoring communities more closely. We also want to reflect on how to foster greater resiliency in emerging adulthood so emerging adults' formation for mission continues unimpeded. We will explore an illustration that ties together many of the concepts raised in the book. Last, we want to highlight areas where significant research is still needed.

WHAT COMPRISES A
MENTORING COMMUNITY?

Often when we think of mentoring, the picture of a one-to-one relationship comes to mind. An older, more seasoned person with a lot of life experience imparts it to a younger person so he or she can avoid unnecessary mistakes. However, Sharon Daloz Parks takes the idea further into a community of relationships founded on purpose, dialogue, substantive questions, and other essential components. Mentoring communities challenge emerging adults to reach their potential. They are places where people listen, seek to understand, and are willing to be affected and change their minds.[1] They are interwoven with significant questions about issues such as personal calling, social justice, what faithfulness looks like in a broken world, and so on.

Mentoring communities provide living examples of humans sharpening one another (Prov 27:17). They provide safe places to "reach for the ideal" and begin to imagine how life might be different. Without the challenge of meaningful and significant questions, emerging adults can default into living their lives "busy and stressed but distracted from matters worthy of their interest, concern, and practical engagement."[2] They become "vulnerable to the all-pervasive influence of media, advertising, and consumer culture" at "the very time when a future-driven anticipation should be beckoning them forth to kingdom living."[3]

A mentoring community is a network of belonging that provides physical, emotional, intellectual, and spiritual support in tangible ways. Mentoring communities might last for brief periods of time, or they may extend for years. Despite how long they last, they can be extremely influential. The features of mentoring communities include networks of belonging, big-enough questions, encounters with otherness, specific habits of the mind, and vision for the future. We recognize these features in many of the chapters that have been shared in this text. Encounters with otherness provide transformative moments of perspective taking and opportunities for examining deeply held but often tacit assumptions. These can be facilitated through intercultural experiences, service-learning opportunities, local outreach, engagement in racial reconciliation, and so on. The specific habits of mind necessary are those needed to create "habits of discourse and inclusion that invite genuine dialogue, strengthen critical thought, encourage connective-holistic awareness, and develop the contemplative mind."[4]

FOSTERING GREATER RESILIENCY

However, as several of the stories in the various chapters illustrate, emerging adulthood is a season where past spiritual development or engagement in a mentoring community does not ensure ongoing missional development. Emerging adulthood is a season fraught with vulnerability. With each transition friendships, spiritual practices, and faith communities can be altered in ways that destabilize routines and relationships that fostered prior growth.[5] Added to that mix is the reality that newer research shows many in Gen Z are struggling to develop resiliency and grit, having been sheltered by parents from disappointing and hurtful experiences more than prior generations.[6]

TEACH THEM TO FISH

While we believe mentoring communities provide safe spaces to experiment, learn, and grow from failures and successes, often we stop short if we only create mentoring communities *for* emerging adults and they are not also taught *how to create these for themselves* in the next phases of their lives. In research with emerging adults two to four years after graduation from university, participating in a mentoring community was strongly linked to their ability to thrive and continue to grow in their missional formation.[7] But if they ended up in a mentoring community, it tended to be attributed to luck. They could tell they had found something that many of their peers did not have, but it was most often created for them by others.

Some found a mentoring community within their church's small group ministry. However, the phrase "small group" can mean virtually anything. Small groups can be places that include just one or multiple of the following components: fellowship, Bible study, prayer, shared meals, and so on. All of these activities are good, but these types of small groups may or may not incorporate the other features that Parks identifies are present in mentoring communities. More intentionality needs to be placed on not just developing mentoring communities for emerging adults, but helping them imagine and anticipate how to create them for themselves and others, especially as they navigate a variety of moves, work transitions, family transitions, and so on.

HELP THEM CONNECT WITH OTHERS

Emerging adult formation happens best in community, but with all the professional and personal transitions happening at this stage of life, people can often feel isolated from others. Even if at one time emerging adults had close and meaningful relationships that were catalytic for their personal or missional growth, a year later they can find themselves in a situation where no one they trust is nearby. Greater intentionality is needed to find ways to help emerging adults connect with others like themselves who also want to keep growing in their missional formation. In some ways it is odd to have to mention this in a world that is so virtually connected, but many still struggle with feelings of isolation and a lack of genuine community.

SET REALISTIC EXPECTATIONS

As Jeffrey Arnett explains in his research, emerging adults across diverse socioeconomic groups tend to be a hopeful about the future even in the face of "formidable obstacles."[8] Added to this is the message many hear in higher education. It is virtually impossible to count the number of university graduation ceremonies that focus on "following your dreams" and say, "Do what you love and you will never work a day in your life." But life can be quite hard, and disappointment can abound. Optimism fades at times when emerging adults encounter a world that is not nearly as rosy and full of promise as they were led to believe.

Transitioning to a faith community can be one of those moments. Finding new groups of friends who are passionate about

God's purposes in the world can be difficult, and even if they are identified, job schedules can make meeting on a regular basis even more challenging. Those supporting emerging adults in their missional development need to help them think carefully through the obstacles they are likely to face and practice encountering some of those obstacles before they transition to the next phase of life. Experimentation can happen during summer breaks, when they are away from their friends, during holiday breaks, and so on. Then it is possible to debrief those experiences when they return and envision how to move forward without their current community if it is time bound and linked to their educational journey.[9]

A CLOSING ILLUSTRATION

In our research at the Wheaton College Billy Graham Center on the unchurched and churches reaching them, we heard several stories that illustrate the potency of mentoring communities and many of the issues we have discussed in the preceding chapters. For example, in our interviews with sixty previously unchurched emerging adults, one of them was Keith.[10] He was a football player on a local college team who connected with a local church, committed to Christ, and started a mentoring community that reached many of his friends.

Sean was instrumental in mentoring Keith. Sean was an emerging adult leader who partnered with a local church and Fellowship of Christian Athletes, and he reached out to the football team. Bridge people like Sean are key in developing relationships with unchurched emerging adults outside the four walls of a church. Sean began to attend football practices before the season started, cheering the players on and beginning to get to know them. Because he had a strong sports background himself, he built trust easily as they talked about shared athletic experiences. When the season started, Sean was at every football game.

He also began to have lunch with a few of them at the college, opening space to talk about questions and concerns that were important to them. He began to care for them and try to help in practical ways, such as offering to pray, giving them a ride, or helping them find a part-time job.

Over time the guys started to trust Sean more and, as their trust grew, they shared more deeply about their concerns and challenges. Keith asked Sean for help around relationship issues he faced. Sean's church had an emerging adult group that was planning a series on internet dating and moving toward healthy relationships. Sean invited Keith to attend. He tried it out and liked it. The senior pastor at the church spoke at one of the sessions, and Sean introduced him to Keith. The senior pastor took time to listen and then later asked whether Keith would ever be willing to have coffee with him, to help the pastor understand the needs of college students better. They exchanged cell numbers, met occasionally, and got to know each other more.

Sean continued the mentoring community with Keith and his friends, talking about many life issues, and pointing conversations when appropriate toward faith. Keith also began to attend the Sunday church service as well as the church's emerging adult ministry group in response to the pastor's invitation. After one of the services, the pastor had coffee again with Keith on campus to ask how he thought the service would be perceived by Keith's friends. He was asking Keith for advice, and mentoring was mutual.

Next, Sean invited Keith to help host a discovery Bible study on campus with some of Keith's friends on the football team. Sean explained to Keith that he saw tremendous leadership potential in him and that he wanted to mentor Keith to reach that potential. They started that group after football season was over, when most of the guys had time to attend. Many teammates were interested in opportunities to keep connecting and maintaining their friendships during the offseason. Before Keith had even committed to

Christ, Sean also asked Keith to help him plan a service event for the emerging adult group in a sister church that served meals to people living on the streets in an urban neighborhood. Keith invited a few of his friends to come to that as well.

During a painful relationship breakup, Sean challenged Keith to give his life to Christ, and Keith made that commitment. Next Sean asked whether Keith would be willing share his story with the emerging adult group. As Keith shared his story, he was engaging in the process of narrative identity formation. Keith began inviting other members of his football team to the emerging adult ministry, and Sean challenged him to start a weekly Bible study with a few of them, now that the discovery Bible study was no longer going. Sean offered to mentor him in leading that study.

Ultimately, that Bible study became a new mentoring community, which Keith embraced and led. He saw family members and several football players connect to the congregation through that group, and also through his personal invitations and storytelling. Some of his family members and his football teammates later committed to Christ. And since the football team was multiracial, the mentoring community that Keith led had many opportunities for learning and gaining new perspectives from others with different experiences.

In this way, mentoring communities and the many issues raised in prior chapters provide pathways to facilitate emerging adult formation for mission for believers, but also for those who do not yet believe but are open to exploring faith. Mentoring has achieved its goal when those who were initially mentored begin to have their own mentoring communities and invest in others. In our research, this kind of process was illustrated time and again for many different kinds of emerging adult contexts in the churches that were most effectively reaching and developing emerging adult disciples and leaders.[11]

WHERE IS MORE RESEARCH NEEDED?

There are so many contexts in which additional research is needed that is can be hard to know how to best focus when you have limited time and resources. Here are some categories and areas to consider as you think through future research.

WHO IS MOST AT RISK?

Who are the emerging adults you are working with right now who are most at risk of not continuing to develop and fulfill God's calling and purposes for their lives? Are they people who will be moving away? Are they emerging adults with substance-abuse tendencies? Are they people prone to lose themselves in their work? What are the risk factors you are seeing in the next leg of their journeys? Through action research, qualitative research, or quantitative research, get crystal clear about these risk factors. Work with emerging adults and other key stakeholders to identify solutions that can lessen those risks. For example, perhaps many are going to an area that there are few churches. Would it be possible to partner with a church-planting organization so they can be involved in addressing that lack and through the process continue to grow in their own mission formation?

WHAT APPROACHES ARE MORE FRUITFUL?

Another area of research is uncovering what educational interventions are most fruitful for facilitating emerging adult missional formation now. Several have been highlighted in this book; however, countless more are possible. What factors are in place when emerging adults' missional formation is flourishing? What are creative ways to multiply those so more can experience similar growth? What factors are causing emerging adults' missional formation to get stalled or derailed now? What are new ways go about addressing those issues that are hindering them? Focused research in these areas has the potential to uncover new and creative methods to develop more emerging adults in their formation for mission, or to take those engaged in the process further.

WHAT IS THE IMPACT OF RACE AND CONTEXT?

The impact of race, ethnicity, and context is significant. While grand theories were commonplace in the twentieth century, emerging adults are living in a world that is more racially and ethnically diverse than previous generations.[12] Racial, ethnic, and socioeconomic issues cannot be subsumed into larger narratives.[13] Many of these realities are distinct, needing different strategies and approaches for the development of emerging adult missional formation. This is an area that needs much broader exploration.

THE POWER OF CARING

So where do we go from here? How can we find the capacity and resolve to keep moving forward in the midst of such significant complexity, competing priorities, and limited resources? We think the answer lies in the nature of the one we serve. Our God is love. Love finds a way when the path gets difficult, when circumstances are inconvenient, and when sacrifice is needed to move things forward. Scripture explains that love enables us to keep believing, enduring, and persevering (1 Cor 13). For this reason, we believe that we can take heart. If we love emerging adults, and if we keep seeking God for wisdom (Jas 1:5), we will find what we need to help them in their formation for mission. It is a worthy aim. The world is going to need them to grow to their full potential and faithfully live out God's purposes in their lives.

QUESTIONS FOR DIALOGUE

1. What types of mentoring communities are most effective for your context and why?

2. What questions are emerging adults in your context asking? Are there ways to tie these to bigger questions that are also worthy of exploration?

3. What are some of the biggest risks emerging adults in your context face that put their ongoing missional formation at risk? What are steps that can be taken to mitigate these risks?

4. Which areas of research are most intriguing to you?

BIBLIOGRAPHY

Arnett, Jeffrey Jensen. "Does Emerging Adulthood Theory Apply across Social Classes? National Data on a Persistent Question." *Emerging Adulthood* 4, no. 4 (2016): 227–35.

———. "Emerging Adulthood: A Theory of Development from the Late Teens through the Twenties." *American Psychologist* 55, no. 5 (2000): 469–80.

———. *Emerging Adulthood: The Winding Road from the Late Teens through the Twenties.* 2nd ed. New York: Oxford University Press, 2015.

———. "The Psychology of Globalization." *American Psychologist* 57, no. 10 (2002): 774–83.

Duckworth, Angela. *Grit: The Power of Passion and Perseverance.* New York: Scribner, 2016.

Elmore, Tim, and Andrew McPeak. *Generation Z Unfiltered: Facing Nine Hidden Challenges of the Most Anxious Population.* Atlanta: Poet Gardner, 2019.

Lederleitner, Mary. "Transition Journeys in Emerging Adulthood as InterVarsity Students Seek to Connect with Faith Communities after Graduation: A Qualitative Study with Educational and Sociological Implications." PhD diss., Trinity Evangelical Divinity School, 2014.

Parker, Kim, and Ruth Igielnik. "On the Cusp of Adulthood and Facing and Uncertain Future: What We Know about Gen Z So Far." Pew Research Center. 2020. https://www. pewresearch.org/social-trends/2020/05/14/on-the-cusp-of-adulthood-and-facing-an-uncertain-future-what-we-know-about-gen-z-so-far-2/.

Parks, Sharon Daloz. *Big Questions, Worthy Dreams: Mentoring Young Adults in Their Search for Meaning, Purpose, and Faith*. San Francisco: Jossey-Bass, 2000.

———. *Big Questions, Worthy Dreams: Mentoring Young Adults in Their Search for Meaning, Purpose, and Faith*. Rev. 10th anniv. ed. San Francisco: Jossey-Bass, 2011.

———. *Common Fire: Leading Lives of Commitment in a Complex World*. Boston: Beacon, 1997.

Phinney, Jean. "Understanding Development in Cultural Contexts: How Do We Deal with the Complexity?" *Human Development* 53 (2010): 33–38.

Richardson, Rick. *You Found Me: New Research on How Unchurched Nones, Millennials, and Irreligious Are Surprisingly Open to Christian Faith*. Downers Grove, IL: InterVarsity Press, 2019.

Setran, David P., and Chris A. Kiesling. *Spiritual Formation in Emerging Adulthood: A Practical Theology for College and Young Adult Ministry*. Grand Rapids: Baker Academic, 2013.

Smith, Christian, Kari Christoffersen, Hilary Davidson, and Patricia Snell Herzog. *Lost in Transition: The Dark Side of Emerging Adulthood*. Oxford: Oxford University Press, 2011.

Smith, Christian, and Patricia Snell. *Souls in Transition: The Religious and Spiritual Lives of Emerging Adults*. Oxford: Oxford University Press, 2009.

Appendix

Emerging Adults' Historic Impact in Mission

Allen Yeh

· · · · ·

Quien no recuerda la historia está condenado a repetirla.[1]
—Spanish philosopher George Santayana, *The Life of Reason*

As someone who is both a college professor and a new parent, I often ponder and analyze the differences between generations,[2] and they are stark. When I recall my childhood, it is notable that parents these days (myself included!) will cringe when I recount that—for six years of my life—I walked to elementary school a mile each way, every day, unsupervised, without a cell phone. The fear of kidnapping, abuse, neglect, and so on are all too legitimate. Fast-forward to my teen years: I remember getting my driver's license as soon as I could, right on my sixteenth birthday, and driving myself everywhere, such as going to the mall to hang out with my friends, with my parents not always even being aware of where I was (again, without a cell phone; in fact, I did not get a cell phone until I was in grad school!). And I think, now that I am a parent, there is *no way* I would ever let my child do any of what I did. Yet, those experiences made me what I am. I am the better for it, in terms of perseverance, independence, maturing, "learning to fish" (instead of just being "given a fish"), and developing *grit*— what University of Pennsylvania professor Angela Duckworth cites as the number-one indicator of success in life.[3]

This difference in generations is a double-edged sword. Children these days are statistically safer than in my day. But is it because the world is a safer place? No, there is a good case to argue that it is actually more dangerous. But kids are safer because of the safeguards that their Gen X parents have put in place (which is ironic, because the very thing that Gen Z's parents did are the very things that are now disallowed by said parents). But this "snowplow" or "lawnmower" style of parenting has detrimental side effects as well, namely, developmental delay.[4] Millennials and Gen Z are usually four years slower to mature than Boomers or Gen X. The younger generations usually don't even get their driver's license until age twenty or twenty-one—and even then they don't necessarily even desire it, it's the push from their parents to get them out the door that initiates it.[5] But it's also a self-fulfilling prophecy, because the parents were the ones who discouraged their children from getting their drivers' licenses at sixteen in the first place, for fear of the dangers of immaturity in operating heavy machinery (which, again, is legitimate). It seems a quandary: How do we balance these different generational impulses, which often seem to be at odds with one another? And how do we—as this chapter addresses—navigate this impasse to a meaningful mobilization of young adults and mission?

HAND IN GLOVE: THE "FIT" OF
EMERGING ADULTS AND MISSIONS

As a missiologist, I have often argued that there is perhaps no demographic better suited for mission than young adults, particularly of the university student variety. A number of factors make them so: health (they are physically in the prime of their life and well-suited for the rigors of adapting to new cultures, climates, and foods), intelligence (college-educated, making them critical and broad thinkers), flexibility (usually do not yet have family commitments such as a spouse or children), passion (their zeal has not yet been tempered by cynicism or weariness), and open-mindedness (usually good about cross-cultural situations without too many preconceived judgments).

All this is fantastic, of course, but times and people change. As a Gen Xer, I hear many complaints from Gen Zers that it is my generation that has ruined them (even though "OK Boomer" tends to roll off the tongue more easily).[6] Because Gen X tend to be the parents of Gen Z, "we" are seen to have left them with the legacies of climate change, scarce resources, political polarization, rising inequality, unaffordable college tuition, pushing them toward return on investment, and they being the first generation to have a lower quality of life than the generation before them. And yet, it is the older generations that continue to mock the younger generation, calling them "narcissists," referring to "slacktivism," "virtue signaling," being "entitled," needing "safe spaces" and "participant trophies" (which we gave them, mind you), and calling them "snowflakes" (but consider a certain recent White House occupant who—armed with Twitter—constantly demonstrated that he was Snowflake-in-Chief, tweeting defensively every time he was criticized, so this is certainly not just a characteristic of the young). David Kinnaman warns older generations to be vigilant against self-righteousness.[7] Jason Dorsey says that the number-one characteristic that influences Gen Z is not—as popularly assumed—screen time (which is why they have often been dubbed "iGen"), but rather parenting.[8]

As we have moved from the twentieth to twenty-first century, we have seen the shift of generational cultures, from boomers, to Gen X, to millennials, and now to Gen Z.[9] Are college students (or, more broadly, emerging adults) today just as suited to missions

as in years gone by, especially given the aforementioned developmental delay? Does this principle still hold true, and can we (or
should we) encourage young adults for missions? And if so, how
should we shift our strategy to engage them, because even though
the goal may be the same, perhaps the method should adapt to
the modern context? I believe that George Santayana's maxim of
learning from history needs to be modified in this case. It is not
so much a warning that we need to heed, but rather a recognition
that we can learn positively from history and not need to reinvent
the wheel.

EMERGING ADULTS AND MISSIONS: DESCRIPTIVE CONNECTIONS

There is much historical evidence for young/emerging adults' positive impact on the mission field. Much of the impetus for this
came from universities themselves, which were often founded for
the training up of ministers (e.g., Oxbridge and the Ivy Leagues).[10]
In fact, fully half of the missionaries in the early twentieth century were young people from universities.[11]

David Bebbington, professor of church history at the University
of Stirling, Scotland, famously came up with a definition of the
word "evangelical" based on historical description, not prescriptive mandate. Evangelicals are people who are biblicist, crucicen-
trist, conversionist, and activist.[12] This became such a standard
definition of evangelical that it eventually came to be named after
him, the Bebbington quadrilateral.

Similarly, is there a multipronged historical description of
emerging adults in mission? They all seem to have encompassed
at least these four common characteristics:[13]

1. Prayer. The first major Protestant missionary, Count Nikolaus
Ludwig von Zinzendorf (1700-1760), the leader of the Moravians,
initiated a prayer chain that lasted over one hundred years.[14] There
is a direct correlation of this kind of faithful relationship with the

Lord of the harvest sending laborers into the field. The work that the Moravians did was vast, going literally to the ends of the earth in places such as Greenland, South Africa, the northern reaches of Finland, and Suriname in South America. When I went to visit IHOP (International House of Prayer, not Pancakes!) in Kansas City, I was pleased to note that—at the back of their 24/7 worship and prayer sanctuary—they had painted the words: "The fire on the altar shall never go out ... Leviticus 6:13 (Count Zinzendorf)." For the American missionary movement, it started with the Haystack Prayer Meeting.[15] In August 1806, at Williams College in western Massachusetts, five students took shelter from a rainstorm in a haystack and decided to pray fervently for missions as they waited out the storm. These were Samuel Mills, James Richards, Francis Robbins, Harvey Loomis, and Byram Green. They dubbed themselves the Society of Brethren, which eventually led directly to the formation of the American Board of Commissioners for Foreign Mission (ABCFM), which sent out the first US missionaries to other continents.

2. Postdenominationalism. Emerging adults have often been concerned for ecumenical unity, choosing to identify more with parachurch organizations than ecclesiastical structures. Ralph Winter, founder of the U.S. Center for World Missions, called the former sodalities (from the Latin sodalis, meaning "comrade"), and advocated for them over and against the latter, which were known as modalities (from "mode," or the standard way of doing something).[16] This idea originally arose from William Carey, the "father of modern missions," who advocated for sodalities in his An Enquiry in 1792.[17] Carey realized that Catholic missionaries had an advantage, structurally, over Protestants in that they could avail themselves of their monastic societies, such as the Jesuits, Franciscans, and Dominicans, which all became de facto mendicant missionary orders. Directly as a result of An Enquiry sprang the LMS (London Missionary Society), the BMS (Baptist Missionary Society), CIM (China Inland Mission), SIM (Sudan

Interior Mission), and other mission societies. Adoniram and Ann Judson, the first intercontinental missionaries from the United States, were sent out by the ABCFM in 1812 to Burma.[18] Judson met Samuel Mills when they were classmates at Andover Theological Seminary,[19] and this mutual chemistry led to a springboard for missions. This comradeship also manifested itself in conferences, for example, Edinburgh 1910 and Tokyo 2010, which were also focused on sodalities. And missionaries such as Lesslie Newbigin became ever more convinced that imposing Western denominations was a form of colonialism and instead advocated for a three-self church[20] of indigenous leadership. Newbigin himself even left his own Presbyterian denomination to join the Church of South India, convinced of its right to self-govern.

3. Christian educational integration. Much of this young adult missionary impulse came out of the Anglo-American world. Renowned world evangelist D. L. Moody's revival campaigns on both sides of the North Atlantic led to the creation of the Student Volunteer Movement for Foreign Missions (SVM) in 1887 and the World's Student Christian Federation in 1895.[21] The SVM, in particular, arose out of Mount Hermon, Massachusetts, expanding from a pledge of one hundred students to over twenty thousand some sixty years later.[22] The students of the YMCA and the YWCA were organized by John Mott, who later was the chief architect of the Edinburgh 1910 World Missionary Conference, which had the watchword "the evangelization of the world in this generation."[23] The direction that these English-speaking Westerners often set their sights toward was Asia, particularly China and India.[24] This is not to suggest that only one geography or culture can reach another, but what was the natural inclination of the students that moved them in such a direction? It was their training in liberal arts.

The great philosophical traditions of Confucianism, Daoism, Hinduism, and Buddhism were a fertile soil for the engagement with Western higher thinking. In the past, missionaries were mostly trained at Bible colleges, such as Moody Bible Institute or BIOLA (formerly an acronym standing for Bible Institute of Los Angeles), but eventually many of these institutions shifted toward being universities, where they studied not only Bible, but instead a multitude of subjects. The educational philosophy here is called *integration*—that "all truth is God's truth" and anything that does not directly contradict the Bible, even if it is from a "secular" source, is something that we can learn from. This is basically the idea behind what St. Augustine said about "plunder[ing] the Egyptians for their gold" (itself was drawn from Exod 3:22).[25] It is ironic that much of Western Christian theology is actually built on pagan Greek philosophy, but when it comes to Asian philosophy (the *Analects*, the *Bhagavad Gita*, the *Dao De Jing*, or the vedas, just to name a few), those are rejected wholesale. In contrast, these missionary university students were not afraid to engage robustly and radically with international schools of thought, expanding beyond an unnuanced idea of *sola Scriptura*.[26] It is quite something that the best and brightest—some might think of Borden of Yale, C. T. Studd, and Samuel Zwemer[27]—took their skills and intelligence to propagate the gospel in "heathen" lands instead of seeking to line their own pockets with financially lucrative careers.

4. Grassroots. This refers to a bottom-up or diffuse leadership style. This is no longer the romantic era of heroes where all the power is vested in one person; it is a period of teamwork.[28] Just to name some notable groups of young missionaries, the Cambridge Seven were among the most renowned, but there was also the St. Andrews Seven from Scotland,[29] and of course William Carey worked together with Joshua Marshman and William Ward to form the Serampore Trio. And Adoniram Judson was commissioned with his compatriots of Luther Rice, Samuel Newell, Samuel Nott, and Gordon Hall at the Tabernacle Church in Salem, Massachusetts (although he did not ultimately set sail with them but rather with his wife, Ann). This descriptive connection has several implications: first, it is not the administrators or the older adults who are doing the leading, but rather

the students have their own initiative. Second, young adults take their own initiative to either raise support or become tentmakers and can function very well independently. Third, it also means that women—such as Ann Judson, Lottie Moon, Amy Carmichael, and Gladys Aylward, among others—were empowered to serve as much as men. Evidence of this comes from the fact that Protestant women have actually outnumbered men two-to-one on the mission field in history.

The realization that emerging adults—especially of the undergraduate university students variety—have had an impact on missions like no other has been historically true, despite the shifting generational cultures that often seem to be keen to highlight more how things have changed. But this leads us to the next section, where I will show that if the focus is only on the differences, we will miss out on the great number of similarities, which should give us hope.

EMERGING ADULTS AND MISSIONS: PRESCRIPTIVE CONNECTIONS

So the question remains: Can we rely on the above-named descriptors to remain consistent? Can we map our understanding of young adults and missions, historically, onto the present day? In other words, does the glove still fit the hand? The answer is: yes, though modification and adaptability are necessary.[30]

1. Prayer is still efficacious, although today the impetus comes from the Majority World, aka the Two-Thirds World or the Global South.[31] When one thinks about early-morning Korean simultaneous prayer, or much of the tongues and prophesying that comes out of global Pentecostalism (e.g., Brazil, China, Africa), prayer is still vibrant unless one thinks only of the West and its "flaw of the excluded middle."[32] The shift of the center of gravity of Christianity to Africa, Asia, and Latin America, or in the United States to ethnic minorities and immigrants, means that fervent

prayer is still alive and well today. But, because of universities,[33] the world has come to the West, so campuses remain centers of revival. Western universities used to be training centers to send out missionaries, but now they *are* a major mission field. Christian students are very open to Pentecostalism and signs and wonders—for example, over one hundred thousand young people filled the LA Memorial Coliseum on April 9, 2016, for Azusa Now, celebrating the 110th anniversary of the Azusa Street Revival[34] with corporate prayer and worship revival. Also, IHOP has been engaged in nonstop prayer since 1999, so while that is still a far cry from the Moravians (and they have said they are explicitly not trying to compete against Zinzendorf but instead are wanting just to be inspired by him), it shows that the importance of deep intercessory prayer still has key remnants in the West.

It is interesting that Gen Z—despite its love of transience (Facebook and Instagram "stories," Snapchat, TikTok, "gig" economies)[35]—also embraces certain things of permanence (tattoos, liturgy). I think this betrays a thirst for foundations in a constantly shifting culture. While one way that emerging adults exhibit this is through embracing "high church," this shows that appealing to ancient Christian practices such as *lectio divina* or the Prayer of Examen can help win their hearts in their thirst for meaningfulness and a lasting legacy. In fact, Jason Dorsey recommends that we begin with the end in mind. If we want buy-in from younger generations, we need to not ask them to just trust us on faith, but to show them where we're going first.[36]

2. Postdenominationalism is often expressed in a subtler way by emerging adults. It is usually seen in their *omission* of certain identification markers rather than their outright *rejection* of them. Most young adults, when queried, not only do not identify with a particular denomination, but cannot even articulate the differences between them when pressed. This is not a lacuna in theological education so much as an ecumenical unity that supersedes the divisions of yesteryear. Similar to how most Christians today

are not arguing over the minute differences in *filioque* or *homoou-sios*, as was so important in the patristic era, so today most young Christians are not so invested in the differences between paedo-baptism and credobaptism, or pre- versus post- versus a-millen-nialism, or church polity. Instead, they are very happy expressing their faith through parachurch organizations such as campus min-istries (e.g., Cru, InterVarsity, Navigators) or missions organiza-tions (e.g., OMF, UWM, SIM), and attending mass conferences such as the triennial Urbana (sponsored by IFES, the International Fellowship of Evangelical Students) or Passion, or in Catholic cir-cles there is World Youth Day. As such, young adults in missions really lean into sodalities—they would make William Carey or Ralph Winter extremely happy! Despite the divisiveness that social media often creates in populations, it seems that young adults do long to see healing and restoration in this world. However, they may not know how to properly cultivate it. While they may have high CQ, they perhaps need to work on their EQ[37]—something that is not new, but the Bible simply calls wisdom. Zeal for justice is great, but knowing how to express it without becoming incendi-ary is something that requires practice, being trained to interact not just through screen time (Zoom or instant messaging), but through in-person reading of nonverbals. As a concrete example, the 2010 Boston conference leveraged an ecumenical unity of the various theological schools and Christian denominational tradi-tions that appealed to this generation that longs for reconciliation.[38]

3. Integration is a more complicated topic, as it is perhaps in this area that college students have morphed most profoundly. It has been said that there has been more change in higher edu-cation in the last ten years than in the last fifty years prior. I can attest to this, as I have personally seen students shifting away from liberal arts and humanities majors toward greater return-on-investment majors such as STEM (science, technology, engineer-ing, and math) and business. However, the development of whole people is still the purview of Christian colleges.[39] Rather than just

being content with the lower levels of Maslow's hierarchy of needs, namely, money and physiological survival, the aim of a Christian college education is still to holistically build up character development, emotional intelligence, and spiritual formation, not just head knowledge.

However, this erosion of liberal arts education is having impact worldwide. Vinoth Ramachandra, IFES theologian from Sri Lanka, observes: "China and India together produce more science and engineering graduates every year than North America and Europe combined. But Asian mission studies dissertations and the bulk of articles in mission studies journals focus on historical studies of religious sects and denominations, traditional tribal cultures or exotic new religious movements."[40] This is both a good and a bad thing. First, it does show that Asia is not just philosophical but can engage with the best of the world in the hard sciences. However, has the pendulum swung too far in the opposite direction? Lesslie Newbigin laments in his *The Gospel in a Pluralist Society* that the West has exported relativism worldwide.[41] Perhaps it can be said that much of the Majority World has lost its liberal arts foundations and has imbibed this return on investment–only mentality from the West, to its detriment. Certainly Covid-19 has only exacerbated this tendency. One way to mitigate such a trend is to remind emerging adults that their stability is not just in money (or fear of lack of it), but in something more eternal. Missionary Jim Elliot famously said, "He is no fool who gives up what he cannot keep to gain what he cannot lose."

4. Grassroots/bottom-up organization is ever more relevant. Emerging adults tend to distrust authoritarian power that is not shared and have become disenchanted with leaders who fail. It must be pointed out that Gen Z is different from millennials because they don't feel entitled (e.g., the need to be CEO of a company immediately upon graduating from college) but rather insecure. However, the same principle applies to both of those generations: do not denigrate them. For millennials, allow them

to try, to fail, and to pick themselves back up, with a renewed sense of reality. For Gen Z, they need confidence to be activated. They need encouragement to step out on their own, but once they do, they will find that they can fly—they just don't know it yet. At Biola, we have our Student Missionary Union, which is the last remnant of the old SVM. It is the largest student-run missions organization in the world, and through it I have seen what students can do when given a long runway and a lot of confidence in them. In addition to all this, grassroots structuring also implies the mobilization of urban areas. In 2008, the world's population shifted to become more than 50 percent in urban areas,[42] and this has only increased as time marches on. The recognition of how to minister in densely packed diverse places is ever more needed as the world's influence has also shifted to cities.[43]

While the generations may be different today, having encountered different traumas that have shaped them (instead of World War II or the Vietnam War, it might be 9/11 or the 2008 financial crisis or Covid-19),[44] young people in many ways remain the same—they are still brave, resilient, smart, hungry, and willing. The descriptive history has relevance to the prescriptive present.

CLOSING ADMONITION

It is not easy being an emerging adult today. Certainly saying "back in my day ..." in a dismissive way is immensely unhelpful, because then the endless cycle of older denigrating younger, and younger rebelling against (or at the very least, rolling their eyes at) older, continues. Generations understanding each other is really an intercultural problem. Rather, millennials and Gen Z need the support, encouragement, and resources of the older generations. And the older generations need to learn from the younger generations in turn, as they have much to offer. However, at the end of the day, we have to also look at our similarities, not just our differences. Young people of any era are wired in a certain way and therefore have similarities that transcend time. If the similarities can be unpacked and even leveraged, perhaps understanding can occur, and then we can really get something done. C. S. Lewis wrote of friendship as opposed to romantic love: "*Lovers are normally face to face, absorbed in each other; Friends, side by side, absorbed in some common interest.*"[45] If younger and older Christians can see each other as friends and partners to win the world for Christ, rather than as antagonists who struggle against each other, perhaps the world can be truly transformed by the unity that occurs.

BIBLIOGRAPHY

Barna and Impact 360 Institute. *Gen Z: The Cultures, Beliefs, and Motivations Shaping the Next Generation*. Ventura, CA: Barna Group, 2018.

Bebbington, David. *Evangelicalism in Modern Britain*. London: Unwin Hyman, 1989.

Carey, William. *An Enquiry into the Obligations of Christians to Use Means for the Conversion of the Heathens*. Leicester, UK: Ann Ireland, 1792.

Dorsey, Jason. "Generational Clues Uncovered." August 13, 2019. https://globalleadership.org/articles/leading-organizations/jason-dorsey-generational-clues-uncovered/.

Duckworth, Angela. *Grit: The Power of Passion and Perseverance*. New York: Scribner, 2016.

Hiebert, Paul. *Anthropological Reflections on Missiological Issues*. Grand Rapids: Baker, 1994.

Hunt, Rosalie Hall. *Bless God and Take Courage: The Judson History and Legacy*. Valley Forge, PA: Judson Press, 2005.

Jenkins, Philip. *The Next Christendom: The Coming of Global Christianity*. Oxford: Oxford University Press, 2002.

Johnson, Todd M., Rodney L. Petersen, Gina A. Bellofatto, and Travis L. Myers. *2010Boston: The Changing Contours of*

World Mission and Christianity. Eugene, OR: Pickwick, 2012.

Keller, Timothy. *Why God Made Cities.* New York: City to City, 2013.

Kim, Kirsteen, and Andrew Anderson, eds. *Mission Today and Tomorrow.* Oxford: Regnum, 2011.

Knickerbocker, Brad. "World First: In 2008, Most People Will Live in Cities." *Christian Science Monitor*, January 12, 2007. https://www.csmonitor.com/2007/0112/p25s02-wogi.html.

Lee, Rachael. "'Azusa Now': Some 100,000 Pray for Revival at Los Angeles Memorial Coliseum." *Christianity Daily*, April 11, 2016. http://www.christianitydaily.com/articles/7963/20160411/azusa-now-more-100-000-pray-revival-los-angeles-memorial.htm.

Lewis, C. S. *The Four Loves: The Much Beloved Exploration of the Nature of Love.* New York: Harcourt, Brace, 1960.

Lorenz, Taylor. "'OK Boomer' Marks the End of Friendly Generational Relations." *New York Times*, October 29, 2019. https://www.nytimes.com/2019/10/29/style/ok-boomer.html.

Lukianoff, Greg, and Jonathan Haidt. *The Coddling of the American Mind: How Good Intentions and Bad Ideas Are Setting Up a Generation for Failure.* New York: Penguin, 2018.

Newbigin, Lesslie. *The Gospel in a Pluralist Society.* Grand Rapids: Eerdmans, 1989.

Payne, J. D. *Strangers Next Door: Immigration, Migration, and Mission.* Downers Grove, IL: InterVarsity Press, 2012.

Piggin, Stuart, and John Roxborogh. *The St. Andrews Seven: The Finest Flowering of Missionary Zeal in Scottish History.* Edinburgh: Banner of Truth Trust, 1985.

Pollock, John. *The Cambridge Seven: The True Story of Ordinary Men Used in No Ordinary Way.* Fearn, UK: Christian Focus, 2006.

Rah, Soong-Chan. *The Next Evangelicalism: Freeing the Church from Western Cultural Captivity*. Downers Grove, IL: InterVarsity Press, 2009.

Richards, Thomas Cole. *The Haystack Prayer Meeting: An Account of Its Origin and Spirit*. Williamstown, MA: Haystack Centennial Committee, 1906.

Rouse, Ruth, and Stephen Charles Neill. *A History of the Ecumenical Movement*. 3rd ed. Vol. 1. Geneva: World Council of Churches, 1986.

Santayana, George. *The Life of Reason, or The Phases of Human Progress*. New York: Scribner's Sons, 1905–6.

Stanley, Brian. *Christianity in the Twentieth Century*. Princeton: Princeton University Press, 2018.

Tarr, Leslie K. "A Prayer Meeting That Lasted 100 Years." *Decision*, 1977. Repr., *Christianity Today*. https://www. christianitytoday.com/history/issues/issue-1/prayer-meeting-that-lasted-100-years.html.

Tucker, Ruth A. *From Jerusalem to Irian Jaya: A Biographical History of Christian Missions*. Grand Rapids: Zondervan, 2004.

Twenge, Jean. *iGen: Why Today's Super-Connected Kids Are Growing Up Less Rebellious, More Tolerant, Less Happy—and Completely Unprepared for Adulthood*. New York: Atria, 2017.

Walls, Andrew. "In Quest of the Father of Mission Studies." *International Bulletin of Mission Studies* (July 1999): 98–104.

Winter, Ralph. "The Two Structures of God's Redemptive Mission." *Perspectives on the World Christian Movement*. 1973. http://frontiermissionfellowship.org/uploads/documents/two-structures.pdf.

Yeh, Allen. *Polycentric Missiology: Twenty-First Century Mission from Everyone to Everywhere*. Downers Grove, IL: IVP Academic, 2016.

Yeh, Allen, and Tite Tiénou, eds. *Majority World Theologies: Theologizing from Africa, Asia, Latin America, and the Ends of the Earth*. Pasadena, CA: William Carey, 2018.

List of Contributors

• • • • •

EDITORS

Mary T. Lederleitner (PhD, Trinity Evangelical Divinity School) is founder and executive director of Missional Intelligence LLC and author of *Cross-Cultural Partnerships* and *Women in God's Mission: Accepting the Invitation to Serve and Lead.*

Andrew MacDonald (PhD Candidate, Trinity Evangelical Divinity School) is associate director of the research institute at the Wheaton College Billy Graham Center.

Rick Richardson (PhD, Trinity International University) is professor of evangelism and leadership at Wheaton College, director of the church evangelism and research institutes for the Wheaton College Billy Graham Center, and an Anglican priest. He is author of *You Found Me: New Research on How Unchurched Nones, Millennials, and Irreligious Are Surprisingly Open to Christian Faith.*

CONTRIBUTORS

Kplang'at Cheruiyot Bii (MA, Taylor University) is the director of Taylor World Outreach.

Marcos Canales (MDiv, Fuller Theological Seminary) is a pastor at La Fuente Ministries.

Peter Cha (PhD, Northwestern University) is the professor of Church, Culture and Society and director of Mosaic Ministries at Trinity Evangelical Divinity School.

Jenny Collins (PhD Candidate, Concordia Theological Seminary) is an associate professor of Intercultural Studies at Taylor University.

Deborah A. Colwill (PhD, Education, Trinity Evangelical Divinity School; PhD, Organization Development, Benedictine University) is the Chair of the Department of Educational Ministries and associate professor Educational and Leadership Studies at Trinity Evangelical Divinity School.

Jamie Goodwin (PhD, Indiana University) is an assistant professor of Humanitarian and Disaster Leadership at Wheaton College.

Daniel Hartman (MDiv, Trinity Evangelical Divinity School) is the ministries director of Mosaic Ministries at Trinity Evangelical Divinity School.

Patricia Snell Herzog (PhD, University of Notre Dame) is the Melvin Simon Chair and associate professor of Philanthropic Studies in the Lilly Family School of Philanthropy at Indiana University–Purdue University Indianapolis.

Russell Jeung (PhD, UC Berkeley) is the professor of Asian American Studies at San Francisco State University and a leader of Stop AAPI Hate.

Juan F. Martínez (PhD, Fuller Theological Seminary) is the president of Centro Hispano de Estudios (Estudios) Teológicos.

Dwight A. Radcliff, Jr. (PhD, Fuller Theological Seminary) is the academic dean for the Pannell Center for Black Church Studies and assistant professor of Mission, Theology and Culture at Fuller Theological Seminary.

David Setran (PhD, Indiana University) is the Price-LeBar Chair of Christian Formation and Ministry at Wheaton College.

Charles E. (Chuck) Stokes (PhD, University of Texas at Austin) is an associate professor of sociology at Samford University.

Kevin Turner (DPM, Southern Methodist University) is the minister of music and worship at Davidson United Methodist Church.

Allen Yeh (DPhil, University of Oxford) is an associate professor of Intercultural Studies and Missiology at Biola University.

Notes

· · · · ·

Chapter 1. What Are We Talking About?

1. The opening quote is paraphrased due to space constraints. The story comes from Mary Lederleitner's research about what is helping and hindering missional twenty-somethings from transitioning into churches after graduation. Mary Lederleitner, "Transition Journeys in Emerging Adulthood as InterVarsity Students Seek to Connect with Faith Communities after Graduation: A Qualitative Study with Educational and Sociological Implications" (PhD diss., Trinity Evangelical Divinity School, 2014), https://search.proquest.com/openview/3f13b701def4a8576c-c030a35881fdc3/1?pq-origsite=gscholar&cbl=18750&diss=y. See pages 132–33; 155–56; 167.

2. Sharon Daloz Parks, *Big Questions, Worthy Dreams: Mentoring Young Adults in Their Search for Meaning, Purpose, and Faith* (San Francisco: Jossey-Bass, 2000), 11.

3. Jeffrey Jensen Arnett, "Does Emerging Adulthood Theory Apply across Social Classes? National Data on a Persistent Question," *Emerging Adulthood* 4, no. 4 (2016): 228–29.

4. Manuela du Bois-Reymond, "Emerging Adulthood Theory and Social Class," in *The Oxford Handbook of Emerging Adulthood*, ed. Jeffrey Jensen Arnett (Oxford: Oxford University Press 2016), 47–61; Moin Syed and Lauren L. Mitchell, "Race, Ethnicity, and Emerging Adulthood: Retrospect and Prospects," *Emerging Adulthood* 1, no. 2 (2013): 83–95.

5. Arnold Van Gennep, *The Rites of Passage*, 2nd ed. (Chicago: University of Chicago Press, 2019).

6. Pew Research Center, "U.S. Decline of Christianity Continues at a Rapid Pace: Update on America's Changing Religious Landscape," 2019, https://www.pewforum.org/2019/10/17/in-u-s-decline-of-christianity-continues-at-rapid-pace/; Pew Research Center, "America's Changing Religious Landscape," 2015, https://www.pewforum.org/2015/05/12/americas-changing-religious-landscape/.

7. This data comes from the 2018/2019 edition of Pew's ongoing Religious Landscape Study, with this chart reflecting a compilation of data from pages 3-4, 22 of the full report. Pew Research Center, Oct. 17, 2019, "In U.S., Decline of Christianity Continues at Rapid Pace."

8. Christian Smith and Patricia Snell, *Souls in Transition: The Religious and Spiritual Lives of Emerging Adults* (Oxford: Oxford University Press, 2009); David Kinnaman and Aly Hawkins, *You Lost Me: Why Young Christians Are Leaving the Church … and Rethinking Faith* (Grand Rapids: Baker, 2011).

9. Robert Wuthnow, *After the Baby Boomers: How Twenty-and Thirty-Somethings Are Shaping the Future of American Religion* (Princeton: Princeton University Press, 2007), 12.

10. Jeffrey Jensen Arnett, "Emerging Adulthood: A Theory of Development from the Late Teens through the Twenties," *American Psychologist* 55, no. 5 (2000): 469–80.

11. Jeffrey Jensen Arnett, *Emerging Adulthood: The Winding Road from the Late Teens through the Twenties* (Oxford: Oxford University Press, 2004), 8.

12. Jeffrey Jensen Arnett et al., *Debating Emerging Adulthood: Stage or Process?* (New York: Oxford University Press, 2011), 126–27.

13. Arnett, *Emerging Adulthood*, 13–14.

14. James Côté and John M. Bynner, "Changes in the Transition to Adulthood in the UK and Canada: The Role of Structure and Agency in Emerging Adulthood," *Journal of Youth Studies* 11, no. 3 (2008): 251; Marion Kloep and Leo B. Hendry, "A Systematic Approach to the Transitions to Adulthood," in Arnett et al., *Debating Emerging Adulthood*, 53–75.

15. On moral intuitionism, see Eric Silver, "Students' Attitudes toward College Drinking: A Moral Intuitionist Approach," *Deviant Behavior* 41, no. 8 (2020):1033–51; Smith and Snell, *Souls in Transition* (Oxford: Oxford University Press, 2009). On identity being shaped by postmodern secular and political culture, see Don Everts and Doug Schaupp, *I Once Was Lost: What Postmodern Skeptics Taught Us about Their Path to Jesus* (Downers Grove, IL: IVP Books, 2008); Christian Smith et al., *Lost in Transition: The Dark Side of Emerging Adulthood* (Oxford: Oxford University Press, 2011). On social media influences, see Smith and Snell, *Souls in Transition*; Barna Group, *Gen Z: The Culture, Beliefs, and Motivations Shaping the Next Generation* (Barna Group Publishers, 2018).

16. Rick Richardson, *You Found Me: New Research on How Unchurched Nones, Millennials, and Irreligious Are Surprisingly Open to Christian Faith* (Downers Grove, IL: InterVarsity Press, 2019).

17. Barna Group, "Millennial Non-Christians Show Greater Spiritual Curiosity Than Older Adults," 2019, https://www.barna.com/research/millennial-spiritual-curiosity.

18. Richardson, *You Found Me*, 110.

Chapter 2. *The Role of Identity Formation*

1. This young woman found a significant disparity between what she was taught she could be and do in the world, and what she encountered after she graduated from university.

2. A pseudonym has been used as requested by the research participant.

3. Mary Lederleitner, "Transition Journeys in Emerging Adulthood as InterVarsity Students Seek to Connect with Faith Communities after Graduation: A Qualitative Study with Educational and Sociological Implications" (PhD diss., Trinity Evangelical Divinity School, 2014), 130.

4. Ruthellen Josselson, "Theory of Identity Development and the Question of Intervention," in *Interventions for Adolescent Identity Development*, ed. Sally L. Archer (Thousand Oaks, CA: Sage, 1994), 12–16.

5. Erik Erikson, *Identity and the Life Cycle* (New York: W. W. Norton, 1959); Erikson, *Identity: Youth and Crisis* (New York: W. W. Norton, 1968); Erikson, *The Life Cycle Completed* (New York: W. W. Norton, 1997).

6. Erikson, *Identity: Youth and Crisis*, 17.

7. Erikson, *Identity: Youth and Crisis*, 217-18, 245.

8. Erikson, *Identity: Youth and Crisis*, 24, 211.

9. Erikson, *Identity: Youth and Crisis*, 22-23, 217-18.

10. Sally L. Archer, "A Feminist's Approach to Identity Research," in *Adolescent Identity Formation*, ed. Gerald R. Adams, Thomas P. Gullotta, and Raymond Montemayor (Newbury Park, CA: Sage, 1992), 25-29.

11. Archer, "Feminist's Approach," 29.

12. James E. Marcia, "Development and Validity of Ego-Identity Status," *Journal of Personality and Social Psychology* 3, no. 5 (1966): 551.

13. Marcia, "Development and Validity," 551-52.

14. James E. Marcia, "Identity and Psychotherapy," in Archer, *Interventions for Adolescent Identity Development*, 40-41.

15. Marcia, "Development and Validity," 552.

16. Josselson, "Theory of Identity Development," 16, 20.

17. Marcia, "Identity and Psychotherapy," 41, 552.

18. Seth J. Schwartz, "The Evolution of Eriksonian and Neo-Eriksonian Identity Theory and Research: A Review and Integration," *Identity: An International Journal of Theory and Research* 1, no. 1 (2001): 12; John Paul McKinney, "Identity: A Construct Comes of Age and Starts to Work," in Archer, *Interventions for Adolescent Identity Development*, 248.

19. Urie Bronfenbrenner, ed., *The Ecology of Human Development: Experiments by Nature and Design* (Cambridge: Harvard University Press, 1979); Bronfenbrenner, *Making Human Beings Human: Bioecological Perspectives on Human Development* (Thousand Oaks, CA: Sage, 2005).

20. Bronfenbrenner, *Ecology of Human Development*, 9, 21.

21. Bronfenbrenner, *Ecology of Human Development*, 4, 6.

22. Bronfenbrenner, *Ecology of Human Development*, 56-67.

23. Bronfenbrenner, *Ecology of Human Development*, 41-42, 212, 214-15.

24. Jean Phinney, "Ethnic Identity in Adolescents and Adults: Review of Research," *Psychological Bulletin* 3, no. 3 (1990): 499.

25. Henri Tajfel, "Social Psychology of Intergroup Relations," *Annual Review of Psychology* 33 (1982): 1-39; Phinney, "Ethnic Identity in Adolescents," 502.

26. Phinney, "Ethnic Identity in Adolescents," 503.

27. Phinney, "Ethnic Identity in Adolescents," 27.

28. Jean Phinney, "Identity Formation across Cultures: The Interaction of Personal, Societal, and Historical Change," *Human Development* 43 (2000): 28.

29. Jean Phinney, "Understanding Development in Cultural Contexts: How Do We Deal with the Complexity?," *Human Development* 53 (2010): 33-34.

30. Phinney, "Understanding Development," 36.

31. Eugene H. Peterson, "Spirituality/Spiritual Formation," in *Dictionary for Theological Interpretation of the Bible*, ed. Kevin J. Vanhoozer (Grand Rapids: Baker Books, 2005), 768.

32. Peterson, "Spirituality/Spiritual Formation," 768.

33. Christopher J. H. Wright, *The Mission of God's People: A Biblical Theology of the Church's Mission* (Grand Rapids: Zondervan, 2010), 23.

34. James Côté, "Emerging Adulthood as an Institutionalized Moratorium: Risks and Benefits to Identity Formation," in *Emerging Adults in America: Coming of Age in*

the 21st Century, ed. Jeffrey Jensen Arnett and Jennifer Lynn Tanner (Washington, DC: American Psychological Association, 2006), 99.

35. Erikson, *Identity: Youth and Crisis*, 31; Josselson, "Theory of Identity Development," 235-36; Christian Smith and Patricia Snell, *Souls in Transition: The Religious and Spiritual Lives of Emerging Adults* (Oxford: Oxford University Press, 2009), 152.

36. Robert Wuthnow, *After the Baby Boomers: How Twenty- and Thirty-Somethings Are Shaping the Future of American Religion* (Princeton: Princeton University Press, 2007), 12-13, 216.

Chapter 3. Emerging Adult Sexuality and Discipleship

1. Elizabeth Kwiatkowski, "'Married at First Sight' Star Iris Caldwell: I Get So Much Hate and Feel Misjudged, When Did Virginity Become a Bad Thing?!," RealityTVWorld.com, November 18, 2019.

2. Mark Yarhouse, *Understanding Sexual Identity: A Resource for Youth Ministry* (Grand Rapids: Zondervan, 2013).

3. Mark D. Regnerus, and Jeremy Uecker, *Premarital Sex in America: How Young Americans Meet, Mate, and Think about Marrying* (New York: Oxford University Press, 2010), 113.

4. Regnerus and Uecker, *Premarital Sex in America*.

5. Regnerus and Uecker, *Premarital Sex in America*; Mark D. Regnerus, *Cheap Sex: The Transformation of Men, Marriage, and Monogamy* (New York: Oxford University Press, 2017); Regnerus, *The Future of Christian Marriage* (New York: Oxford University Press, 2020).

6. Brad Wilcox, "When Marriage Disappears: The New Middle America," Report by Institute for American Values and National Marriage Project, 2010.

7. Regnerus, *Cheap Sex*.

8. Brad Wilcox and Lyman Stone, "The Happiness Recession," *The Atlantic*, April 4, 2019.

9. Abigail Haworth, "Why Have Young People in Japan Stopped Having Sex?," *The Observer*, October 19, 2013.

10. The most esteemed professor I had as a PhD student, a ninety-something-year-old living legend in social theory and an avowed secularist, said the two most influential inventions in human history were the numeral zero and the birth control pill.

11. Regnerus, *Cheap Sex*.

12. In *Mere Christianity*, C. S. Lewis has a prophetic discussion on how the sex drive becomes disordered as we separate sexuality from its organic orientations toward procreation and marital unity. He first presented this argument in the 1940s, two decades before the birth control pill.

13. For more information on the dual-thinking systems in our brains, see Daniel Kahneman, *Thinking, Fast and Slow* (New York: Farrar, Straus, and Giroux, 2011).

14. While it sometimes seems that Christian denominations can't agree on much, the "Nicene orthodoxy" on the incarnation of Christ and resurrection of the body is still held by nearly every evangelical Protestant denomination, as well as Catholic and Orthodox churches.

15. For more see N. T. Wright, *Surprised by Hope: Rethinking Heaven, the Resurrection, and the Mission of the Church* (New York: HarperCollins, 2008); Christopher West, *Theology of the Body for Beginners: Rediscovering the Meaning of Life, Love, Sex, and Gender* (North Palm Beach, FL: Beacon, 2018).

16. Bessel Van Der Kolk, *The Body Keeps the Score: Brain, Mind, and Body in the Healing of Trauma* (New York: Penguin, 2014).

17. Scripture quotations in this chapter follow the NIV.

18. Parents can see, for more, the unapologetic but compassionate "Tips for Talking to Your Kids about Sex" from CanaVox, 2020.

19. Abraham Kuruvilla, "Celibacy and the Gospel," in *Sanctified Sexuality*, ed. Sandra Glahn and C. Gary Barnes (Grand Rapids: Kregel Academic, 2020).

20. According to sociological research, the most common signs of an increase in commitment are (1) marriage, (2) having a child together, or (3) long-term cohabitation.

21. G. K. Chesterton, *What's Wrong with the World?* (New York: Dodd, Mead & Co, 1910), 48.

Chapter 4. Tackling What Impedes Church Involvement

1. Xander is Latino. His real first name was used per his request.

2. A pseudonym has been used as requested by the research participant.

3. Christian Smith and Patricia Snell, *Souls in Transition: The Religious and Spiritual Lives of Emerging Adults* (Oxford: Oxford University Press, 2009), 75.

4. Beth Seversen, *Not Done Yet: Reaching and Keeping Unchurched Emerging Adults* (Downers Grove, IL: InterVarsity Press, 2020); David Kinnaman and Mark Matlock, *Faith for Exiles: Five Ways for a New Generation to Follow Jesus in a Digital Babylon* (Grand Rapids: Baker Books, 2019); Kara Powell, Jake Mulder, and Brad Griffin, *Growing Young: Six Essential Strategies to Help Young People Discover and Love Your Church* (Grand Rapids: Baker Books, 2016).

5. Jeffrey Jensen Arnett, *Emerging Adulthood: The Winding Road from the Late Teens through the Twenties* (Oxford: Oxford University Press, 2004), 176.

6. Smith and Snell, *Souls in Transition*, 73.

7. InterVarsity Press, "About InterVarsity Press," http://www.ivpress.com/about/, 2013.

8. InterVarsity Press, "About InterVarsity Press," http://www.ivpress.com/about/, 2020.

9. Mary Lederleitner, "Transition Journeys in Emerging Adulthood as InterVarsity Students Seek to Connect with Faith Communities after Graduation: A Qualitative Study with Educational and Sociological Implications" (PhD diss., Trinity Evangelical Divinity School, 2014).

10. Michael Quinn Patton, *Qualitative Research and Evaluation Methods*, 3rd ed. (Thousand Oaks, CA: Sage, 2002), 96.

11. Kathy Charmaz, "Grounded Theory: Objectives and Constructivist Methods," in *Handbook of Qualitative Research, Second Edition*, ed. N. K. Denzin and Y. S. Lincoln (Thousand Oaks, CA: Sage, 2000), 525.

12. Urie Bronfenbrenner, ed., *The Ecology of Human Development: Experiments by Nature and Design* (Cambridge: Harvard University Press, 1979), 4, 6, 56, 65.

13. Bronfenbrenner, *Ecology of Human Development*, 212, 214–15.

14. Bronfenbrenner, *Ecology of Human Development*, 41–42.

15. Nancy K. Schlossberg, "Marginality and Mattering: Key Issues," in *Designing Campus Activities to Foster a Sense of Community*, ed. Dennis C. Roberts (San Francisco: Jossey-Bass, 1989), 6.

16. Sandra P. Thomas, "Editorial: What Is Mattering and How Does It Relate to Mental Health?," *Issues in Mental Health Nursing* 32 (2011): 485.

FORMATION FOR MISSION

17. Morris Rosenberg and B. Claire McCullough, "Mattering: Inferred Significance to Parents and Mental Health among Adolescents," *Research in Community & Mental Health* 2 (1981): 164–65.

18. Nancy K. Schlossberg, *Counseling Adults in Transition* (New York: Springer, 1984), 28; Schlossberg, "Marginality and Mattering," 9.

19. Schlossberg, "Marginality and Mattering," 8.

20. Schlossberg, "Marginality and Mattering," 7–10.

21. Schlossberg, *Counseling Adults in Transition*, 35.

22. Victor Turner, "Liminality and Communitas," in *Sociology of Religion: A Reader*, ed. Susanne C. Monahan, William A. Mirola, and Michael O. Emerson (Upper Saddle River, NJ: Prentice-Hall, 2001), 48.

23. Schlossberg, *Counseling Adults in Transition*, 35.

24. Nancy K. Schlossberg, Ann Q. Lynch, and Arthur W. Chickering, *Improving Higher Education Environments for Adults: Responsive Programs and Services from Entry to Departure* (San Francisco: Jossey-Bass, 1991), 173.

25. Alexander Astin, "Student Involvement: A Developmental Theory for Higher Education," *Journal of College Student Personnel* 25, no. 4 (1984): 306.

26. Alexander Astin, *Preventing Students from Dropping Out* (San Francisco: Jossey-Bass, 1975).

27. Nancy Ammerman, Carroll Jackson, Carl S. Dudley, and William McKinney, eds., *Studying Congregations* (Nashville: Abingdon, 1998), 23–39.

28. Powell, Mulder, and Griffin, *Growing Young*, 163–95.

29. Seversen, *Not Done Yet*, 92–105.

30. Powell, Mulder, and Griffin, *Growing Young*, 50–87.

31. Kinnaman and Matlock, *Faith for Exiles*, 175–203.

32. Powell, Mulder, and Griffin, *Growing Young*, 126–62.

33. Seversen, *Not Done Yet*, 150–69.

34. Kinnaman and Matlock, *Faith for Exiles*, 143–68.

35. Sharon Daloz Parks, *Big Questions, Worthy Dreams: Mentoring Young Adults in Their Search for Meaning, Purpose, and Faith*, rev. 10th anniv. ed. (San Francisco: Jossey-Bass, 2011).

36. Ann S. Masten, Jelena Obradovic, and Keith B. Burt, "Resilience in Emerging Adulthood: Developmental Perspectives on Continuity and Transformation," in *Emerging Adults in America: Coming of Age in the 21st Century*, ed. Jeffrey Jensen Arnett and Jennifer Lynn Tanner (Washington, DC: American Psychological Association, 2006), 188.

Chapter 5. Living a Better Story in Emerging Adulthood

1. Christian Smith and Patricia Snell, *Souls in Transition: The Religious and Spiritual Lives of Emerging Adults* (New York: Oxford University Press, 2009), 154.

2. Nicholas Wolterstorff, *Educating for Responsible Action* (Grand Rapids: Eerdmans, 1980), 4.

3. Scripture quotations in this chapter follow the NIV.

4. James K. A. Smith, *Desiring the Kingdom: Worship, Worldview, and Cultural Formation* (Grand Rapids: Baker Academic, 2009), 54.

5. Dan P. McAdams and Kate C. McLean, "Narrative Identity," *Current Directions in Psychological Science* 22, no. 3 (2013): 236.

6. Dan P. McAdams, "The Problem of Narrative Coherence," *Journal of Constructivist Psychology* 19, no. 2 (2006): 115–16. Some note that this new capacity reflects the emergence of Piagetian formal operational thinking, in which

individuals begin to think abstractly, hypothetically, and inferentially. See McAdams and McLean, "Narrative Identity," 236.

7. Smith, *Desiring the Kingdom*, 127.

8. Kate C. McLean and Andrea V. Breen, "Selves in a World of Stories in Emerging Adulthood," in *The Oxford Handbook on Emerging Adulthood*, ed. Jeffrey Jensen Arnett (New York: Oxford University Press, 2016), 385–400.

9. Dan P. McAdams, *The Redemptive Self: Stories Americans Live By* (New York: Cambridge University Press, 2006).

10. Cornelius Plantinga Jr., *Engaging God's World: A Christian Vision of Faith, Learning, and Living* (Grand Rapids: Eerdmans, 2002).

11. Lewis R. Rambo, *Understanding Religious Conversion* (New Haven: Yale University Press, 1993).

12. James K. A. Smith, *Imagining the Kingdom: How Worship Works* (Grand Rapids: Baker Academic, 2013), 109–10, 139.

13. Dallas Willard, *The Divine Conspiracy: Rediscovering Our Hidden Life with God* (New York: HarperCollins, 1998), 321–22.

14. Miroslav Volf, *The End of Memory: Remembering Rightly in a Violent World* (Grand Rapids: Eerdmans, 2006), 98–99.

15. Christian Smith, *Lost in Transition: The Dark Side of Emerging Adulthood* (New York: Oxford University Press, 2011), 234.

16. David Kinnaman and Aly Hawkins, *You Lost Me: Why Young Christians Are Leaving the Church ... and Rethinking Faith* (Grand Rapids: Baker Books, 2011).

17. Smith, *Lost in Transition*, 234.

18. Sharon Daloz Parks, *Big Questions, Worthy Dreams: Mentoring Young Adults in Their Search for Meaning, Purpose, and Faith* (San Francisco: Jossey-Bass, 2000), 121.

19. Peter Berger and Thomas Luckmann, *The Social Construction of Reality: A Treatise in the Sociology of Knowledge* (New York: Anchor Books, 1967), 158.

20. Albert Bandura, "Self-Efficacy: Toward a Unifying Theory of Behavioral Change," *Psychological Review* 84, no. 2 (1977): 191–215.

21. Rebecca K. DeYoung, *Glittering Vices: A New Look at the Seven Deadly Sins and Their Remedies* (Grand Rapids: Brazos, 2009), 9.

22. Kate C. McLean, "Late Adolescent Identity Development: Narrative Meaning Making and Memory Telling," *Developmental Psychology* 41, no. 4 (2005): 684.

23. Amanda Hontz Drury, *Saying Is Believing: The Necessity of Testimony in Adolescent Spiritual Development* (Downers Grove, IL: IVP Academic, 2015).

24. Keith Anderson and Randy Reese, *Spiritual Mentoring: A Guide for Seeking and Giving Direction* (Downers Grove, IL: InterVarsity Press, 1999), 41.

25. Frederick Buechner, *The Sacred Journey* (San Francisco: HarperSanFrancisco, 1982), 95.

26. James W. Fowler, *Becoming Adult, Becoming Christian: Adult Development and Christian Faith* (San Francisco: Jossey-Bass, 1999), 113, 117.

Chapter 6. Developing Emerging Missional Leaders: No Greater Joy

1. Ellen Van Velsor, Cynthia McCauley, and Marian Ruderman, *The Center for Creative Leadership Handbook of Leadership Development*, 3rd ed. (San Francisco: Jossey-Bass, 2010).

2. D. Scott DeRue and Kristina M. Workman, "Toward a Positive and Dynamic Theory of Leadership Development," in *The Oxford Handbook of Positive*

Organizational Scholarship, ed. Kim S. Cameron and Gretchen M. Spreitzer (New York: Oxford University Press, 2013), 784–97.

3. David V. Day et al., "Advances in Leader and Leadership Development: A Review of 25 Years of Research and Theory," *The Leadership Quarterly* 25, no. 1 (2014): 63–82.

4. S. T. Hannah and B. J. Avolio, "The Locus of Leader Character," *The Leadership Quarterly* 22, no. 5 (2011): 979.

5. Bernard M. Bass and Ruth Bass, *The Bass Handbook of Leadership: Theory, Research, and Managerial Applications,* 4th ed. (New York: Free Press, 2008), 220.

6. Day et al., "Advances in Leader and Leadership Development."

7. David V. Day and Lisa Dragoni, "Leadership Development: An Outcome-Oriented Review Based on Time and Levels of Analyses," *Annual Review of Organizational Psychology and Organizational Behavior* 2 (2015): 134.

8. Day et al., "Advances in Leader and Leadership Development," 64.

9. Peter G. Northouse, *Introduction to Leadership: Concepts and Practice,* 5th ed. (Los Angeles: Sage, 2021), 102, 104, 109.

10. Cynthia D. McCauley et al., *Experience-Driven Leader Development: Models, Tools, Best Practices, and Advice for On-the-Job Development,* 3rd ed. (San Francisco: Jossey-Bass, 2013).

11. Cynthia D. McCauley, "Identifying Development-in-Place Opportunities," in *Experience-Driven Leader Development: Models, Tools, Best Practices, and Advice for On-the-Job Development,* 3rd ed., ed. Cynthia D. McCauley, D. Scott DeRue, Paul R. Yost, and Sylvester Taylor (San Francisco: Jossey-Bass, 2013), 21–24.

12. McCauley, "Identifying Development-in-Place Opportunities," 21.

13. McCauley, "Identifying Development-in-Place Opportunities," 21–22.

14. DeRue and Workman, "Toward a Positive and Dynamic Theory," 787.

15. McCauley, "Identifying Development-in-Place Opportunities," 23.

16. McCauley, "Identifying Development-in-Place Opportunities," 23.

17. DeRue and Workman, "Toward a Positive and Dynamic Theory," 788.

18. Gretchen Spreitzer et al., "A Socially Embedded Model of Thriving at Work," *Organization Science* 16, no. 5 (2005): 538.

19. Bass and Bass, *Bass Handbook of Leadership,* 219.

20. Hannah and Avolio, "Locus of Leader Character," 983.

21. Robert Clinton, *The Making of a Leader: Recognizing the Lessons and Stages of Leadership Development,* rev. ed. (Colorado Springs: NavPress, 2012), 23, 28.

22. Clinton, *Making of a Leader,* 145.

23. DeRue and Workman, "Toward a Positive and Dynamic Theory," 792.

24. Gretchen Spreitzer, "Leadership Development Lessons from Positive Organizational Studies," *Organizational Dynamics* 35, no. 4 (2006): 313.

25. Spreitzer et al., "Socially Embedded Model," 544.

26. Clinton, *Making of a Leader,* 115.

27. Deborah A. Colwill, *Conflict, Power, and Organizational Change.* (New York: Routledge, 2021).

28. James M. Kouzes and Barry Z. Posner, *Learning Leadership: The Five Fundamentals of Becoming an Exemplary Leader* (Hoboken, NJ: Wiley, 2016), 156.

29. Kouzes and Posner, *Learning Leadership,* 152.

30. Colwill, *Conflict, Power, and Organizational Change.*

31. Susan R. Komives and Wendy Wagner, *Leadership for a Better World: Understanding the Social Change Model of Leadership Development,* 2nd ed. (San Francisco: Jossey-Bass, 2017), 25.

32. Spreitzer et al., "Socially Embedded Model," 541.

33. Clinton, *Making of a Leader*.

34. McCauley et al., *Experience-Driven Leader Development*.

35. Colwill, *Conflict, Power, and Organizational Change*.

36. William Isaacs, *Dialogue: The Art of Thinking Together* (New York: Currency, 1999), 101.

37. Kouzes and Posner, *Learning Leadership*, 52.

38. Clinton, *Making of a Leader*.

39. Stephen Seamands, *Ministry in the Image of God: The Trinitarian Shape of Christian Service* (Downers Grove, IL: IVP Books, 2005).

Chapter 7. How Churches Reach and Develop Emerging Adults

1. Rick Richardson, *You Found Me: New Research on How Unchurched Nones, Millennials, and Irreligious Are Surprisingly Open to Christian Faith* (Downers Grove, IL: InterVarsity Press, 2019), 7.

2. The term conversion community comes from *Breaking the Huddle: How Your Community Can Grow Its Witness*, by Don Everts, Doug Schaupp, and Val Gordon (Downers Grove, IL: IVP Books, 2016). I have adapted its use to fit my research findings.

3. Richardson, *You Found Me*, 110.

4. Adapted from Figure 5.1 in Richardson, *You Found Me*, 107.

5. Richardson, *You Found Me*, 69–70.

6. You can get the full story about how to become a conversion community from my book *You Found Me*. You can also learn more about our work at the Church Evangelism Institute at the Wheaton College Billy Graham Center by visiting us online at https://www.ceicohorts.com. If you are interested in being in a cohort that helps churches become conversion communities, you can register your interest on that site.

7. Beth Seversen, *Not Done Yet: Reaching and Keeping Unchurched Emerging Adults* (Downers Grove, IL: InterVarsity Press, 2020), 106–20.

8. I learned these missional practices in my former church, Community Christian Church, where Rev. Dave Ferguson and Rev. Jon Ferguson pastor. Their book that outlines how this model works is in the reference list.

9. Seversen, *Not Done Yet*, 76–105.

10. Seversen, *Not Done Yet*, 179.

11. Seversen, *Not Done Yet*, 152.

Chapter 8. Singing Together Missionally

1. David Kinnaman and Hawkins, *You Lost Me: Why Young Christians Are Leaving Church … and Rethinking Faith* (Grand Rapids: Baker Books, 2011), 21.

2. Kinnaman and Hawkins, *You Lost Me*, 22.

3. Pew Research Center, "U.S. Decline of Christianity Continues at a Rapid Pace: Update on America's Changing Religious Landscape," 2019, https://www.pewforum.org/2019/10/17/in-u-s-decline-of-christianity-continues-at-rapid-pace/.

4. Christian Smith and Melinda Lundquist Denton, *Soul Searching: The Religious and Spiritual Lives of American Teenagers*, (Oxford: Oxford University Press, 2005); Christian Smith and Patricia Snell, *Souls in Transition: The Religious and Spiritual Lives of Emerging Adults* (Oxford: Oxford University Press, 2009); Smith et al. 2011.

5. Doug Gay, *Remixing the Church: The Five Moves of Emerging Ecclesiology* (Norwich, UK: SCM Press, 2011), 82.

6. Jeffrey Jensen Arnett, "Emerging Adulthood: A Theory of Development from the Late Teens through the Twenties," *American Psychologist* 55, no. 5 (2000): 469–80; Arnett, *Emerging Adulthood: The Winding Road from the Late Teens through the Twenties*, 2nd ed. (New York: Oxford University Press, 2015).

7. Brad Harper and Paul Louis Metzger, *Exploring Ecclesiology: An Evangelical Introduction* (Grand Rapids: Brazos, 2009), 118.

8. Diana Butler Bass, *Christianity after Religion: The End of Church and the Birth of a New Spiritual Awakening* (New York: HarperCollins, 2012), 47.

9. Richard R. Dunn and Jana L. Sundene, *Shaping the Journey of Emerging Adults: Life-giving Rhythms for Spiritual Transformation* (Downers Grove, IL: InterVarsity Press, 2012), 25.

10. David P. Setran and Chris A. Kiesling, *Spiritual Formation in Emerging Adulthood: A Practical Theology for College and Young Adult Ministry* (Grand Rapids, MI: Baker Academic, 2013), 99.

11. Kurt Bestor, "Prayer of the Children: The Story behind the Song," accessed December 14, 2019, http://www.kurtbestor.com/story-behind-prayer-of-the-children.

12. Pope Francis, *The Joy of the Gospel: Evangelii Gaudium* (Vatican City: United States Conference of Catholic Bishops, 2013), 24.

13. Pope Francis, *Joy of the Gospel*, 24.

14. Setran and Kiesling, *Spiritual Formation in Emerging Adulthood*.

15. Setran and Kiesling, *Spiritual Formation in Emerging Adulthood*, 101.

16. Robert Wuthnow, *After the Baby Boomers: How Twenty- and Thirty-Somethings Are Shaping the Future of American Religion* (Princeton: Princeton University Press, 2007), 232.

Chapter 9. Practicing Racial Reconciliation

1. William F. Frey, "The Millennial Generation: A Demographic Bridge to America's Diverse Future," Brookings Institute, January 2018, https://www.brookings.edu/research/millenials/.

2. Kara Powell, Jake Mulder, and Brad Griffin, *Growing Young: Six Essential Strategies to Help Young People Discover and Love Your Church* (Grand Rapids: Baker Books, 2016).

3. Anthony Giddens, *Modernity and Self-Identity: Self and Society in the Late Modern Age* (Stanford: Stanford University Press, 1991).

4. Kenneth Gergen, *Relational Being*, rev. ed. (New York: Oxford University Press, 2011); Gergen, *The Saturated Self: Dilemmas of Identity in Contemporary Life*, rev. ed. (New York: Basic Books, 2000); Sherry Turkle, *Reclaiming Conversation* (New York: Penguin Books, 2015).

5. Sheila Rowe, *Healing Racial Trauma: The Road to Resilience* (Downers Grove, IL: IVP Books, 2020).

6. Park, Kyeyoung. "'I Really Do Feel I'm 1.5': The Construction of Self and Community by Young Korean Americans," *Amerasia Journal* 25, no. 1 (1999), 139–64; Peter Cha, "Constructing New Intergenerational Ties, Cultures, and Identities among Korean American Christians: A Congregational Case Study," in *This Side of Heaven: Race, Ethnicity, and Christian Faith*, ed. Robert Priest and Alvaro Nieves (New York: Oxford University Press, 2006); Gergen, *Relational Being*.

7. Powell, Mulder, and Griffin, *Growing Young*, 166.

8. Miroslav Volf, *Exclusion and Embrace: A Theological Exploration of Identity, Otherness, and Reconciliation* (Nashville: Abingdon, 1996).

9. Sharon Parks, *Big Questions, Worthy Dreams: Mentoring Young Adults in Their Search for Meaning, Purpose, and Faith*, rev. 10th anniversary ed. (San Francisco: Jossey-Bass, 2011); Powell, Mulder, and Griffin, *Growing Young.*

10. Ticola Caldwell Ross, "Exploring the Relationships between Youth Activism, Developmental Assets, and Sociopolitical Consciousness in Emerging Adulthood," PhD diss. (North Carolina State University, 2015).

11. Powell, Mulder, and Griffin, *Growing Young*; Rick Richardson, *You Found Me: New Research on How Unchurched Nones, Millennials, and Irreligious Are Surprisingly Open to Christian Faith* (Downers Grove, IL: InterVarsity Press, 2019); Beth Seversen, *Not Done Yet: Reaching and Keeping Unchurched Emerging Adults* (Downers Grove, IL: InterVarsity Press, 2020).

12. Powell, Mulder, and Griffin, *Growing Young*, 169.

13. Edgar H. Schein, *Organizational Culture and Leadership*, rev. 4th ed. (San Francisco: Jossey-Bass, 2010).

14. Jackson W. Carroll et al., *Being There: Culture and Formation in Two Theological Schools* (New York: Oxford University Press, 1997).

15. Trinity International University, "About Trinity Evangelical Divinity School (TEDS)," accessed September 20, 2020, https://www.tiu.edu/divinity/about-teds/.

16. Emmanuel Katongole and Chris Rice, *Reconciling All Things: A Christian Vision for Justice, Peace, and Healing*, Resources for Reconciliation (Downers Grove, IL: IVP Books, 2008), 125–26.

17. Katongole and Rice, *Reconciling All Things.*

18. Katongole and Rice, *Reconciling All Things*, 133.

Chapter 10. Participating in Service-Learning Trips

1. A pseudonym is used instead of the student's real name.

2. Corey Seemiller and Meghan Grace, *Generation Z Goes to College* (San Francisco: Jossey-Bass, 2016) 17, 40.

3. Pew Research Center, "On the Cusp of Adulthood and Facing an Uncertain Future: What We Know about Gen Z So Far," accessed September 30, 2020, https://www.pewsocialtrends.org/essay/on-the-cusp-of-adulthood-and-facing-an-uncertain-future-what-we-know-about-gen-z-so-far, 4, 8.

4. Tim Elmore and Andrew McPeak, *Generation Z Unfiltered: Facing Nine Hidden Challenges of the Most Anxious Population* (Atlanta: Poet Gardner, 2019).

5. Elmore and McPeak, *Generation Z Unfiltered*, 64.

6. Dominique Burrows, Stephen J. Snyder, and Andrew Ferro, "Perceived Longitudinal Effects of SLMTs," *Journal of Psychology and Theology* 46, no. 3 (2018): 168–83.

7. Burrows, Snyder, and Ferro, "Perceived Longitudinal Effects."

8. Burrows, Snyder, and Ferro, "Perceived Longitudinal Effects."

9. Burrows, Snyder, and Ferro, "Perceived Longitudinal Effects."

10. Burrows, Snyder, and Ferro, "Perceived Longitudinal Effects," 177.

11. Seemiller and Grace, *Generation Z Goes to College.*

12. Pew Research Center, "On the Cusp of Adulthood."

13. Barna Group, *Spiritual Conversations in the Digital Age* (Ventura, CA: Barna Group, 2018), 71.

14. Barna Group, *The Future of Mission: Ten Questions about Global Ministry the Church Must Answer with the Next Generation* (Ventura, CA: Barna Group, 2020), 75–76.

15. Barna Group, *Future of Mission*, 28–29, 33–35.

16. James Emery White, *Meet Generation Z: Understanding and Reaching the New Post-Christian World* (Grand Rapids: Baker Books, 2017).

17. Thomas E. Bergler, "Generation Z and Spiritual Maturity," *Christian Education Journal* 17, no. 1 (2020): 85.

18. Seemiller and Grace, *Generation Z Goes to College*.

19. Corey Seemiller and Meghan Grace, *Generation Z: A Century in the Making* (New York: Routledge, 2019).

20. InterVarsity, "Engaging Gen Z: Urbana 18 Exhibitor Webinar with Jolene Erlacher," video, 2018, https://urbana.org/engaging-gen-z.

21. InterVarsity, "Engaging Gen Z."

22. Barna Group, *Spiritual Conversations in the Digital Age*.

23. Elmore and McPeak, *Generation Z Unfiltered*; Jean M. Twenge, *iGen* (New York: Atria Books, 2017).

24. Elmore and McPeak, *Generation Z Unfiltered*.

Chapter 11. Growing through Philanthropy

1. Christian Smith and Patricia Snell, *Souls in Transition: The Religious and Spiritual Lives of Emerging Adults* (New York: Oxford University Press, 2009), 13–14.

2. Smith and Snell, *Souls in Transition*, 19, 25.

3. Smith and Snell, *Souls in Transition*, 26–30.

4. Christian Smith, Kari Christoffersen, Hilary Davidson, and Patricia Snell Herzog, *Lost in Transition: The Dark Side of Emerging Adulthood* (New York: Oxford University Press, 2011).

5. Marianne Cooper, *Cut Adrift: Families in Insecure Times* (Berkeley: University of California Press, 2014).

6. Jeffrey Jensen Arnett, *Emerging Adulthood: The Winding Road from the Late Teens through the Twenties*, 2nd ed. (New York: Oxford University Press, 2015).

7. Ofra Mayseless and Einat Keren, "Finding a Meaningful Life as a Developmental Task in Emerging Adulthood: The Domains of Love and Work across Cultures," *Emerging Adulthood* 2, no. 1 (2014): 63–73, https://doi.org/10.1177/2167696813515446; Carolyn McNamara Barry and Mona M. Abo-Zena, *Emerging Adults' Religiousness and Spirituality: Meaning-Making in an Age of Transition* (Oxford: Oxford University Press, 2014); Ian A. Gutierrez, and Crystal L. Park, "Emerging Adulthood, Evolving Worldviews: How Life Events Impact College Students' Developing Belief Systems," *Emerging Adulthood* 3, no. 2 (2015): 85–97.

8. Heather L. Lawford and Heather L. Ramey, "'Now I Know I Can Make a Difference': Generativity and Activity Engagement as Predictors of Meaning Making in Adolescents and Emerging Adults." *Developmental Psychology* 51, no. 10 (2015): 1395–1406.

9. Melissa Chan, Kim M. Tsai, and Andrew J. Fuligni, "Changes in Religiosity across the Transition to Young Adulthood," *Journal of Youth and Adolescence* 44 (2014): 1555–66, https://doi.org/10.1007/s10964-014-0157-0.

10. David P. King, "Millennials, Faith and Philanthropy: Who Will Be Transformed?," *Bridge/Work* 1, no. 1 (2016): 2.

11. Emily Barman, "The Social Bases of Philanthropy," *Annual Review of Sociology* 43, no. 1 (2017): 271–90, https://doi.org/10.1146/annurev-soc-060116-053524.

12. Robert L. Payton and Michael P. Moody, *Understanding Philanthropy: Its Meaning and Mission* (Bloomington: Indiana University Press, 2008).

13. Jason Franklin, "Placing Social Justice Philanthropy in a Historical Context: Key Moments from 20th Century U.S. Political & Philanthropic History," Bolder Giving, Sustainable Agriculture & Food Systems Funders (SASF) (blog), 2011, http://www.safsf.org/documentsold/2011Forum_BolderGiving_Overview.pdf; Dorian O. Burton and Brian C. B. Barnes, "Shifting Philanthropy from Charity to Justice (SSIR)," Stanford Social Innovation Review (SSIR) (blog), January 3, 2017, https://ssir.org/articles/entry/shifting_philanthropy_from_charity_to_justice.

14. Patricia Illingworth, Thomas Pogge, and Leif Wenar, eds., *Giving Well: The Ethics of Philanthropy* (New York: Oxford University Press, 2012).

15. Susan Phillips and Steven Rathgeb Smith, "Public Policy for Philanthropy: Catching the Wave or Creating a Backwater," in *The Routledge Companion to Philanthropy*, ed. Tobias Jung, Susan D. Phillips, and Jenny Harrow (Philadelphia: Routledge, 2016), 213–28.

16. Henrietta Grönlund and Anne Birgitta Pessi, "The Influence of Religion on Philanthropy across Nations," in *The Palgrave Handbook of Global Philanthropy*, ed. Pamala Wiepking and Femida Handy (London: Palgrave Macmillan UK, 2015), 558–69.

17. Steven T. Yen, and Ernest M. Zampelli, "What Drives Charitable Donations of Time and Money? The Roles of Political Ideology, Religiosity, and Involvement," *Journal of Behavioral and Experimental Economics* 50 (2014): 58–67, https://doi.org/10.1016/j.socec.2014.01.002; Kevin F. Forbes and Ernest M. Zampelli, "Volunteerism: The Influences of Social, Religious, and Human Capital," *Nonprofit & Voluntary Sector Quarterly* 43, no. 2 (2014): 227–53, https://doi.org/10.1177/0899764012458542.

18. E.g., Stijn Ruiter and Nan Dirk De Graaf, "National Context, Religiosity and Volunteering: Results from 53 Countries," *American Sociological Review* 71, no. 2 (2006): 191–210; Noah D. Drezner et al., *Philanthropy in Israel 2016: Patterns of Individual Giving* (Tel Aviv: Tel Aviv University, 2016).

19. Ram Cnaan and Stephanie C. Boddie, *The Invisible Caring Hand: American Congregations and the Provision of Welfare* (New York: New York University Press, 2002); Sabith Khan, "New Styles of Community Building and Philanthropy by Arab-American Muslims," *Voluntas: International Journal of Voluntary & Nonprofit Organizations* 27, no. 2 (2016): 941–57, https://doi.org/10.1007/s11266-015-9553-7.

20. E.g., Graham Perkins, "The Teaching Excellence Framework (TEF) and Its Impact on Academic Identity Within A Research-Intensive University." *Higher Education Policy; London* 32 (2): 297–319, http://dx.doi.org.proxy.ulib.uits.iu.edu/10.1057/s41307-018-0082-z.

21. Alan Skelton, *Understanding Teaching Excellence in Higher Education: Toward a Critical Approach* (New York: Routledge, 2005).

22. Skelton, *Understanding Teaching Excellence*, 33.

23. Benjamin S. Bloom, *Taxonomy of Educational Objectives, Handbook 1: Cognitive Domain*, 2nd ed. (New York: Addison-Wesley Longman, 1956); Lorin W. Anderson et al., *A Taxonomy for Learning, Teaching, and Assessing: A Revisions of Bloom's Taxonomy of Educational Objectives* (New York: Longman, 2001).

24. L. Dee. Fink, *Creating Significant Learning Experiences: An Integrated Approach to Designing College Courses*, rev. and updated ed. (San Francisco: Jossey-Bass, 2013).

25. Richard C. Turner, "Philanthropic Studies as a Central and Centering Discipline in the Humanities," *International Journal of the Humanities* 2, no. 3 (2004): 2083–86.

26. Sarah L. Ash and Patti H. Clayton, "Generating, Deepening, and Documenting Learning: The Power of Critical Reflection in Applied Learning," *Journal of Applied Learning in Higher Education* 1, no. 1 (2009): 25–48.

27. Richard Bach, *The Bridge across Forever: A True Love Story* (New York: William Morrow Paperbacks, 2006). Richard Bach: "You don't want a million answers as much as you want a few forever questions. The questions are diamonds you hold in the light. Study a lifetime and you see different colors from the same jewel."

28. Payton and Moody, *Understanding Philanthropy*.

29. Patricia Snell Herzog, *The Science of Generosity: Causes, Manifestations, and Consequences*, Palgrave Studies in Altruism, Morality, and Social Solidarity (London: Palgrave Macmillan, 2019).

30. Patricia Snell Herzog and Heather Price, *American Generosity: Who Gives and Why* (New York: Oxford University Press, 2016).

Chapter 12. Latinx Migration and Mission

1. We are a sojourning species, We do not have belongings only baggage, We travel along with the wind like the pollen, Alive because we are in movement. Never still, we are nomadic, We are parents, children, grandchildren, and great-grand children of immigrants, What I dream, it's more mine than what I can touch. I am not from here but neither are you. From nowhere at all and from everywhere a little bit. (Translation our own.)

2. All names have been changed for confidentiality purposes.

3. *Departamento* is the term use by the Salvadorian government to delineate the fourteen provinces and administrative divisions that make up the republic of El Salvador.

4. Throughout this chapter, we will use the term "Latinx" as a gender-neutral alternative. We recognize that this is a more recent term used in the fields of scholarship, marketing, and community organizing. We acknowledge the linguistic complexities that it presents for a gendered language such as Spanish, and its essentializing pan-ethnic label. At the same time, the awareness and usage of this term in the generational cohort we are describing represents a need for its incorporation in our discussion. Thus, unless otherwise noted as female or male, "Latinx" will be used to refer to all those who are or relate to Latin American origin or descent (see Pew Research Center, "About One-in-Four U.S. Hispanics Have Heard of Latinx, but Just 3% Use It"). While recognizing its limited scope to fully encompass the Latina reality of adults between the ages of eighteen and twenty-nine, for the purpose of this chapter we will use the term "emerging adults" in order to maintain coherence with the present project.

5. U.S. Census Bureau, "Racial and Ethnic Diversity in the United States: 2010 Census and 2020," 2020, https://www.census.gov/library/visualizations/interactive/racial-and-ethnic-diversity-in-the-united-states-2010-and-2020-census.htmlj.

6. U.S. Census Bureau, "65 and Older Population Grows Rapidly as Baby Boomers Age," 2020, https://www.census.gov/newsroom/press-releases/2020/65-older-population-grows.html. See also Mark Hugo Lopez, Jens Manuel Krogstad, and Antonio Flores, "Key facts about young Latinos, one of the nation's fastest-growing populations." Pew Research Center, September 13, 2018. https://pewrsr.ch/2x9Ucvj.

7. What do we do with Latinx young people?

8. God, what kind of missional imagination have you given our Latinx youth?

9. International Organization for Migration and United Nations, "World Migration Report," 2020, https://www.un.org/sites/un2.un.org/files/wmr_2020.pdf, 19.

10. Mark Charles and Soong-Chan Rah, *Unsettling Truths: The Ongoing, Dehumanizing Legacy of the Doctrine of Discovery* (Downers Grove, IL: InterVarsity Press, 2019).

11. Juan González, *Harvest of Empire: A History of Latinos in America* (New York: Penguin Books, 2001). In a more recent history, the United States' intervention throughout Latin America in order to defend (i.e., impose) democratic values, institutions, and governments aligned with United States' foreign policy (i.e., economic interests) has created continuous migratory patterns with a south-to-north flow.

12. Caroline Brettell and James Frank Hollifield, *Migration Theory: Talking across Disciplines*, 2nd ed. (New York: Routledge, 2008).

13. Juan Francisco Martínez, *The Story of Latino Protestants in the United States* (Grand Rapids: Eerdmans, 2018), 197.

14. Daniel A. Rodriguez, *A Future for the Latino Church : Models for Multilingual, Multigenerational Hispanic Congregations* (Downers Grove, IL: IVP Academic, 2011).

15. Nancy L. Galambos and Jeffrey Jensen Arnett, eds., *Exploring Cultural Conceptions of the Transition to Adulthood*, New Directions for Child and Adolescent Development 100 (San Francisco: Jossey-Bass, 2003), 74.

16. Juan Francisco Martínez, *Walk with the People: Latino Ministry in the United States* (Nashville: Abingdon, 2008).

17. Martínez, *Walk with the People*, 19–23. These subcultures include Nuclear, Bicultural, Marginal, Fleeing, Returning, Assimilated, and New Nuclear (becoming part of another minority culture).

18. Ken Johnson-Mondragón and National Study of Youth & Religion (U.S.), *Pathways of Hope and Faith among Hispanic Teens: Pastoral Reflections and Strategies Inspired by the National Study of Youth and Religion*, Pathways and Journeys for a New Generation 5.1 (Stockton, CA: Instituto Fe y Vida, 2007), 33–39.

19. Andrea Dyrness and Enrique Sepúlveda III, *Border Thinking: Latinx Youth Decolonizing Citizenship* (Minneapolis: University of Minnesota Press, 2020).

20. We recognize that other descriptors such as "Latinx millennials" or "Hispanic millennials" may also inform this discussion on identity formation processes. Latinx millennials, while a subset of this generational cohort, do possess internal differences such as US born versus foreign born, a reality that influences their sense of the American dream, markers of success, financial solvency, and cultural assimilation (see Sensis and Think Now Research, "Hispanic millennial Project," 2014–2015, http://www.hispanicmillennialproject.com/waves). *Jóvenes* is a term used within local Latina churches to identify ministry to Latinx young people in relationship to their marital status, deeply rooted within cultural expectations of adulthood. See Carmen M. Cervantes and Ken Johnson-Mondragón, *Pastoral Juvenil Hispana, Youth Ministry, and Young Adult Ministry: An Updates Perspective on Three Different Pastoral Realities* (Stockton, CA: Instituto Fe y Vida, 2007).

21. Allan Yeh, in his book *Polycentric Missiology: 21st-Century Mission from Everyone to Everywhere* (Downers Grove, IL: IVP Academic, 2016), argues that God as the primary agent of mission is concerned with people much more than places; this missiological shift creates a multiplicity of active "hubs" where the Triune God is at work throughout the Two-Thirds world. Yeh reaches this conclusion as he thoroughly analyzes and reflects upon the global missiological consultations that took place to commemorate the Missions Conference of Edinburgh 1910 in its

hundredth anniversary—a major conference that influenced the focus of missions in the twentieth century in terms of theology, methodology, and scope of world missions.

22. Jóvenes CLADE V, "Youth, Actors for Transformation," Pastoral letter, 2012, https://jovenescladev.files.wordpress.com/2012/07/carta-pastoral-de-la-consulta-de-jovenes-ingles.pdf.

23. Loida I. Martell-Otero, Zaida Maldonado Pérez, and Elizabeth Conde-Frazier, *Latina Evangélicas: A Theological Survey from the Margins* (Eugene, OR: Cascade Books, 2013), 68–71.

24. Martell-Otero, Maldonado Pérez, and Conde-Frazier, *Latina Evangélicas*, 71.

25. "My daughter or son."

26. Natalia Kohn, Noemi Quiñones Vega, and Kristy Garza Robinson, *Hermanas: Deepening Our Identity and Growing Our Influence* (Downers Grove, IL: InterVarsity Press, 2019).

27. Kohn, Quiñones Vega, and Garza Robinson, *Hermanas*, 49–58.

28. A point of reference for this adaptability may be seen through the usage, proficiency, retention, and rise of both Spanish and English among the Latinx population. See a more detailed study by Pew Research Center, "English Proficiency on the Rise among Latinos: US Born Driving Language Changes," May 12, 2015 https://www.pewresearch.org/hispanic/2015/05/12/english-proficiency-on-the-rise-among-latinos/.

29. Oscar García-Johnson. *Spirit Outside the Gate: Decolonial Pneumatologies of the American Global South* (Downers Grove, IL: IVP Academic, 2019), 258.

30. Elizabeth Tamez Méndez, "Rethinking Latino Youth Ministry: Frameworks That Provide Roots and Wings for Our Youth," *Apuntes* 37, no. 2 (2017): 86–91.

31. Elizabeth Conde-Frazier, "Jovenes Latin@s: Children of the Basilea," *Apuntes* 37, no. 2 (2017): 98–99.

32. Juana Bordas, *The Power of Latino Leadership: Culture, Inclusion, and Contribution*, A Bk Business Book (San Francisco: Berrett-Koehler, 2013).

33. Marcos Canales and Jennifer Guerra Aldana, *Understanding and Relating to Latino/a Youth: A Bilingual and Intergenerational Conversation Toolkit* (Pasadena, CA: Fuller Youth Institute, 2018).

34. See Robert Chao Romero, *Brown Church: Five Centuries of Latina/o Social Justice, Theology, and Identity* (Downers Grove, IL: IVP Academic, 2020).

35. Included but not limited to racism, mass incarceration, poverty, unjust immigration laws, creation care, underresourced schools, policing, and police brutality.

Chapter 13. Hip-Hop in Missional Formation

1. This quote is from page 115 of Dwight Radcliff's dissertation. The rest of this chapter contains excerpts from his scholarly research, with the exception of some minor editing to meet space limitations. To view the work in its entirety and read more about his research methodology, see Dwight Radcliffe, "The Message: A Hip Hop Hermeneutic As A Missiological Model," (PhD diss., Fuller Theological Seminary, 2019), https://search.proquest.com/docview/2231128523?pq-origsite=gscholar&fromopenview=true.

2. Radcliff, D. A., Jr. (2019). *The Message: A Hip Hop Hermeneutic as a Missiological Model* (13883491), 80.

3. Daniel White Hodge, *The Soul of Hip Hop: Rims, Timbs and a Cultural Theology* (Downers Grove, IL: IVP Books, 2010); Efrem Smith and Phil Jackson, *The Hip-Hop Church: Connecting with the Movement Shaping Our Culture* (Downers Grove, IL: InterVarsity Press, 2005); Alonzo Westbrook, *Hip Hoptionary TM: The Dictionary of Hip Hop Terminology* (New York: Harlem Moon, 2002).

4. Frederick L. Ware, "Methodologies in African American Theology," in Oxford Handbook of African American Theology online, 2014, http://www.oxfordhand books.com.fuller.idm.oclc.org/view/10.1093/oxfordhb/9780199755653.001.0001/ oxfordhb-9780199755653-e-008.

5. Scott W. Sunquist, *Understanding Christian Mission: Participation in Suffering and Glory*, Kindle ed. (Grand Rapids: Baker Academic, 2013), 254.

6. Smith and Jackson, *Hip-Hop Church*, 47.

7. Ralph Watkins, "From Black Theology and Black Power to Afrocentric Theology and Hip Hop Power: An Extension and Socio-Re-theological Conceptualization of Cone's Theology in Conversation with the Hip Hop Generation," *Black Theology* 8, no. 3 (2015): 327–40.

8. Smith and Jackson, *Hip-Hop Church*, 68.

9. Charles H. Kraft, *Communication Theory for Christian Witness*, Kindle ed. (Maryknoll, NY: Orbis Books, 1991), 23, 25.

10. Andrew F. Walls, *The Missionary Movement in Christian History: Studies in the Transmission of Faith*, Kindle ed. (Maryknoll, NY: Orbis Books, 1996), loc2. 328, 341.

11. Andrew F. Walls, "The Translation Principle in Christian History," in *Bible Translation and the Spread of the Church: The Last 200 Years*, ed. P. C. Stine (Boston: Brill, 1990).

12. Andrew F. Walls, *The Cross-Cultural Process in Christian History: Studies in the Transmission and Appropriation of Faith*, Kindle ed. (Maryknoll, NY: Orbis, 2002), loc. 668.

13. Lamin O. Sanneh, *Translating the Message: The Missionary Impact on Culture*, rev ed. (Maryknoll, NY: Orbis Books, 2009), 1.

14. Robert E. Hood, *Must God Remain Greek: Afro Cultures and God-Talk* (Minneapolis: Fortress, 1990).

15. Sanneh, *Translating the Message*, 121.

16. Sanneh, *Translating the Message*, 56.

17. Cleophus James LaRue, *I Believe I'll Testify: The Art of African American Preaching* (Louisville, KY: Westminster John Knox, 2011), 61.

18. Henry H. Mitchell, *Black Preaching: The Recovery of a Powerful Art*, Kindle ed. (Nashville: Abingdon, 1990), 66.

19. LaRue, *I Believe I'll Testify*, 60.

20. Ralph Watkins, *Hip-Hop Redemption: Finding God in the Rhythm and the Rhyme* (Grand Rapids: Baker Academic, 2011).

21. Karen Snell and Johan Söderman, *Hip-Hop within and without the Academy* (Lanham, MD: Lexington Books, 2014).

22. Mitchell, *Black Preaching*, 15.

Chapter 14. Chinese American Emerging Adults

1. Pew Research Center, "Asian Americans: A Mosaic of Faiths," 2012; Pew Research Center, "The Rise of Asian Americans (Updated Edition, 4/4/2013)," 2013.

2. Julie J. Park, "I Needed to Get Out of My Korean Bubble: An Ethnographic Account of Korean American Collegians Juggling Diversity in a Religious Context," *AEQ Anthropology & Education Quarterly* 42, no. 3 (2011): 193–212.

3. The overall findings are from Russell Jeung, Seanan Fong, and Helen Kim's *Family Sacrifices: The Worldviews and Ethics of Chinese Americans* (New York, Oxford University Press, 2019) and its sample of 58 Chinese American families nationwide, and an analysis of the 2012 National Asian American Survey of 728 Chinese Americans.

4. The findings on Chinese American Christians stem from Michael Karim's dissertation, "Keeping the Faith by Second Generation Chinese American Freshmen: A Morphogenetic Analysis of Reflexive Mediation of the Christian Faith over the First Year of University Life" (2020) and its sample of 25 Chinese American first-year students.

5. Jeung, Fong, and Jin Kim, *Family Sacrifices*, 16.

6. Pew Research Center, "Rise of Asian Americans."

7. D. W. Sue et al., "Racial Microaggressions and the Asian American Experience," *Cultural Diversity & Ethnic Minority Psychology* 13, no. 1 (2007): 72.

8. An excellent example of Jesus as the Way is Mark Scandrette's Ninefold Path of Jesus, a small group practice of following the Beatitudes; see http://www.markscandrette.com/#new-page-2.

9. This Millennial generation has higher rates of activism, commitment to engaging their community, and helping others than ever before. See Kevin Eagen et al., "The American Freshman: National Norms for Fall 2015," Cooperative Institutional Research Program at the Higher Educational Research Institute at UCLA, 2016.

10. Neil G. Ruiz, Juliana Menasce Horowitz, and Christine Tamir, "Many Black and Asian Americans Say They Have Experienced Discrimination amid the COVID-19 Outbreak," Pew Research Center, July 1, 2020, https://www.pewsocialtrends.org/2020/07/01/many-black-and-asian-americans-say-they-have-experienced-discrimination-amid-the-covid-19-outbreak/.

Chapter 15. How Will We Respond?

1. Sharon Daloz Parks, *Big Questions, Worthy Dreams: Mentoring Young Adults in Their Search for Meaning, Purpose, and Faith*, rev. 10th anniv. ed. (San Francisco: Jossey-Bass, 2011), 185.

2. Parks, *Big Questions, Worthy Dreams*, 180, 190–97.

3. David P. Setran, and Chris A. Kiesling, *Spiritual Formation in Emerging Adulthood: A Practical Theology for College and Young Adult Ministry* (Grand Rapids: Baker Academic, 2013), 212.

4. Parks, *Big Questions, Worthy Dreams*, 176–96.

5. Christian Smith and Patricia Snell, *Souls in Transition: The Religious and Spiritual Lives of Emerging Adults* (Oxford: Oxford University Press, 2009), 75.

6. Angela Duckworth, *Grit: The Power of Passion and Perseverance* (New York: Scribner, 2016); Tim Elmore and Andrew McPeak, *Generation Z Unfiltered: Facing Nine Hidden Challenges of the Most Anxious Population* (Atlanta: Poet Gardner, 2019).

7. Mary Lederleitner, "Transition Journeys in Emerging Adulthood as InterVarsity Students Seek to Connect with Faith Communities after Graduation: A Qualitative Study with Educational and Sociological Implications" (PhD diss., Trinity Evangelical Divinity School, 2014), 153–60.

8. Jeffrey Jensen Arnett, "Does Emerging Adulthood Theory Apply across Social Classes? National Data on a Persistent Question," *Emerging Adulthood* 4, no. 4 (2016): 231.

9. Lederleitner, "Transition Journeys in Emerging Adulthood," 193–95.

10. All names mentioned are pseudonyms.

11. Rick Richardson, *You Found Me: New Research on How Unchurched Nones, Millennials, and Irreligious Are Surprisingly Open to Christian Faith* (Downers Grove, IL: InterVarsity Press, 2019), 151–67.

12. Kim Parker and Ruth Igielnik. "On the Cusp of Adulthood and Facing and Uncertain Future: What We Know sbout Gen Z So Far," Pew Research Center, 2020, https://www.pewresearch.org/social-trends/2020/05/14/on-the-cusp-of-adult hood-and-facing-an-uncertain-future-what-we-know-about-gen-z-so-far-2/.

13. Jean Phinney, "Understanding Development in Cultural Contexts: How Do We Deal with the Complexity?," *Human Development* 53 (2010): 33–34.

Appendix

1. "The one who does not remember history is condemned to repeat it."

2. When I first started teaching at Biola University, my students were millennials. Now, over a decade later, they are Gen Z. I have had to change my teaching style accordingly, in numerous ways. In this entire chapter, my characteristics of generational distinctives are all bound by Western culture. For example, Gen Z in the United States would not have the same descriptors as Gen Z in Africa or Asia.

3. Angela Duckworth, *Grit: The Power of Passion and Perseverance* (New York: Scribner, 2016).

4. Greg Lukianoff and Jonathan Haidt, *The Coddling of the American Mind: How Good Intentions and Bad Ideas Are Setting Up a Generation for Failure* (New York: Penguin, 2018), 163–80. "Snowplow" or "lawnmower" parenting is the idea that the parent paves the way in front of the child, removing all obstacles so that the child is not harmed, but consequently the child never learns self-sufficient skills to be able to surmount those obstacles themselves. This is in contrast to helicopter parenting, where the parent hovers over the shoulder of their child, supervising them at every turn. Millennials were more subject to helicopter parenting, while Gen Z is more influenced by snowplow/lawnmower parenting.

5. Jean Twenge, *iGen: Why Today's Super-Connected Kids Are Growing Up Less Rebellious, More Tolerant, Less Happy—and Completely Unprepared for Adulthood* (New York: Atria, 2017), 143–77.

6. Taylor Lorenz, "'OK Boomer' Marks the End of Friendly Generational Relations," *New York Times*, October 29, 2019, https://www.nytimes.com/2019/10/29/style/ok-boomer.html.

7. Barna and Impact 360 Institute, *Gen Z: The Cultures, Beliefs, and Motivations Shaping the Next Generation* (Ventura, CA: Barna Group, 2018), 105.

8. Twenge, *iGen*; Jason Dorsey, "Generational Clues Uncovered," August 13, 2019, https://globalleadership.org/articles/leading-organizations/jason-dorsey-generational-clues-uncovered/.

9. There is an increasing realization that age is a category of culture as much as race or gender or social class. In fact, it is one of the four Pauline categories of culture, as seen in Ephesians 6:1–4 and Colossians 3:20–21. Ephesians and Colossians also unpack the previously mentioned three in Ephesians 3:6 and Colossians 3:11 (race); Ephesians 5:22–33 and Colossians 3:18–19 (gender); and Ephesians 6:5–9

and Colossians 3:22 (class). Though scholars debate about the exact time frame of each generation, it is generally agreed that there are certain historical events that have affected each generation, either affecting their world post-birth or in their consciousness as they have come of age, e.g., millennials with 9/11, and Gen Z with the 2008 financial crisis. Here are some roughly agreed-upon dates for each of these generations: the Greatest Generation (born between 1900 and 1920); The Silent Generation (born between 1920 and 1946); boomers (born between 1946 and 1964); Gen X, aka Busters (born between 1965 and 1979); Gen Y, aka millennials (born between 1980 and 1994, or perhaps 1984 and 2001); Gen Z, aka iGen (born between 1995 and 2015, or perhaps 2002 and 2015).

10. Seven of the eight Ivy League universities were founded to train up ministers. The one exception was Cornell University.

11. Ruth A. Tucker, *From Jerusalem to Irian Jaya: A Biographical History of Christian Missions* (Grand Rapids: Zondervan, 2004), 312.

12. David Bebbington, *Evangelicalism in Modern Britain* (London: Unwin Hyman, 1989), 2–3.

13. Perhaps "Missions and Young Adults" should be known as the MAYA quadrilateral.

14. Leslie K. Tarr, "A Prayer Meeting That Lasted 100 Years," *Decision*, 1977; repr., *Christianity Today*, https://www.christianitytoday.com/history/issues/issue-1/prayer-meeting-that-lasted-100-years.html.

15. Thomas Cole Richards, *The Haystack Prayer Meeting: An Account of Its Origin and Spirit* (Williamstown, MA: Haystack Centennial Committee, 1906).

16. Ralph Winter, "The Two Structures of God's Redemptive Mission," *Perspectives on the World Christian Movement* (1973), http://frontiermissionfellowship.org/uploads/documents/two-structures.pdf, 226–29.

17. William Carey, *An Enquiry into the Obligations of Christians to Use Means for the Conversion of the Heathens* (Leicester, UK: Ann Ireland, 1792).

18. Rosalie Hall Hunt, *Bless God and Take Courage: The Judson History and Legacy* (Valley Forge, PA: Judson Press, 2005).

19. On the campus of the former Andover Seminary (now Phillips Andover Academy, a preparatory high school), there is a plaque engraved on a boulder by the lake, which marks the spot where Mills, Nott, Newell, Hall, Rice, and Judson met on June 29, 1810, forming the American Society for Foreign Missions. Ironically, when I went to seek out this historical marker, I inquired with a number of the current students and nobody had any idea that this even existed right under their very noses!

20. Not to be confused with the TSPM (Three Self Patriotic Movement), which is the Chinese communist government church. Instead, the idea of "three-self" came from missiologists Henry Venn and Rufus Anderson in the nineteenth century. It was a positive philosophy that advocated for Western missionaries to essentially work themselves out of a job, turning over the governing, propagation, and support of Majority World churches to the nationals themselves.

21. Ruth Rouse and Stephen Charles Neill, *A History of the Ecumenical Movement*, 3rd ed. (Geneva: World Council of Churches, 1986), 1:253.

22. Rouse and Neill, *History of the Ecumenical Movement*, 1:328–29. The original site of Moody's vision at Mount Hermon—starting with Green Pastures house in Northfield, Massachusetts—is being turned into the ultimate Christian integration liberal arts institute: the C. S. Lewis College, a place to study Western Great Books with an ecumenical "Mere Christianity" ethos.

23. Rouse and Neill, *History of the Ecumenical Movement*, 1:328.

24. Tucker, *From Jerusalem to Irian Jaya*, 312.

25. Actually, the church father Origen of Alexandria made this connection even earlier than Augustine. Interestingly, Origen was also considered a heretic—though declared such some three centuries after his death at the fifth ecumenical council of Constantinople II in AD 553—due to his apparent universalism, heavy allegory, and doctrine of preexistence of souls (some still dispute whether that posthumous declaration of heterodoxy was fair, especially since Origen was considered orthodox in his day by his fellow patristics). But Andrew Walls calls Origen the "Father of Mission Studies" due to his unflinching engagement of pagan cultures with Christianity. See Andrew Walls, "In Quest of the Father of Mission Studies," *International Bulletin of Mission Studies* (July 1999): 104. Basically, Origen walked the fine line between syncretism (imbibing too much of non-Christian philosophy) and contextualization (evangelizing people with Christianity using their own language and culture).

26. Martin Luther famously said (although it might be more properly attributed to John Calvin at its first utterance, from his *Antidote to the Council of Trent* in 1547): "It is therefore faith alone which justifies, and yet the faith which justifies is not alone." In the same way, taking *sola Scriptura* to simply mean "There is no knowledge to be gleaned outside the Bible" is not what Luther meant. He was indicating the place of the Bible as the Christian's highest authority, but to think that nothing else can be learned outside the Bible goes against Luther's own education. He gleaned much from the humanist Erasmus, who took the best of the classical arts and integrated it with Christianity.

27. Brian Stanley, *Christianity in the Twentieth Century* (Princeton: Princeton University Press, 2018), 175.

28. Allen Yeh, *Polycentric Missiology: Twenty-First Century Mission from Everyone to Everywhere* (Downers Grove, IL: IVP Academic, 2016), 171.

29. John Pollock, *The Cambridge Seven: The True Story of Ordinary Men Used in No Ordinary Way* (Fearn, UK: Christian Focus, 2006); Stuart Piggin and John Roxborogh, *The St. Andrews Seven: The Finest Flowering of Missionary Zeal in Scottish History* (Edinburgh: Banner of Truth Trust, 1985).

30. For example, are young people still suited to adapt to overseas travel, with the changing time zones and different food and climate? Yes, but instead of doing long-term missions they tend to do more short-term missions, with the availability and affordability of air flight making any point on earth literally accessible within a day or two maximum. But there is also a downside, namely, the psychological—not just physical—reason: if emerging adults have a more difficult time having "grit," or if they are more prone to ADHD, or easily get discouraged when obstacles come their way due to their snowplow parents, the lack of stick-to-it-iveness could be the underlying reason for short-term missions. There has been much ink spilled decrying the "voluntourism" and harm to the target culture that short-term missions have created, although it is my estimation that much of this has been overstated, or at the very least there is more positive to be seen in it, even without discounting the negative.

31. Generally, the phrase "Third World" is discouraged as that is not only a relic of the Cold War but also demeaning, to be seen as "third." "Non-Western" is also not advisable, as it still centers the reference frame on the West. "Two-Thirds World" (as in, two-thirds of the world's population lives in Africa, Asia, and Latin America) or "Majority World" (same idea) are used in Christian/missional circles, whereas "Global South" is used more in secular arenas such as the United Nations

(but it seems to be more of an economic term, focused on developing nations and leaving out Asia, which is not in the South).

32. Paul Hiebert, *Anthropological Reflections on Missiological Issues* (Grand Rapids: Baker, 1994), 189–202. This is the idea that most places in the world have three levels of reality: the top level, which is God; the middle level, which are angels, demons, spirits, ancestors, and the like; and the bottom level, which is the material, seen world. Most Western Christians disregard the middle level and do not realize how much this affects Majority World people, and thus miss out on a major way that they can leverage to understand and reach out to people overseas.

33. J. D. Payne, *Strangers Next Door: Immigration, Migration, and Mission* (Downers Grove, IL: InterVarsity Press, 2012), 95–104.

34. Rachael Lee, "'Azusa Now': Some 100,000 Pray for Revival at Los Angeles Memorial Coliseum," *Christianity Daily*, April 11, 2016, http://www.christianitydaily.com/articles/7963/20160411/azusa-now-more-100-000-pray-revival-los-angeles-memorial.htm.

35. This is the idea that—in an effort to pay the bills—they resort to cobbling together numerous short-term jobs such as being an Uber driver or working as a barista in a coffeeshop.

36. Dorsey, "Generational Clues Uncovered."

37. Cultural intelligence and emotional intelligence, respectively. The former is nowadays referred to as intercultural competence, which is being asked of all universities nowadays by college accrediting agencies, although this—the importance of contextualization—has been something that missional Christians have been well aware of for some time.

38. Todd M. Johnson et al., *2010Boston: The Changing Contours of World Mission and Christianity* (Eugene, OR: Pickwick, 2012).

39. Allen Yeh and Tite Tiénou, eds., *Majority World Theologies: Theologizing from Africa, Asia, Latin America, and the Ends of the Earth* (Pasadena, CA: William Carey, 2018), 3–23.

40. Kirsteen Kim and Andrew Anderson, eds., *Mission Today and Tomorrow* (Oxford: Regnum, 2011), 335.

41. Lesslie Newbigin, *The Gospel in a Pluralist Society* (Grand Rapids: Eerdmans, 1989).

42. Brad Knickerbocker, "World First: In 2008, Most People Will Live in Cities," *Christian Science Monitor*, January 12, 2007, https://www.csmonitor.com/2007/0112/p25s02-wogi.html.

43. Timothy Keller, *Why God Made Cities* (New York: City to City, 2013). Shifting to the cities also implies the Majority World, as only three of the world's top twenty largest population metropolises are in the West—New York, Los Angeles, and Moscow. In fact, the world's biggest cities start with Tokyo, Mexico City, New Delhi, Shanghai, and Sao Paulo (depending on how you count the urban area).

44. Many people have asked: What's after Gen Z? Some people have proposed going back to the beginning of the alphabet, or shifting to the Greek alphabet (such as Generation Alpha). Others have proposed (sometimes humorous) names for those affected by the coronavirus, e.g., Gen C or the Coronials.

45. C. S. Lewis, *The Four Loves: The Much Beloved Exploration of the Nature of Love* (New York: Harcourt, Brace, 1960), 61.

Subject Index

Moravians, 256, 257, 261
Mosaic Ministries, 139, 142–52
Multigenerational community.
    See Community
Music, 72, 123–26, 129–45, 203,
    209–13
Musicians. See Music

N

Narrative. See Story
  Learner narrative. See Story
National Study of Youth and
    Religion, 173
Navigators, 261
North American, 124, 202, 203,
    263

O

OMF International (OMF), 261
Oppression. See Marginality
  Minority / minorities. See
    Marginality

P

Passion, 261
Patristics. See Early church
Pentecostal, 117, 210, 259–61
Pew Research Center, 7, 229
Philanthropy, 174–84
Post-denominationalism, 257, 261
Presbyterianism, 127, 258
Purpose, 1, 18, 21, 25–26, 32, 73,
    78, 99, 109, 140–41, 144–45,
    148, 200, 228, 241, 245, 248,
    249

Q

Questioning, 62, 115, 126, 139–42,
    166, 168, 184, 218, 235, 241,
    242

R

Race/ethnicity, 6, 10, 18, 23–25,
    36–39, 49, 80, 103–4,
    109, 118, 139–41, 144, 147,
    149, 151, 156, 162, 179–80,
    191–92, 195, 198–201, 218,
    225–26, 231–35, 249, 260
  Racial. See Race/ethnicity
  Ethnic. See Race/ethnicity
Racial identity, 25, 139–44, 149, 211,
    215–16, 224–26, 231–35
Racial reconciliation, 54, 141–45,
    150–52, 242

S

Same-sex attraction. See Gender
    identity
  LGBTQ+ identity. See Gender
    identity
Schola Cantorum, 124, 129–34
Scripture, 9, 38, 46, 49, 70–80,
    92, 110, 139, 143, 150, 152,
    159, 162–63, 168, 196, 201,
    213–16, 219, 232, 243, 259,
    262
Self-directed learning, 22, 165,
    178
Self-identification. See Identity
Serampore Trio, 259
Sexual desires. See Sexuality
  Sexual behaviors. See
    Sexuality
  Biblical sexuality. See
    Sexuality
Sexual identity, 35, 36, 74, 128
Sexuality, 34–49, 73, 128, 215–16
Sharing faith, 1, 2, 10, 79, 105–6,
    109–11, 114, 131–32, 162–63,
    234, 247
Singleness, 44–46, 49, 74, 102
Spiritual development. See
    Spiritual formation

Author Index

Scripture Index

Old Testament

New Testament